ADVANCE PRAISE FOR *ABINA AND THE IMPORTANT MEN*

Abina and the Important Men engages with thorny issues in World History—human trafficking, colonialism, cultural autonomy, and women's rights. While the stories preserved over time are often those of male leaders, this book brings to life the concerns of a young woman at a pivotal moment in African history. Slavery becomes a contested terrain, as cultural practices interface with an emerging wage economy and British officials turn a blind eye to the presence of underpaid domestic workers in the households of African merchants. Through the multiple voices of a forgotten heroine and a cast of African, European, and Euro-African men, it shows the many perspectives that helped shape our concepts of freedom and independence.

ABENA DOVE OSSEO-ASARE, *University of California, Berkeley*

Abina and the Important Men is an excellent introduction to history and society through an innovative mix of primary text, annotated transcription, and cartoons. It will capture the imagination of new students. It is a must for adoption in first year courses.

PAUL LOVEJOY, *York University*

This is an important departure for Oxford University Press and an excellent combination of research and pedagogy. It is a fine work and I will use it in my teaching. Students today do not easily grasp the difference between a primary and secondary source. This text merges that appreciation—for how historians work—into the fabric of the book.

PAUL S. LANDAU, *University of Maryland*

This is a pioneering work in the narration and representation of African history and will appeal to students of all levels. The book engages in the actual historical process and makes the processes historians go through when compiling such a document very evident for students. The fact that *Abina and the Important Men* highlights the difference between primary and secondary documents, and discusses representation and translation in detail, makes it particularly valid for all history classes.

TIFFANY F. JONES, *California State University, San Bernardino*

This is an excellent project! It is fresh, engaging, and historically sound. I would definitely use this text in my Modern Africa and African Women's History classes. I really like the way that the author and illustrator have divided the book into sections for different levels of analysis. Beginning students can focus on the graphic novel, while more advanced students can also discuss the production of historical knowledge and the larger historiography.

ALICIA D. DECKER, *Purdue University*

W9-ADC-057

Abina and the Important Men is intellectual and accessible at the same time, and the three-level division makes it work. Getz and Clarke make liberal-arts learning integrated, useful, and fun. The characters are all morally ambiguous, something I aim for in my own writing. There's no automatic assumption the good guys will win, because it's always plausibly depicting real people, without white hats on some and black hats on others.

KEN O'DONNELL, *Associate Dean, Academic Programs and Policy, California State University*

I think this is an extraordinarily original and ambitious project. This is a very interesting experiment in using the graphic novel as a means to deliver the life story of someone who is only known to the author through archival material, and in doing so to think more profoundly about how histories are created.

NICOLA FOOTE, *Florida Gulf Coast University*

This is an innovative approach to teaching social history and colonialism in Africa. The graphic history contains beautiful and compelling artwork, and the text closely follows historical documentation. Furthermore, the inclusion of the actual document transcription and historical context make it possible to teach this book on many different levels, getting students to think deeply about the process of how history is made (both in the past and by historians). It would work well in courses on either African history or world history.

ERIN O'CONNOR, *Bridgewater State University*

This is a remarkable feat in scholarship. It tells an equally remarkable story with creativity, historical context, and a deep compassion for the humanity of its subjects. This graphic history charts a new ground for excavating African lives, especially of the seemingly less "important" men (and women), and should be read widely by scholars, students and the general reading public. Trevor Getz and Liz Clarke should be praised, and Abina should be pleased.

KWASI KONADU, *City University of New York*

The project's originality is its main strength; it certainly stands out among other texts on slavery. It also makes the experience of enslavement more immediate, more visual; in other words, it brings it to life.

MAXIM MATUSEVICH, *Seton Hall University*

Academia has finally woken up to the interests of students and Oxford University Press is a willing partner in this awakening. Bravo! This book takes college-level course material in a fresh and invigorating direction. The story—images included—is engrossing, addresses themes regularly featured in our courses, and provides needed insight into a people who still get too little treatment even in world history courses. Also, the author's added commentary on the source material and the general historical context ensure that when students have the book with them at home, they will still recognize the academic qualities of the volume.

JASON RIPPER, *Everett Community College*

This is a very strong and original work. All three sections (the inclusion of the primary source, the historical context section, and the reading guide) allow for a broad range of discussion topics. Students can compare the graphic novel section to the court transcript and discuss how historians develop historical narratives.

JEREMY RICH, *Middle Tennessee State University*

Abina and the Important Men addresses an important gap in the teaching of history, one that recognizes that there are a variety of learning styles

SHARLENE SAYEGH, *California State University, Long Beach*

Through a compelling personal story, *Abina and the Important Men* gets to the heart of the most important issues in 19th century West African history.

LISA LINDSAY, *University of North Carolina, Chapel Hill*

ABINA | AND THE IMPORTANT MEN

A GRAPHIC HISTORY

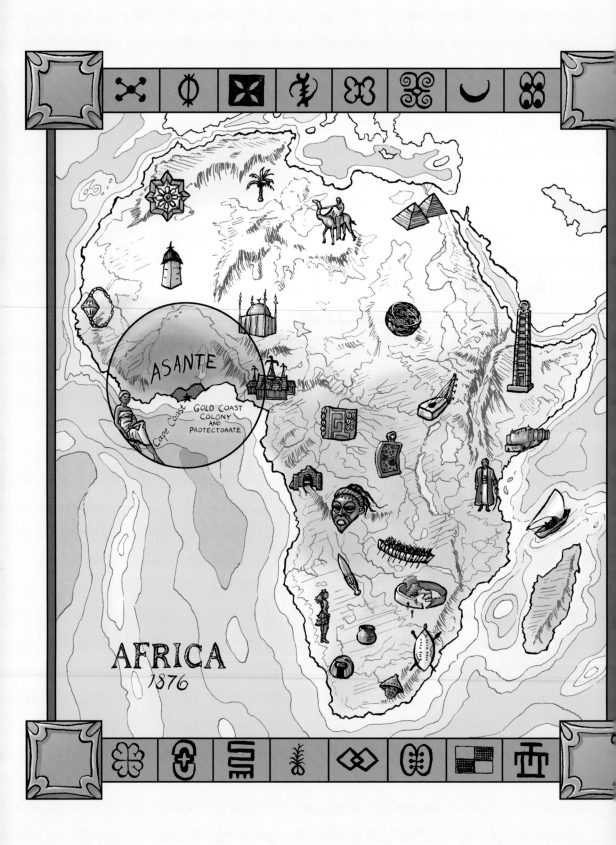

ASANTE

Cape Coast

GOLD COAST
COLONY
AND
PROTECTORATE

AFRICA
1876

ABINA | AND THE IMPORTANT MEN

A GRAPHIC HISTORY

TREVOR R. GETZ

LIZ CLARKE

New York   Oxford
Oxford University Press

Oxford University Press, Inc., publishes works that further Oxford University's objective of excellence in research, scholarship, and education.

Oxford New York
Auckland   Cape Town   Dar es Salaam   Hong Kong   Karachi
Kuala Lumpur   Madrid   Melbourne   Mexico City   Nairobi
New Delhi   Shanghai   Taipei   Toronto

With offices in
Argentina   Austria   Brazil   Chile   Czech Republic   France   Greece
Guatemala   Hungary   Italy   Japan   Poland   Portugal   Singapore
South Korea   Switzerland   Thailand   Turkey   Ukraine   Vietnam

Copyright © 2012 by Oxford University Press, Inc.

Published by Oxford University Press, Inc.
198 Madison Avenue, New York, New York, 10016
http://www.oup.com

Oxford is a registered trademark of Oxford University Press

ISBN 978-0-19-984439-5

Photo on page 124 © *The British Library Board* (HS.74/1099)

Printing number: 9 8 7 6 5 4 3

Printed in the United States of America
on acid-free paper

For Kaela Getz, who—like Abina Mansah—won't be pushed around

CONTENTS

MAPS AND FIGURES

MAPS

FIGURES

LETTER TO THE READER

Dear Reader,

This graphic history recounts the life story of Abina Mansah, a young woman who lived in West Africa during the late nineteenth century. She is representative of the largest group of our human ancestors: those who left little but physical evidence behind to help us to remember them. The histories of all societies, whether passed down orally or in written documents, usually focus on just the major political and social figures. Ordinary peasants and townspeople rarely appear in the record. Even social histories composed by professional historians in the past few decades have tended to focus on everyday people only as a group, instead of as individuals. There are many reasons for this limited perspective on the past. For most of history, men and women of the middle and lower classes were illiterate or wrote little. Even when they left behind written records, these were perceived as having little value and were not carefully preserved. So, their voices faded into oblivion. But historians have also been responsible for this silence: they have tended to see ordinary individuals as less important, and so they have often chosen not to write about them.

In the last few decades, however, historians have developed new strategies for learning about the experiences and perspectives of "people without history." They have learned to use new sources, oral traditions, archaeological remains, and the records of how words and languages have changed over time—to gain insight into the lives of the silent and the forgotten. They have also developed novel ways of finding common peoples' voices in the margins of older sources, such as court cases and newspapers. Many scholarly books and articles have been written about the lives of everyday individuals as a result of these new sources and techniques. Yet, ironically, most of them are not accessible to general audiences today because they are presented in scholarly jargon, published in specialized journals, and designed to be read only by other historians and academics. These works generally seek to be *critical*—that is, to raise complex but sometimes esoteric questions about lived experiences. Those life histories that *are* accessible to the general public tend to be overly simplistic, to cater to nationalist or group-identity goals, or, worse, are simply incorrect. These narratives seek to be *celebratory*—that is, to commemorate a lived experience in order to promote a particular worldview or identity.

Abina and the Important Men is one of a number of projects that seeks to find a middle ground between scholarly and popular histories of regular people. It is not a work of *historical fiction*, but instead a *history* because it aims for accuracy and authenticity even while recognizing that all historical works are at some level speculative and subjective. It is neither completely celebratory nor wholly critical; instead it attempts to show how these two impulses can be linked together. In order to achieve this careful balancing act, it consists of four different approaches to the story. First, at its heart, *Abina* is a graphic history that through pictures and texts presents an interpretation of the life of an African woman, Abina Mansah, based on the single source in which she appeared: the transcript of an 1876 court case. Second, following the graphic history, we also present the transcript itself so that the reader can hear as close as possible Abina's own voice and can evaluate the author's and illustrator's interpretations of her story (presented in original form starting on page 81). Third, this volume includes an historical reconstruction of the world in which Abina lived so that the reader can place the transcript and the graphic history within the context of the time and place in which they are set (beginning on page 95). Finally, rather than seeking to be the final authorities on this story, we invite the reader to question our interpretations in a section that raises key issues about the ways in which historians work to interpret the past (beginning on page 113). We see this work as a conversation we are having with Abina Mansah. We invite you to join in as well.

Trevor Getz
Historian and Author

Liz Clarke
Graphic Artist and Illustrator

ACKNOWLEDGMENTS

The author would like to acknowledge the assistance and support of everyone who read, reviewed, and supported the development of this project: Timothy Carmichael, College of Charleston; Alicia Decker, Purdue University; Nicola Foote, Florida Gulf Coast University; Tiffany Jones, California State University-San Bernardino; Paul Landau, University of Maryland; Maxim Matusevich, Seton Hall University; Erin O'Connor, Bridgewater State University; Jennifer Popiel, St. Louis University; Jonathan Reynolds, Northern Kentucky University; Jeremy Rich, Middle Tennessee State University; Jason Ripper, Everett Community College; Sharlene Sayegh, California State University, Long Beach.

Special thanks are due to Provost Sue Rosser and the Office of Research and Sponsored Programs at San Francisco State University for funding the initial development of this project. Patrick Manning, Jonathan Reynolds, Paul Lovejoy, Candace Goucher, Heather Streets-Salter, Martin Klein, Kwasi Konadu, Abena Osseo-Asare, and Ken O'Donnell reviewed the entire manuscript. Students in the history departments of Northern Kentucky University and San Francisco State tested and commented on the manuscript. At Oxford, project editor Shelby Peak managed the production of the manuscript with grace and agility, and Dan Niver, designer, created a visual setting that captures Abina's spirit and humanity. Finally, this book would not have been possible without the support of Charles Cavaliere, editor extraordinaire at Oxford University Press. Charles immediately recognized the project's potential and has worked tirelessly to see it come it to life.

A NOTE ON GHANAIAN IDEOGRAMS

The symbols that begin each part of this book are Ghanaian ***adinkra*** ideograms. They are each accompanied by the Twi (Akan) language proverb or saying that they represent and an English translation. *Adinkra* are usually employed as metaphors, and that is the role they play here. The reader is invited to ponder the complexities of their meanings in relation to the text that follows.

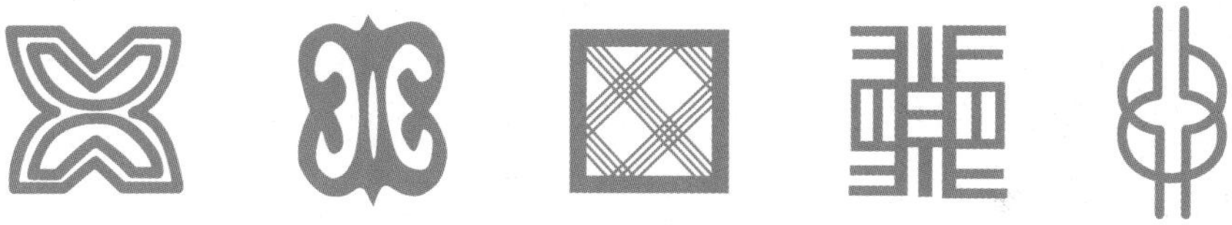

PART I
THE GRAPHIC
HISTORY

FAWOHODIE
"INDEPENDENCE"

CHAPTER 1
ABINA AWAKES

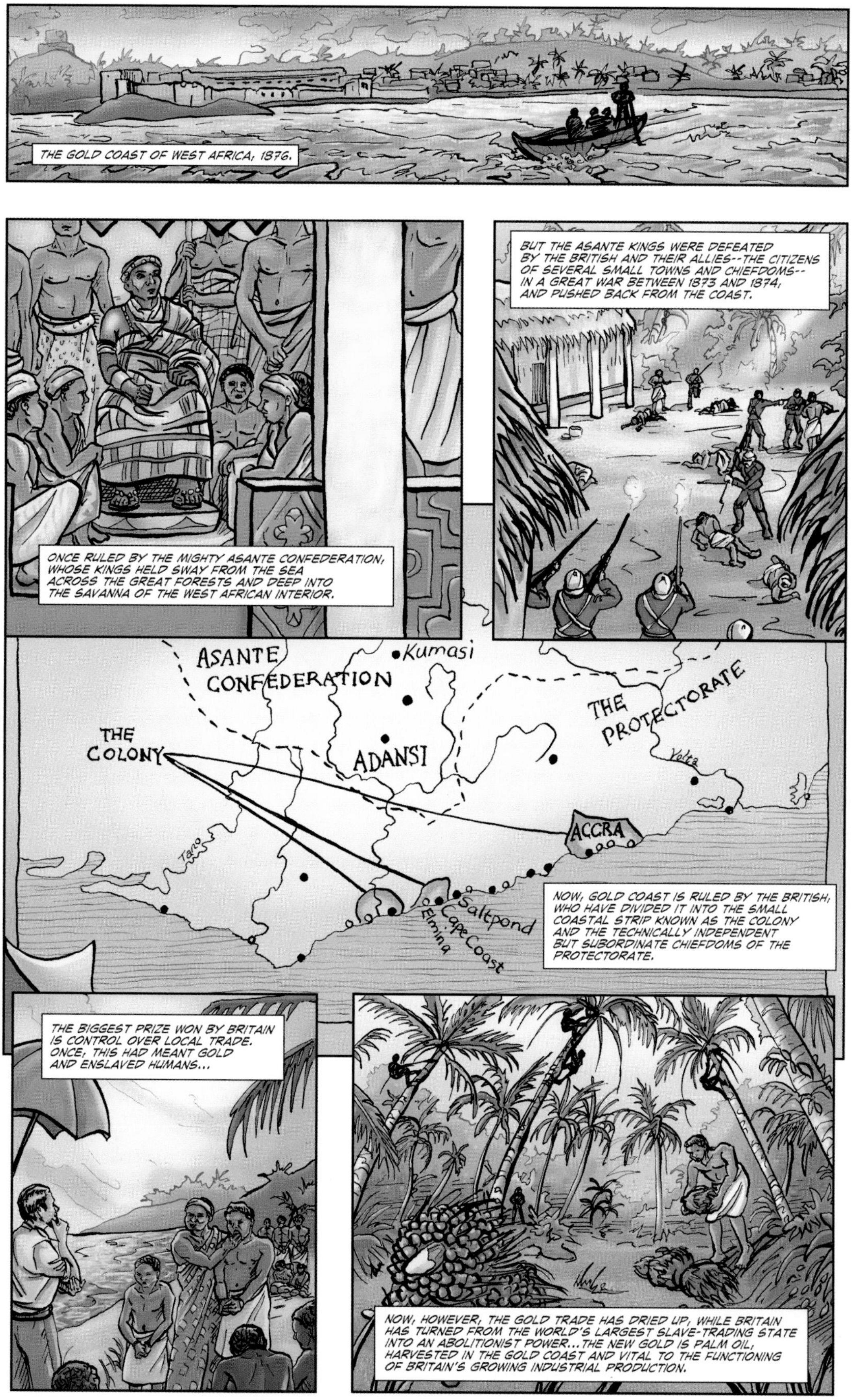
THE GOLD COAST OF WEST AFRICA, 1876.
ONCE RULED BY THE MIGHTY ASANTE CONFEDERATION, WHOSE KINGS HELD SWAY FROM THE SEA ACROSS THE GREAT FORESTS AND DEEP INTO THE SAVANNA OF THE WEST AFRICAN INTERIOR.
BUT THE ASANTE KINGS WERE DEFEATED BY THE BRITISH AND THEIR ALLIES--THE CITIZENS OF SEVERAL SMALL TOWNS AND CHIEFDOMS--IN A GREAT WAR BETWEEN 1873 AND 1874, AND PUSHED BACK FROM THE COAST.
ASANTE CONFEDERATION
Kumasi
THE PROTECTORATE
THE COLONY
ADANSI
Volta
ACCRA
Tano
Saltpond
Cape Coast
Elmina
NOW, GOLD COAST IS RULED BY THE BRITISH, WHO HAVE DIVIDED IT INTO THE SMALL COASTAL STRIP KNOWN AS THE COLONY AND THE TECHNICALLY INDEPENDENT BUT SUBORDINATE CHIEFDOMS OF THE PROTECTORATE.
THE BIGGEST PRIZE WON BY BRITAIN IS CONTROL OVER LOCAL TRADE. ONCE, THIS HAD MEANT GOLD AND ENSLAVED HUMANS...
NOW, HOWEVER, THE GOLD TRADE HAS DRIED UP, WHILE BRITAIN HAS TURNED FROM THE WORLD'S LARGEST SLAVE-TRADING STATE INTO AN ABOLITIONIST POWER...THE NEW GOLD IS PALM OIL, HARVESTED IN THE GOLD COAST AND VITAL TO THE FUNCTIONING OF BRITAIN'S GROWING INDUSTRIAL PRODUCTION.

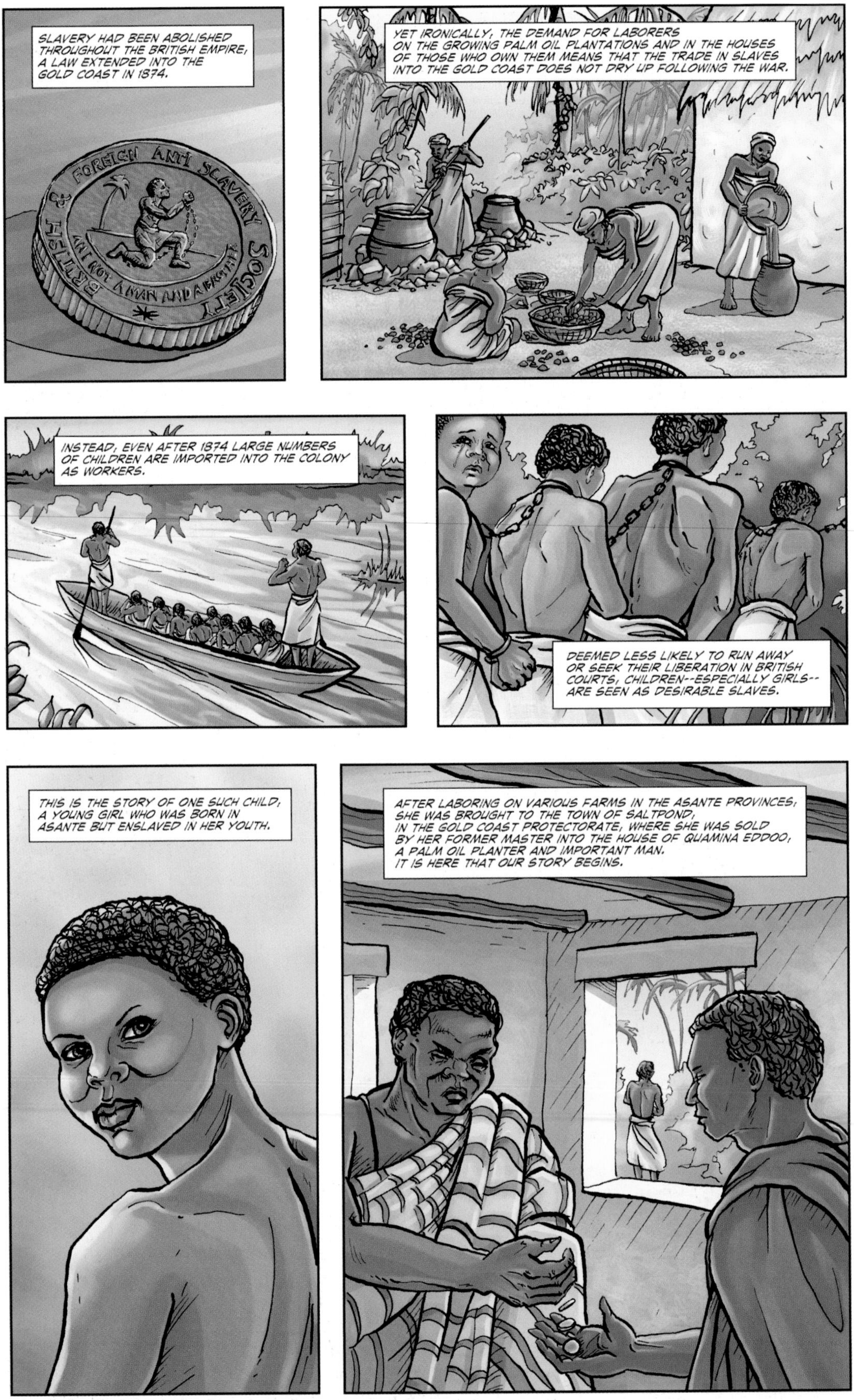
SLAVERY HAD BEEN ABOLISHED THROUGHOUT THE BRITISH EMPIRE, A LAW EXTENDED INTO THE GOLD COAST IN 1874.
BRITISH & FOREIGN ANTI SLAVERY SOCIETY
AM I NOT A MAN AND A BROTHER
YET IRONICALLY, THE DEMAND FOR LABORERS ON THE GROWING PALM OIL PLANTATIONS AND IN THE HOUSES OF THOSE WHO OWN THEM MEANS THAT THE TRADE IN SLAVES INTO THE GOLD COAST DOES NOT DRY UP FOLLOWING THE WAR.
INSTEAD, EVEN AFTER 1874 LARGE NUMBERS OF CHILDREN ARE IMPORTED INTO THE COLONY AS WORKERS.
DEEMED LESS LIKELY TO RUN AWAY OR SEEK THEIR LIBERATION IN BRITISH COURTS, CHILDREN--ESPECIALLY GIRLS--ARE SEEN AS DESIRABLE SLAVES.
THIS IS THE STORY OF ONE SUCH CHILD, A YOUNG GIRL WHO WAS BORN IN ASANTE BUT ENSLAVED IN HER YOUTH.
AFTER LABORING ON VARIOUS FARMS IN THE ASANTE PROVINCES, SHE WAS BROUGHT TO THE TOWN OF SALTPOND, IN THE GOLD COAST PROTECTORATE, WHERE SHE WAS SOLD BY HER FORMER MASTER INTO THE HOUSE OF QUAMINA EDDOO, A PALM OIL PLANTER AND IMPORTANT MAN. IT IS HERE THAT OUR STORY BEGINS.

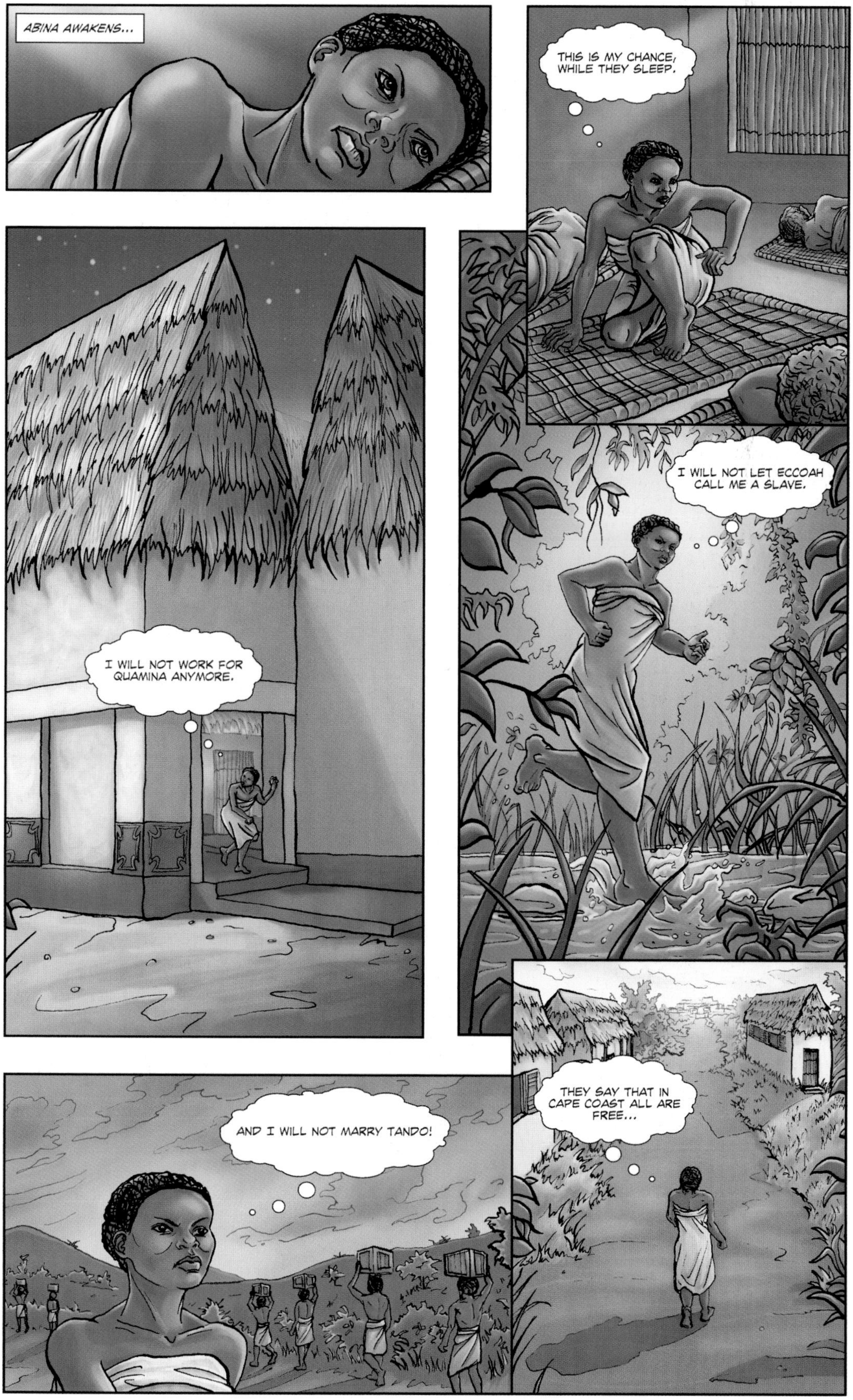
ABINA AWAKENS...
THIS IS MY CHANCE, WHILE THEY SLEEP.
I WILL NOT WORK FOR QUAMINA ANYMORE.
I WILL NOT LET ECCOAH CALL ME A SLAVE.
AND I WILL NOT MARRY TANDO!
THEY SAY THAT IN CAPE COAST ALL ARE FREE...

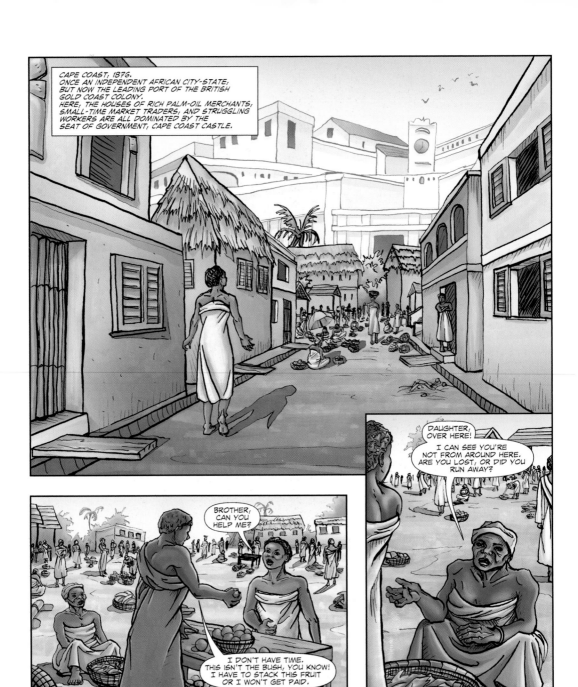

CAPE COAST, 1876.
ONCE AN INDEPENDENT AFRICAN CITY-STATE,
BUT NOW THE LEADING PORT OF THE BRITISH
GOLD COAST COLONY.
HERE, THE HOUSES OF RICH PALM-OIL MERCHANTS,
SMALL-TIME MARKET TRADERS, AND STRUGGLING
WORKERS ARE ALL DOMINATED BY THE
SEAT OF GOVERNMENT; CAPE COAST CASTLE.

DAUGHTER,
OVER HERE!

I CAN SEE YOU'RE
NOT FROM AROUND HERE.
ARE YOU LOST, OR DID YOU
RUN AWAY?

BROTHER,
CAN YOU
HELP ME?

I DON'T HAVE TIME.
THIS ISN'T THE BUSH, YOU KNOW!
I HAVE TO STACK THIS FRUIT
OR I WON'T GET PAID.

I'VE COME HERE
TO BE FREE, AUNTIE.

THEN YOU'LL NEED
PAPERS FROM THE MAGISTRATE.
BUT YOU CAN'T JUST APPROACH HIM.
HE'S AN IMPORTANT MAN.

YOU MUST FIND
SOMEONE TO HELP YOU.
DO YOU KNOW ANYONE HERE?

NO, AUNTIE.

8

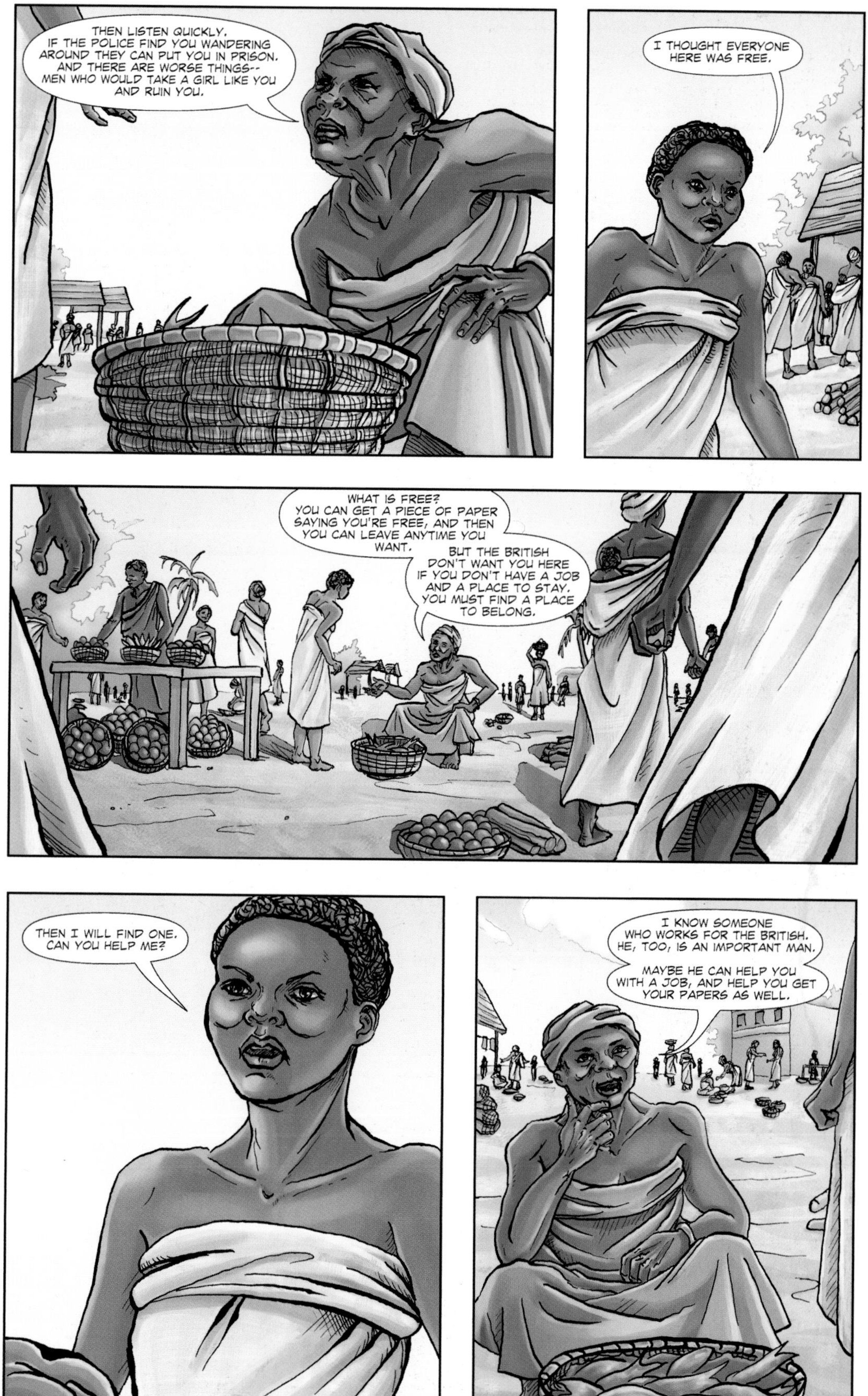
THEN LISTEN QUICKLY. IF THE POLICE FIND YOU WANDERING AROUND THEY CAN PUT YOU IN PRISON. AND THERE ARE WORSE THINGS-- MEN WHO WOULD TAKE A GIRL LIKE YOU AND RUIN YOU.
I THOUGHT EVERYONE HERE WAS FREE.
WHAT IS FREE? YOU CAN GET A PIECE OF PAPER SAYING YOU'RE FREE, AND THEN YOU CAN LEAVE ANYTIME YOU WANT.
BUT THE BRITISH DON'T WANT YOU HERE IF YOU DON'T HAVE A JOB AND A PLACE TO STAY. YOU MUST FIND A PLACE TO BELONG.
THEN I WILL FIND ONE. CAN YOU HELP ME?
I KNOW SOMEONE WHO WORKS FOR THE BRITISH. HE, TOO, IS AN IMPORTANT MAN.
MAYBE HE CAN HELP YOU WITH A JOB, AND HELP YOU GET YOUR PAPERS AS WELL.

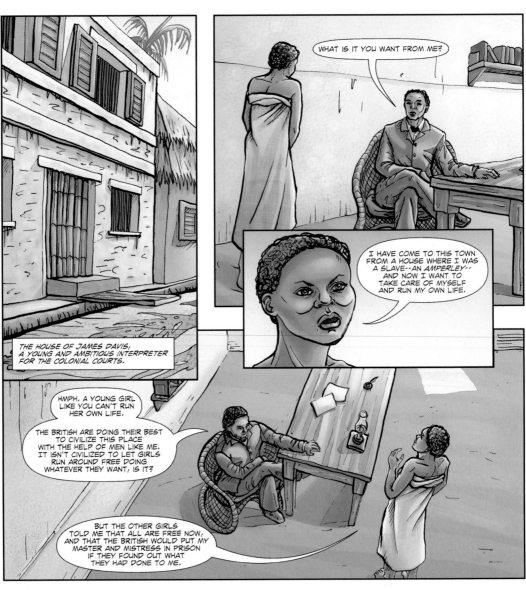

WHAT IS IT YOU WANT FROM ME?

I HAVE COME TO THIS TOWN FROM A HOUSE WHERE I WAS A SLAVE--AN *AMPERLEY*-- AND NOW I WANT TO TAKE CARE OF MYSELF AND RUN MY OWN LIFE.

THE HOUSE OF JAMES DAVIS, A YOUNG AND AMBITIOUS INTERPRETER FOR THE COLONIAL COURTS.

HMPH. A YOUNG GIRL LIKE YOU CAN'T RUN HER OWN LIFE.

THE BRITISH ARE DOING THEIR BEST TO CIVILIZE THIS PLACE WITH THE HELP OF MEN LIKE ME. IT ISN'T CIVILIZED TO LET GIRLS RUN AROUND FREE DOING WHATEVER THEY WANT, IS IT?

BUT THE OTHER GIRLS TOLD ME THAT ALL ARE FREE NOW, AND THAT THE BRITISH WOULD PUT MY MASTER AND MISTRESS IN PRISON IF THEY FOUND OUT WHAT THEY HAD DONE TO ME.

WELL, IT'S TRUE THAT THERE IS NO LEGAL SLAVERY HERE IN CAPE COAST, OR THROUGHOUT THE COLONY AND PROTECTORATE.

BUT LOOK, THE GOVERNMENT DOESN'T HAVE THE MONEY OR THE ABILITY TO ENFORCE THE LAW EVERYWHERE.

COME NOW GIRL, DON'T CRY. I NEED SOMEONE TO HELP OUT AROUND HERE. YOU CAN BE MY MAID, AND MAKE A LITTLE MONEY, AND STAY HERE.

SO LONG AS YOU NEVER LEAVE CAPE COAST, YOU SHOULD BE SAFE FROM YOUR MASTER.

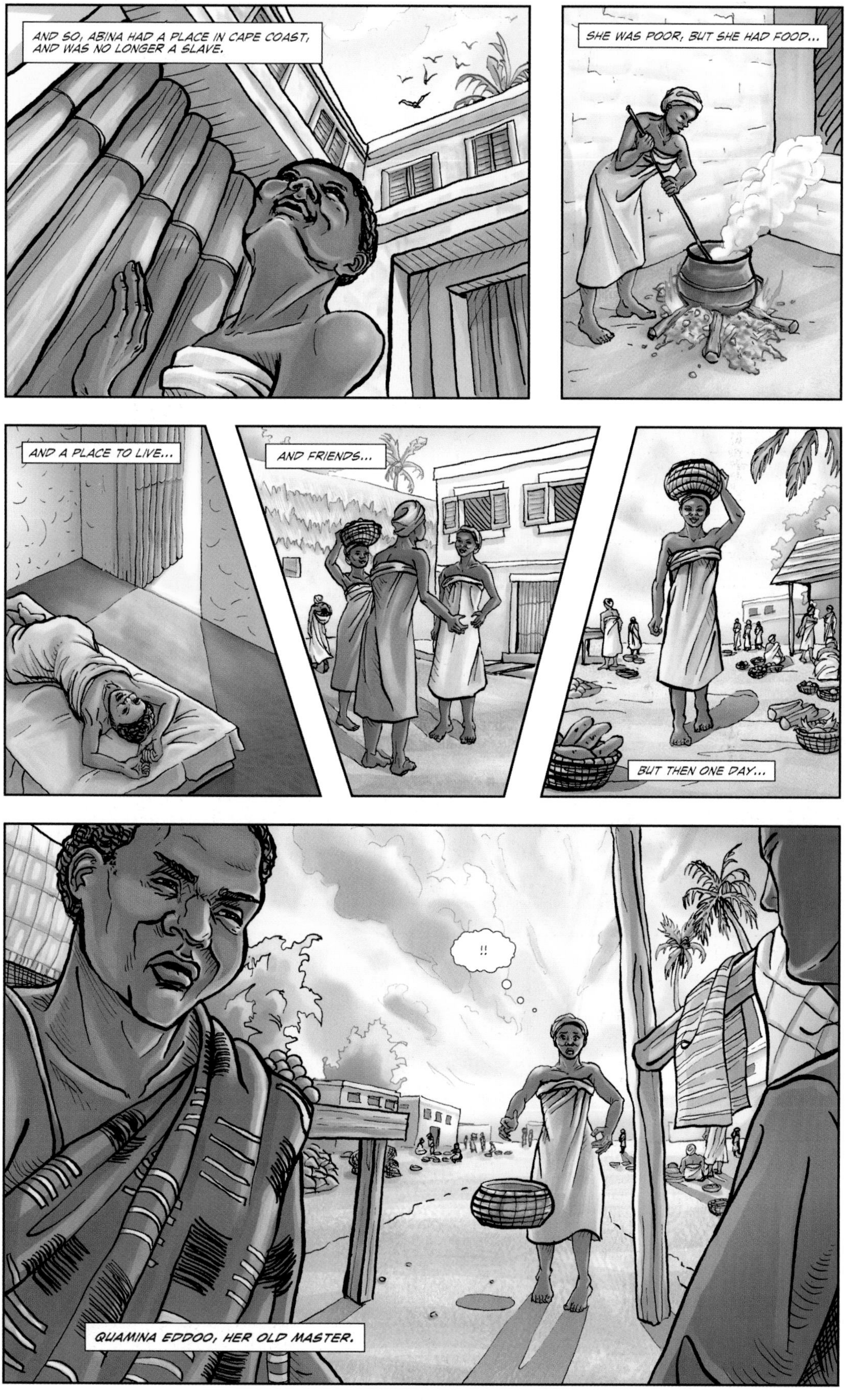
AND SO, ABINA HAD A PLACE IN CAPE COAST, AND WAS NO LONGER A SLAVE.
SHE WAS POOR, BUT SHE HAD FOOD...
AND A PLACE TO LIVE...
AND FRIENDS...
BUT THEN ONE DAY...
!!
QUAMINA EDDOO, HER OLD MASTER.

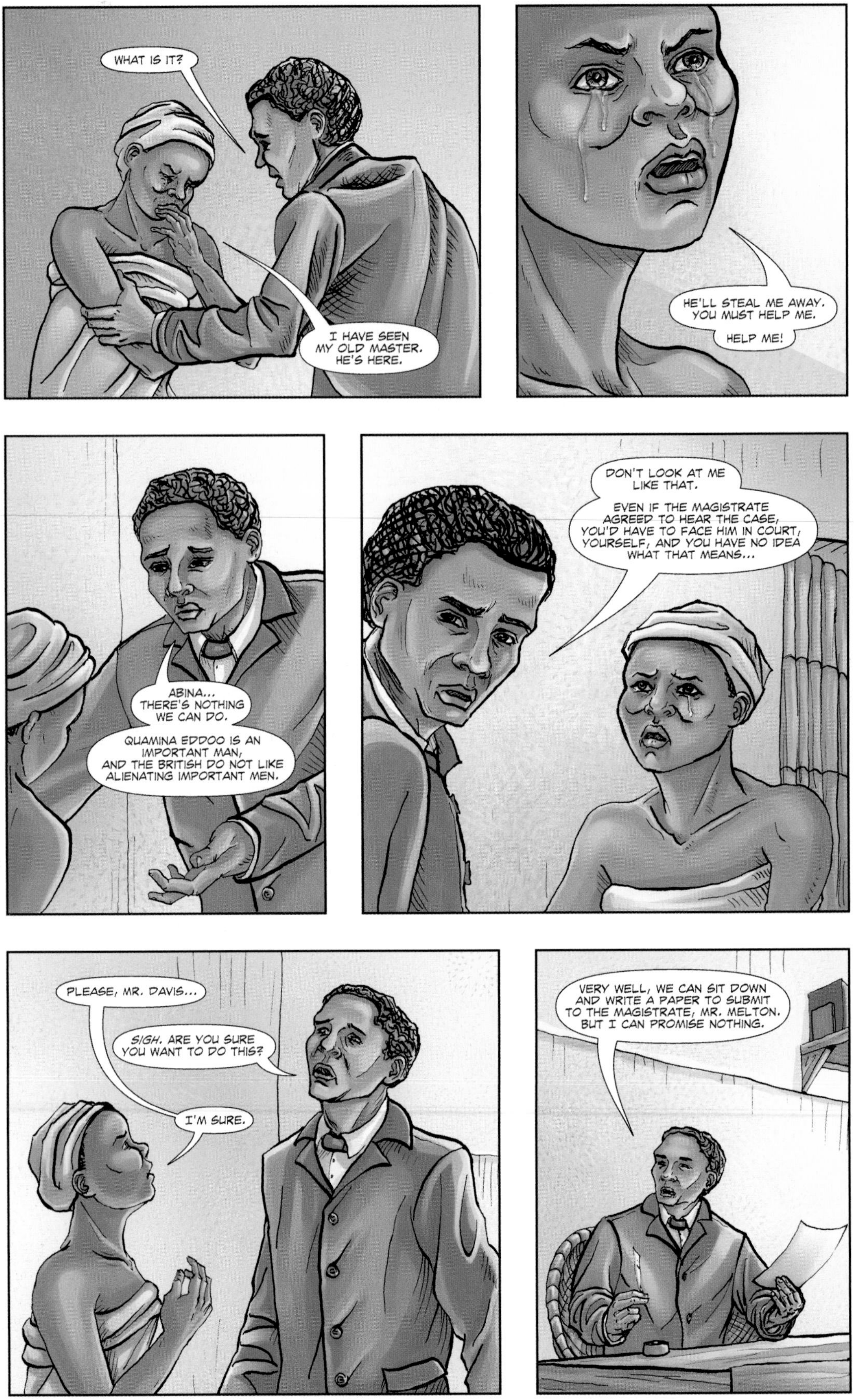
WHAT IS IT?
I HAVE SEEN MY OLD MASTER. HE'S HERE.
HE'LL STEAL ME AWAY. YOU MUST HELP ME.
HELP ME!
ABINA... THERE'S NOTHING WE CAN DO.
QUAMINA EDDOO IS AN IMPORTANT MAN, AND THE BRITISH DO NOT LIKE ALIENATING IMPORTANT MEN.
DON'T LOOK AT ME LIKE THAT.
EVEN IF THE MAGISTRATE AGREED TO HEAR THE CASE, YOU'D HAVE TO FACE HIM IN COURT, YOURSELF, AND YOU HAVE NO IDEA WHAT THAT MEANS...
PLEASE, MR. DAVIS...
SIGH. ARE YOU SURE YOU WANT TO DO THIS?
I'M SURE.
VERY WELL, WE CAN SIT DOWN AND WRITE A PAPER TO SUBMIT TO THE MAGISTRATE, MR. MELTON. BUT I CAN PROMISE NOTHING.

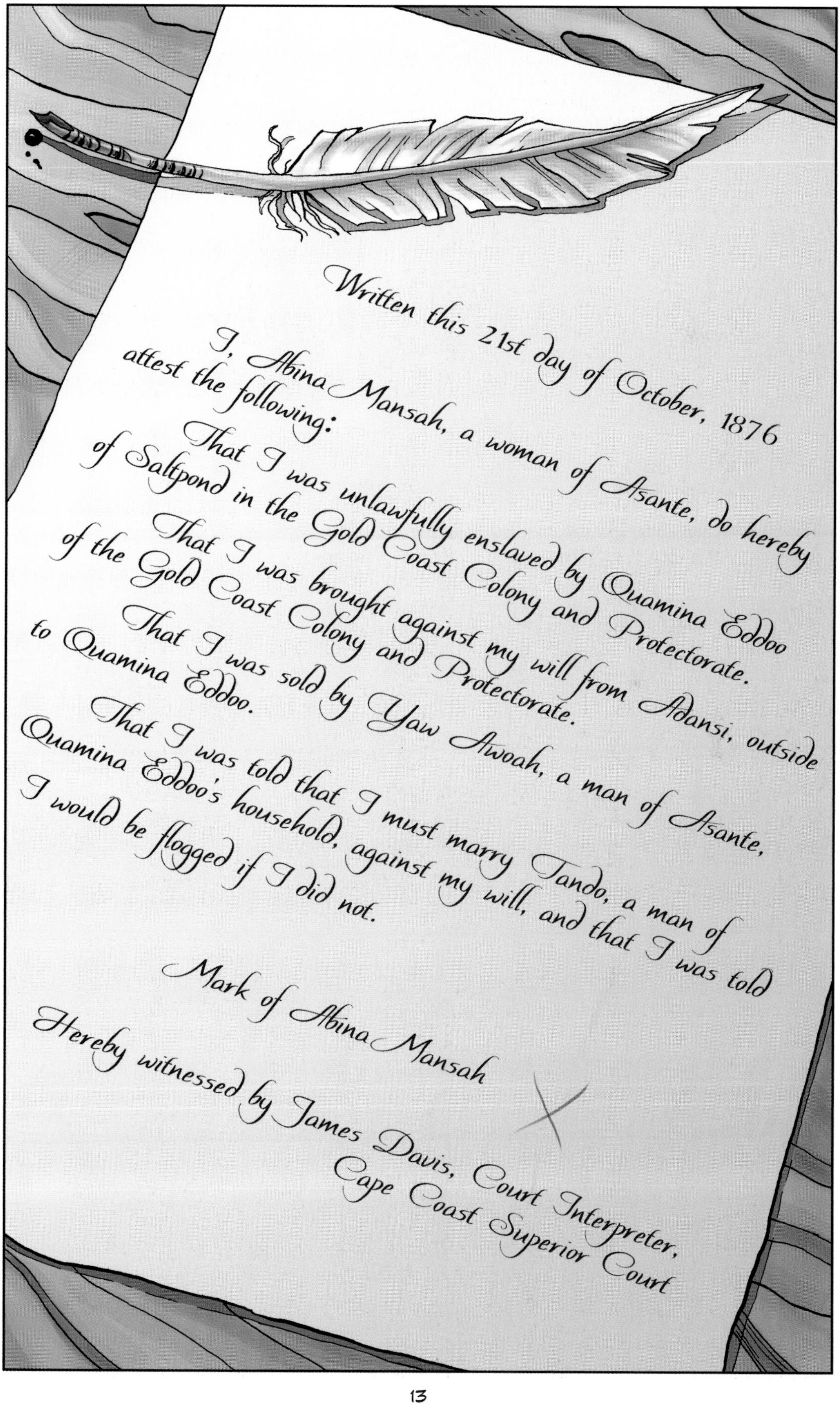
Written this 21st day of October, 1876
I, Abina Mansah, a woman of Asante, do hereby attest the following:
That I was unlawfully enslaved by Quamina Eddoo of Saltpond in the Gold Coast Colony and Protectorate.
That I was brought against my will from Adansi, outside of the Gold Coast Colony and Protectorate.
That I was sold by Yaw Awoah, a man of Asante, to Quamina Eddoo.
That I was told that I must marry Tando, a man of Quamina Eddoo's household, against my will, and that I was told I would be flogged if I did not.
Mark of Abina Mansah
Hereby witnessed by James Davis, Court Interpreter,
Cape Coast Superior Court

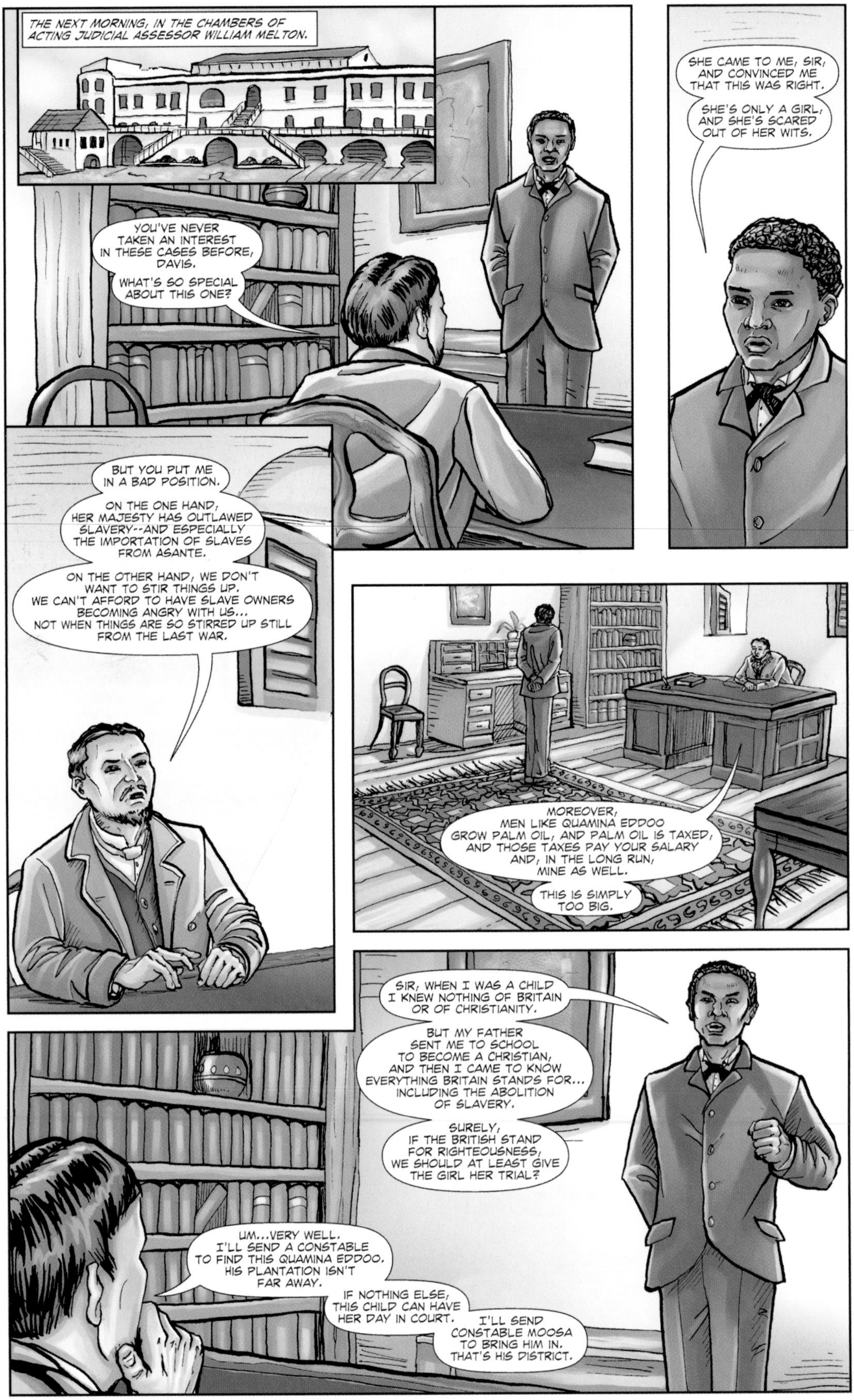

THE NEXT MORNING, IN THE CHAMBERS OF ACTING JUDICIAL ASSESSOR WILLIAM MELTON.
YOU'VE NEVER TAKEN AN INTEREST IN THESE CASES BEFORE, DAVIS.
WHAT'S SO SPECIAL ABOUT THIS ONE?
SHE CAME TO ME, SIR, AND CONVINCED ME THAT THIS WAS RIGHT.
SHE'S ONLY A GIRL, AND SHE'S SCARED OUT OF HER WITS.
BUT YOU PUT ME IN A BAD POSITION.
ON THE ONE HAND, HER MAJESTY HAS OUTLAWED SLAVERY--AND ESPECIALLY THE IMPORTATION OF SLAVES FROM ASANTE.
ON THE OTHER HAND, WE DON'T WANT TO STIR THINGS UP. WE CAN'T AFFORD TO HAVE SLAVE OWNERS BECOMING ANGRY WITH US... NOT WHEN THINGS ARE SO STIRRED UP STILL FROM THE LAST WAR.
MOREOVER, MEN LIKE QUAMINA EDDOO GROW PALM OIL, AND PALM OIL IS TAXED, AND THOSE TAXES PAY YOUR SALARY AND, IN THE LONG RUN, MINE AS WELL.
THIS IS SIMPLY TOO BIG.
SIR, WHEN I WAS A CHILD I KNEW NOTHING OF BRITAIN OR OF CHRISTIANITY.
BUT MY FATHER SENT ME TO SCHOOL TO BECOME A CHRISTIAN, AND THEN I CAME TO KNOW EVERYTHING BRITAIN STANDS FOR... INCLUDING THE ABOLITION OF SLAVERY.
SURELY, IF THE BRITISH STAND FOR RIGHTEOUSNESS, WE SHOULD AT LEAST GIVE THE GIRL HER TRIAL?
UM...VERY WELL. I'LL SEND A CONSTABLE TO FIND THIS QUAMINA EDDOO. HIS PLANTATION ISN'T FAR AWAY.
IF NOTHING ELSE, THIS CHILD CAN HAVE HER DAY IN COURT.
I'LL SEND CONSTABLE MOOSA TO BRING HIM IN. THAT'S HIS DISTRICT.

CHAPTER 2

THE BREAKING OF THE BEADS

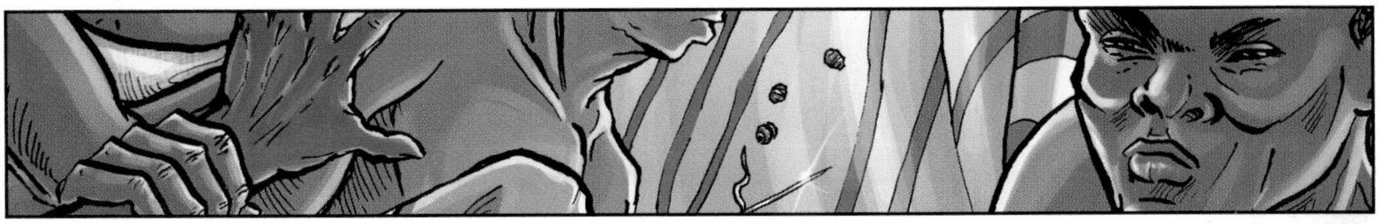

AND SO, A FEW DAYS LATER, AT THE COMPOUND OF QUAMINA EDDOO...

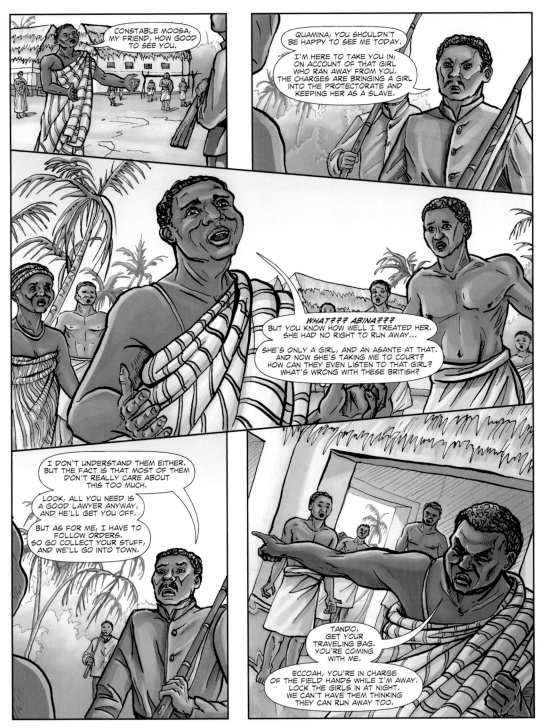

CONSTABLE MOOSA, MY FRIEND, HOW GOOD TO SEE YOU.

QUAMINA, YOU SHOULDN'T BE HAPPY TO SEE ME TODAY.

I'M HERE TO TAKE YOU IN, ON ACCOUNT OF THAT GIRL WHO RAN AWAY FROM YOU. THE CHARGES ARE BRINGING A GIRL INTO THE PROTECTORATE AND KEEPING HER AS A SLAVE.

WHAT??? ABINA??? BUT YOU KNOW HOW WELL I TREATED HER. SHE HAD NO RIGHT TO RUN AWAY...

SHE'S ONLY A GIRL, AND AN ASANTE AT THAT. AND NOW SHE'S TAKING ME TO COURT? HOW CAN THEY EVEN LISTEN TO THAT GIRL? WHAT'S WRONG WITH THESE BRITISH?

I DON'T UNDERSTAND THEM EITHER. BUT THE FACT IS THAT MOST OF THEM DON'T REALLY CARE ABOUT THIS TOO MUCH.

LOOK, ALL YOU NEED IS A GOOD LAWYER ANYWAY, AND HE'LL GET YOU OFF.

BUT AS FOR ME, I HAVE TO FOLLOW ORDERS. SO GO COLLECT YOUR STUFF, AND WE'LL GO INTO TOWN.

TANDO, GET YOUR TRAVELING BAG. YOU'RE COMING WITH ME.

ECCOAH, YOU'RE IN CHARGE OF THE FIELD HANDS WHILE I'M AWAY. LOCK THE GIRLS IN AT NIGHT. WE CAN'T HAVE THEM THINKING THEY CAN RUN AWAY TOO.

17

DON'T WORRY, MY BROTHER. YOU CAN COUNT ON ME.

I'LL MAKE SURE THEY DON'T FOLLOW IN THE FOOTSTEPS OF THAT LITTLE SLAVE!

THE HOME OF JAMES HUTTON BREW, DESCENDANT OF SCOTTISH TRADERS AND AFRICAN CHIEFS. AN EDUCATED MAN, A CHRISTIAN, AND A SOMETIME EMPLOYEE OF THE COLONIAL GOVERNMENT.

HE IS ONE OF THE FEW TRAINED LAWYERS IN ACCRA.

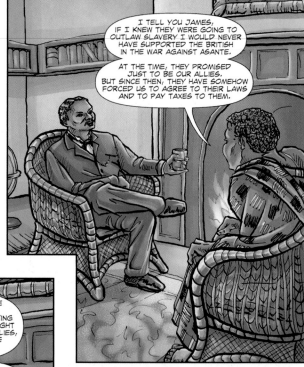

I TELL YOU JAMES, IF I KNEW THEY WERE GOING TO OUTLAW SLAVERY I WOULD NEVER HAVE SUPPORTED THE BRITISH IN THE WAR AGAINST ASANTE.

AT THE TIME, THEY PROMISED JUST TO BE OUR ALLIES. BUT SINCE THEN, THEY HAVE SOMEHOW FORCED US TO AGREE TO THEIR LAWS AND TO PAY TAXES TO THEM.

WELL, YOU HAVE TO BLAME THE AHENFO--THE CHIEFS. ONE MOMENT THEY WERE SAYING THEY WERE JUST GOING TO FIGHT ALONGSIDE THE BRITISH AS ALLIES, AND THE NEXT THEY AGREE TO FOLLOW ALL OF THESE LAWS.

I GUESS IT'S BECAUSE THEY'RE STILL AFRAID OF ASANTE, BUT I ALSO HEAR SOME OF THEM ARE ACCEPTING SALARIES AND GIFTS FROM THE BRITISH.

BUT FOR WHATEVER REASON, THE FACT IS THAT YOUR CHIEF, LIKE THE OTHERS, AGREED THAT SLAVERY IS OUTLAWED AND THAT THE BRITISH COURTS CAN TRY ANYONE WHO KEEPS A SLAVE.

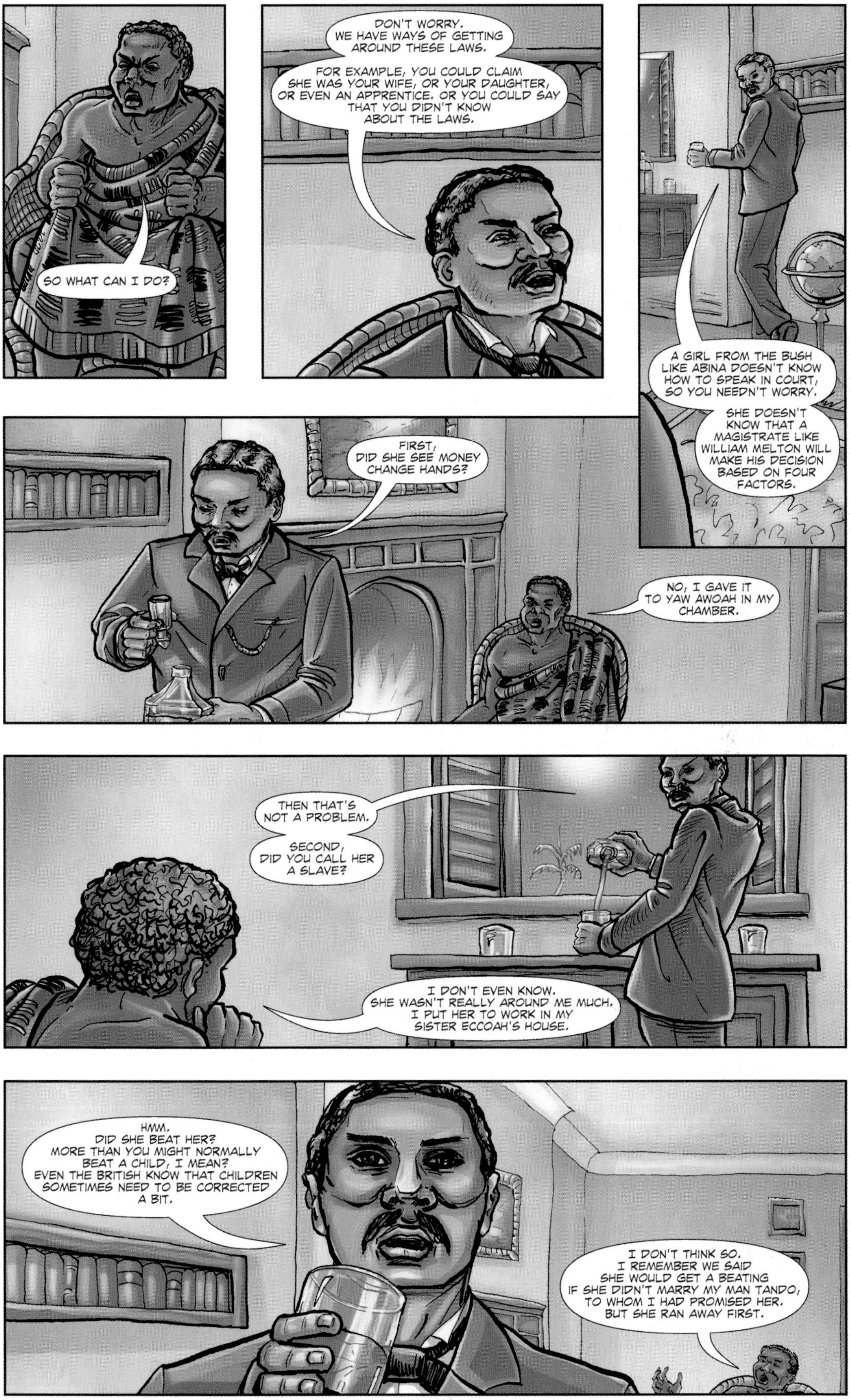
SO WHAT CAN I DO?
DON'T WORRY. WE HAVE WAYS OF GETTING AROUND THESE LAWS.
FOR EXAMPLE, YOU COULD CLAIM SHE WAS YOUR WIFE, OR YOUR DAUGHTER, OR EVEN AN APPRENTICE. OR YOU COULD SAY THAT YOU DIDN'T KNOW ABOUT THE LAWS.
A GIRL FROM THE BUSH LIKE ABINA DOESN'T KNOW HOW TO SPEAK IN COURT, SO YOU NEEDN'T WORRY.
SHE DOESN'T KNOW THAT A MAGISTRATE LIKE WILLIAM MELTON WILL MAKE HIS DECISION BASED ON FOUR FACTORS.
FIRST, DID SHE SEE MONEY CHANGE HANDS?
NO, I GAVE IT TO YAW AWOAH IN MY CHAMBER.
THEN THAT'S NOT A PROBLEM.
SECOND, DID YOU CALL HER A SLAVE?
I DON'T EVEN KNOW. SHE WASN'T REALLY AROUND ME MUCH. I PUT HER TO WORK IN MY SISTER ECCOAH'S HOUSE.
HMM. DID SHE BEAT HER? MORE THAN YOU MIGHT NORMALLY BEAT A CHILD, I MEAN? EVEN THE BRITISH KNOW THAT CHILDREN SOMETIMES NEED TO BE CORRECTED A BIT.
I DON'T THINK SO. I REMEMBER WE SAID SHE WOULD GET A BEATING IF SHE DIDN'T MARRY MY MAN TANDO, TO WHOM I HAD PROMISED HER. BUT SHE RAN AWAY FIRST.

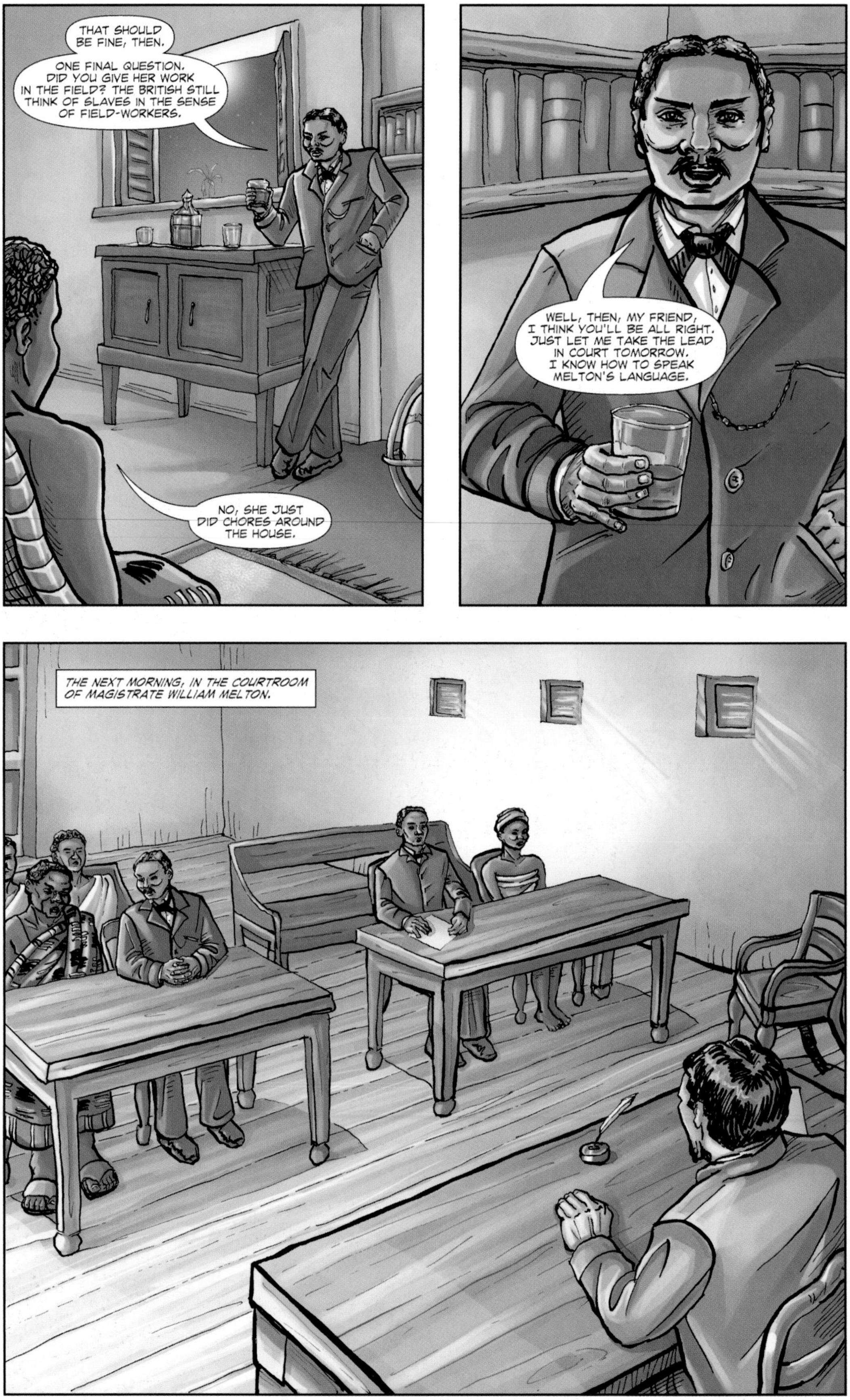
THAT SHOULD BE FINE, THEN.
ONE FINAL QUESTION. DID YOU GIVE HER WORK IN THE FIELD? THE BRITISH STILL THINK OF SLAVES IN THE SENSE OF FIELD-WORKERS.
NO, SHE JUST DID CHORES AROUND THE HOUSE.
WELL, THEN, MY FRIEND, I THINK YOU'LL BE ALL RIGHT. JUST LET ME TAKE THE LEAD IN COURT TOMORROW. I KNOW HOW TO SPEAK MELTON'S LANGUAGE.
THE NEXT MORNING, IN THE COURTROOM OF MAGISTRATE WILLIAM MELTON.

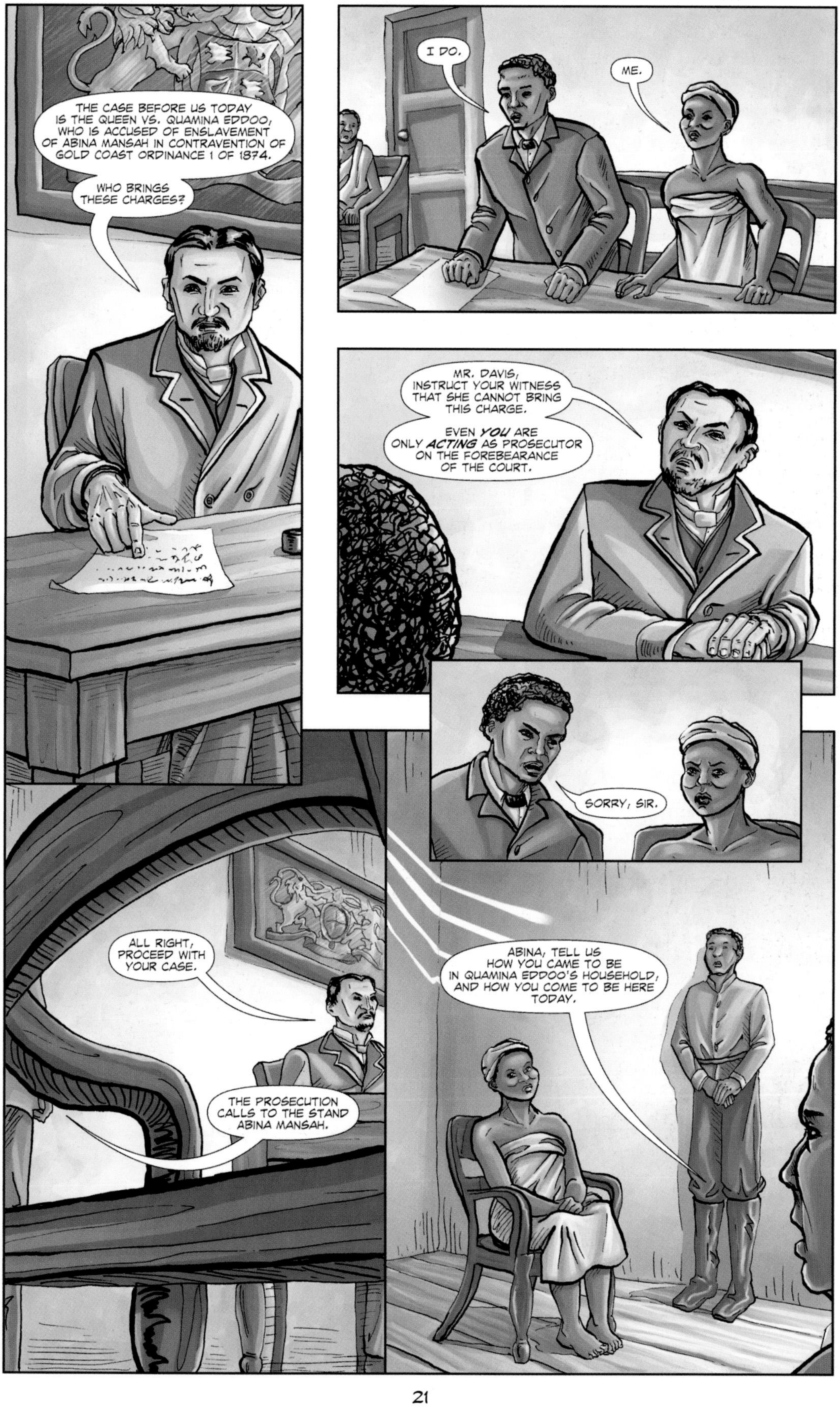
THE CASE BEFORE US TODAY IS THE QUEEN VS. QUAMINA EDDOO, WHO IS ACCUSED OF ENSLAVEMENT OF ABINA MANSAH IN CONTRAVENTION OF GOLD COAST ORDINANCE 1 OF 1874.
WHO BRINGS THESE CHARGES?
I DO.
ME.
MR. DAVIS, INSTRUCT YOUR WITNESS THAT SHE CANNOT BRING THIS CHARGE.
EVEN *YOU* ARE ONLY *ACTING* AS PROSECUTOR ON THE FOREBEARANCE OF THE COURT.
SORRY, SIR.
ALL RIGHT, PROCEED WITH YOUR CASE.
THE PROSECUTION CALLS TO THE STAND ABINA MANSAH.
ABINA, TELL US HOW YOU CAME TO BE IN QUAMINA EDDOO'S HOUSEHOLD, AND HOW YOU COME TO BE HERE TODAY.

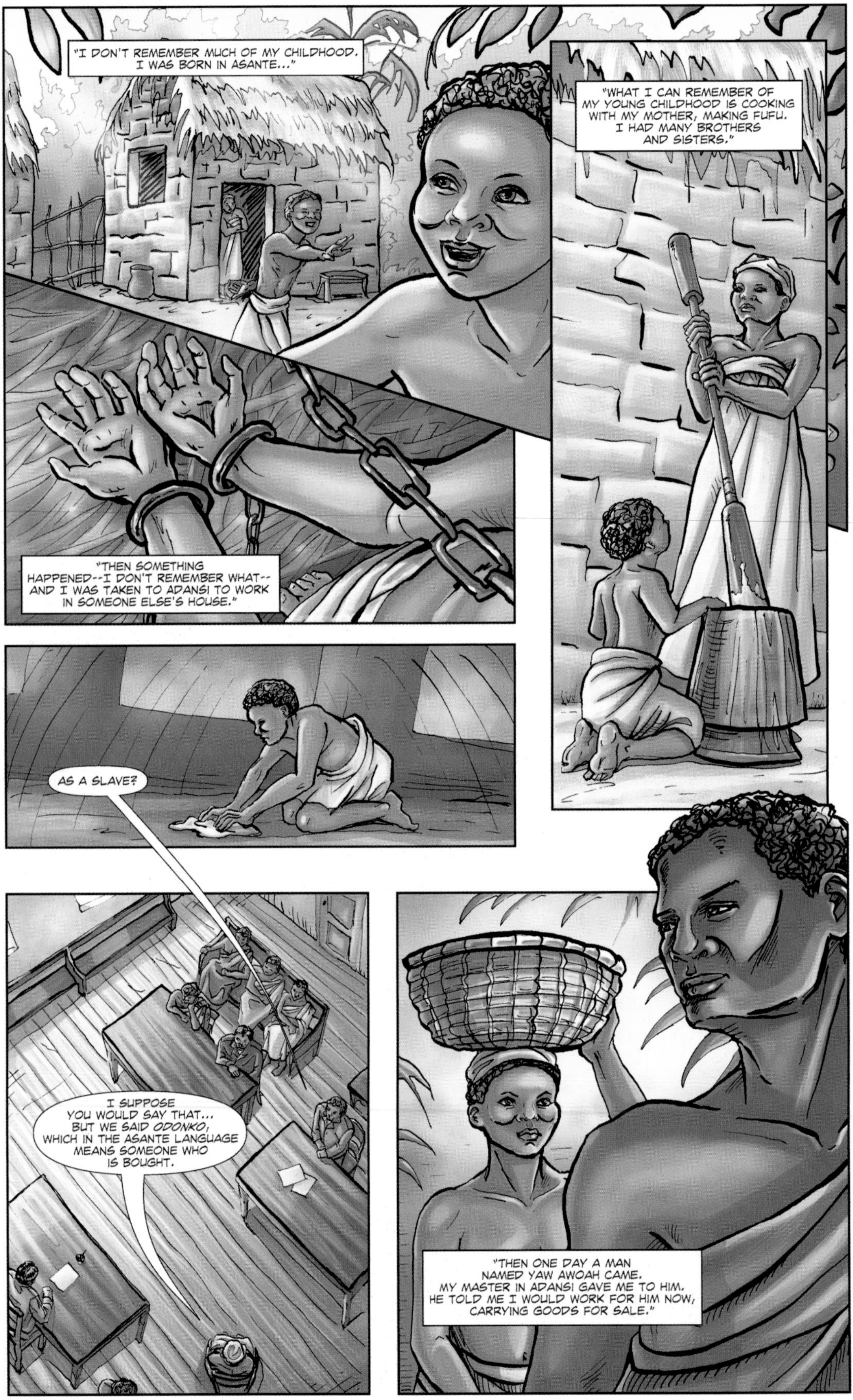
"I DON'T REMEMBER MUCH OF MY CHILDHOOD. I WAS BORN IN ASANTE..."
"WHAT I CAN REMEMBER OF MY YOUNG CHILDHOOD IS COOKING WITH MY MOTHER, MAKING FUFU. I HAD MANY BROTHERS AND SISTERS."
"THEN SOMETHING HAPPENED--I DON'T REMEMBER WHAT--AND I WAS TAKEN TO ADANSI TO WORK IN SOMEONE ELSE'S HOUSE."
AS A SLAVE?
I SUPPOSE YOU WOULD SAY THAT... BUT WE SAID *ODONKO*, WHICH IN THE ASANTE LANGUAGE MEANS SOMEONE WHO IS BOUGHT.
"THEN ONE DAY A MAN NAMED YAW AWOAH CAME. MY MASTER IN ADANSI GAVE ME TO HIM. HE TOLD ME I WOULD WORK FOR HIM NOW, CARRYING GOODS FOR SALE."

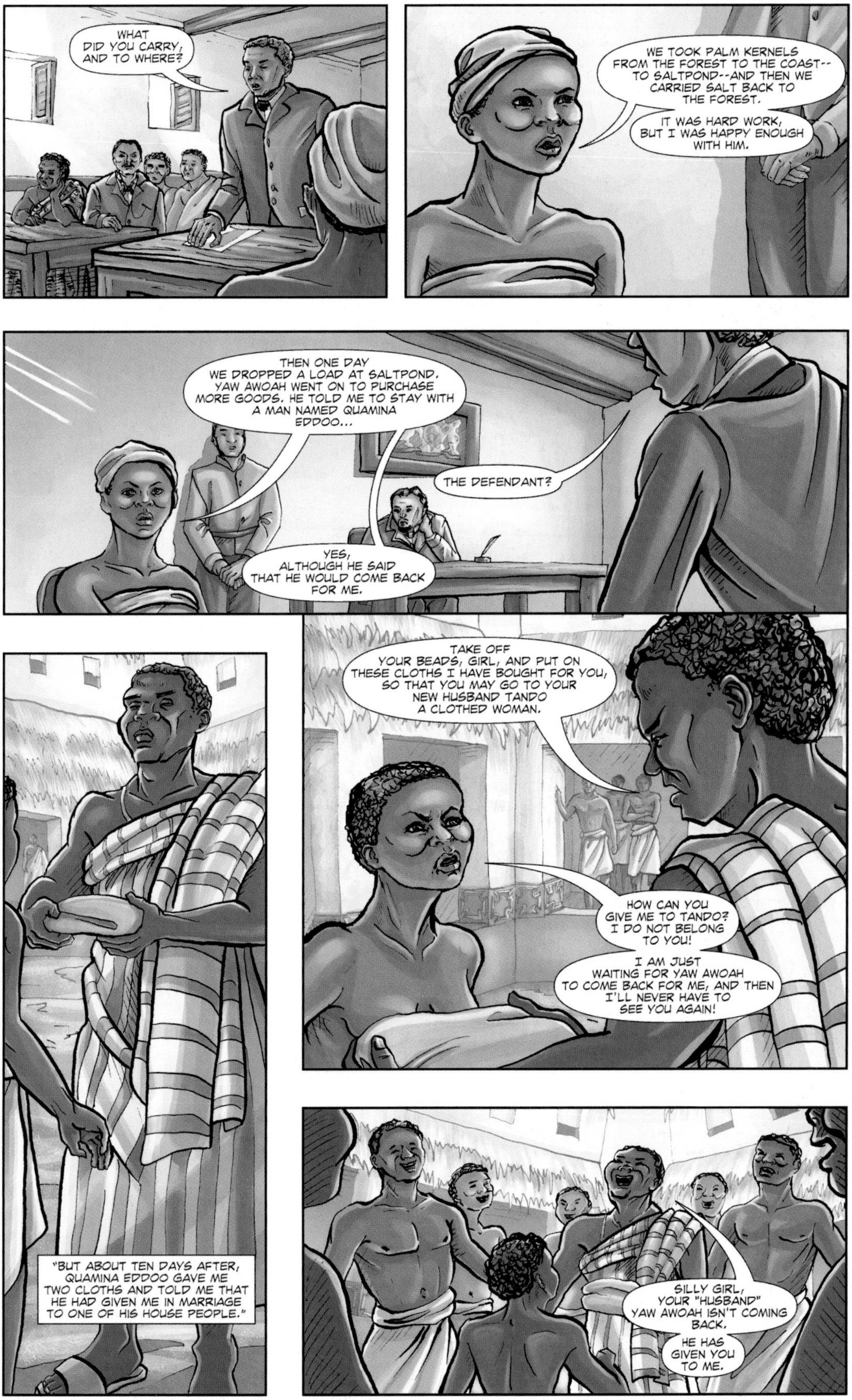
WHAT DID YOU CARRY, AND TO WHERE?
WE TOOK PALM KERNELS FROM THE FOREST TO THE COAST-- TO SALTPOND--AND THEN WE CARRIED SALT BACK TO THE FOREST.
IT WAS HARD WORK, BUT I WAS HAPPY ENOUGH WITH HIM.
THEN ONE DAY WE DROPPED A LOAD AT SALTPOND. YAW AWOAH WENT ON TO PURCHASE MORE GOODS. HE TOLD ME TO STAY WITH A MAN NAMED QUAMINA EDDOO...
THE DEFENDANT?
YES, ALTHOUGH HE SAID THAT HE WOULD COME BACK FOR ME.
"BUT ABOUT TEN DAYS AFTER, QUAMINA EDDOO GAVE ME TWO CLOTHS AND TOLD ME THAT HE HAD GIVEN ME IN MARRIAGE TO ONE OF HIS HOUSE PEOPLE."
TAKE OFF YOUR BEADS, GIRL, AND PUT ON THESE CLOTHS I HAVE BOUGHT FOR YOU, SO THAT YOU MAY GO TO YOUR NEW HUSBAND TANDO A CLOTHED WOMAN.
HOW CAN YOU GIVE ME TO TANDO? I DO NOT BELONG TO YOU!
I AM JUST WAITING FOR YAW AWOAH TO COME BACK FOR ME, AND THEN I'LL NEVER HAVE TO SEE YOU AGAIN!
SILLY GIRL, YOUR "HUSBAND" YAW AWOAH ISN'T COMING BACK.
HE HAS GIVEN YOU TO ME.

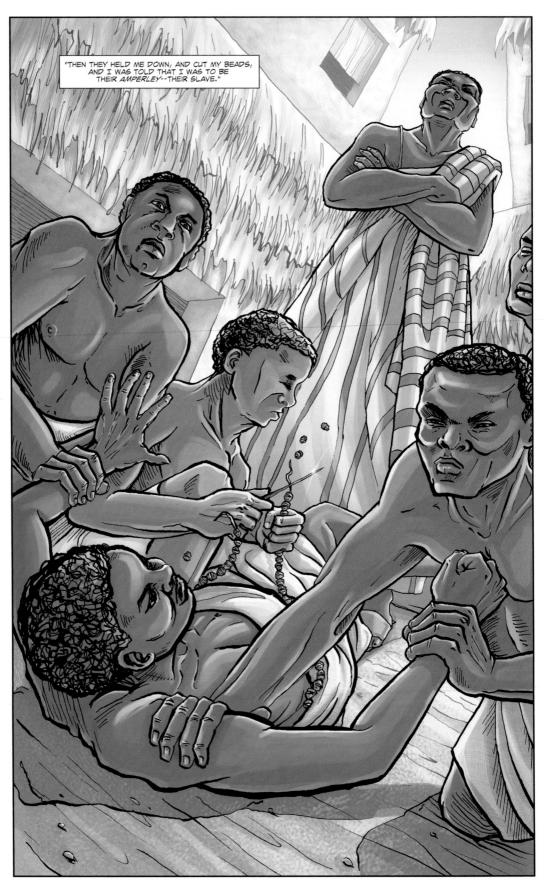

"THEN THEY HELD ME DOWN, AND CUT MY BEADS, AND I WAS TOLD THAT I WAS TO BE THEIR *AMPERLEY*--THEIR SLAVE."

CHAPTER 3
THE TRUTH

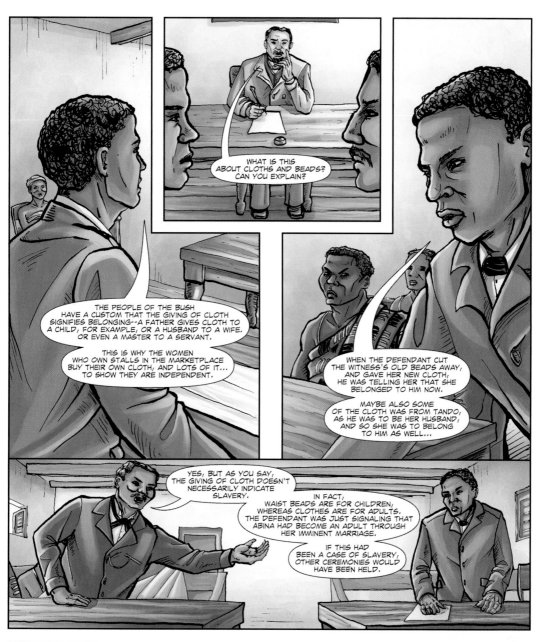

WHAT IS THIS ABOUT CLOTHS AND BEADS? CAN YOU EXPLAIN?

THE PEOPLE OF THE BUSH HAVE A CUSTOM THAT THE GIVING OF CLOTH SIGNIFIES BELONGING--A FATHER GIVES CLOTH TO A CHILD, FOR EXAMPLE, OR A HUSBAND TO A WIFE. OR EVEN A MASTER TO A SERVANT.

THIS IS WHY THE WOMEN WHO OWN STALLS IN THE MARKETPLACE BUY THEIR OWN CLOTH, AND LOTS OF IT... TO SHOW THEY ARE INDEPENDENT.

WHEN THE DEFENDANT CUT THE WITNESS'S OLD BEADS AWAY, AND GAVE HER NEW CLOTH, HE WAS TELLING HER THAT SHE BELONGED TO HIM NOW.

MAYBE ALSO SOME OF THE CLOTH WAS FROM TANDO, AS HE WAS TO BE HER HUSBAND, AND SO SHE WAS TO BELONG TO HIM AS WELL...

YES, BUT AS YOU SAY, THE GIVING OF CLOTH DOESN'T NECESSARILY INDICATE SLAVERY.

IN FACT, WAIST BEADS ARE FOR CHILDREN, WHEREAS CLOTHES ARE FOR ADULTS. THE DEFENDANT WAS JUST SIGNALING THAT ABINA HAD BECOME AN ADULT THROUGH HER IMMINENT MARRIAGE.

IF THIS HAD BEEN A CASE OF SLAVERY, OTHER CEREMONIES WOULD HAVE BEEN HELD.

ABINA, YOU HAVE SEEN HOW SLAVES ARE SOLD, RIGHT? ARE THERE USUALLY CEREMONIES WHEN THEY ARE HANDED OVER?

YES.

WERE ANY OF THESE OBSERVED WHEN YOU WERE ALLEGEDLY SOLD TO EDDOO?

THE ONLY THING THAT WAS DONE WAS THE CUTTING OF THE BEADS.

27

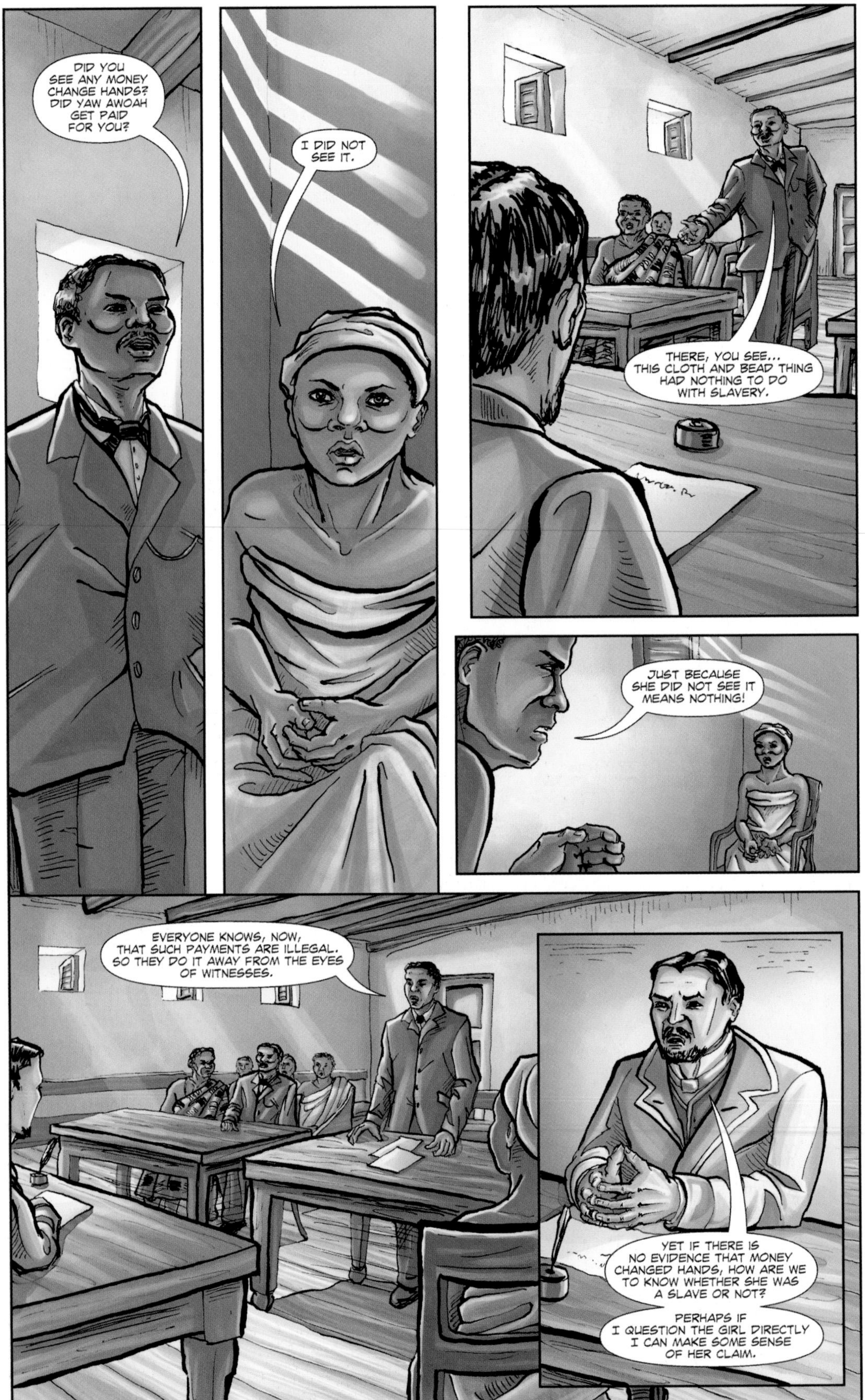
DID YOU SEE ANY MONEY CHANGE HANDS? DID YAW AWOAH GET PAID FOR YOU?
I DID NOT SEE IT.
THERE, YOU SEE... THIS CLOTH AND BEAD THING HAD NOTHING TO DO WITH SLAVERY.
JUST BECAUSE SHE DID NOT SEE IT MEANS NOTHING!
EVERYONE KNOWS, NOW, THAT SUCH PAYMENTS ARE ILLEGAL. SO THEY DO IT AWAY FROM THE EYES OF WITNESSES.
YET IF THERE IS NO EVIDENCE THAT MONEY CHANGED HANDS, HOW ARE WE TO KNOW WHETHER SHE WAS A SLAVE OR NOT?
PERHAPS IF I QUESTION THE GIRL DIRECTLY I CAN MAKE SOME SENSE OF HER CLAIM.

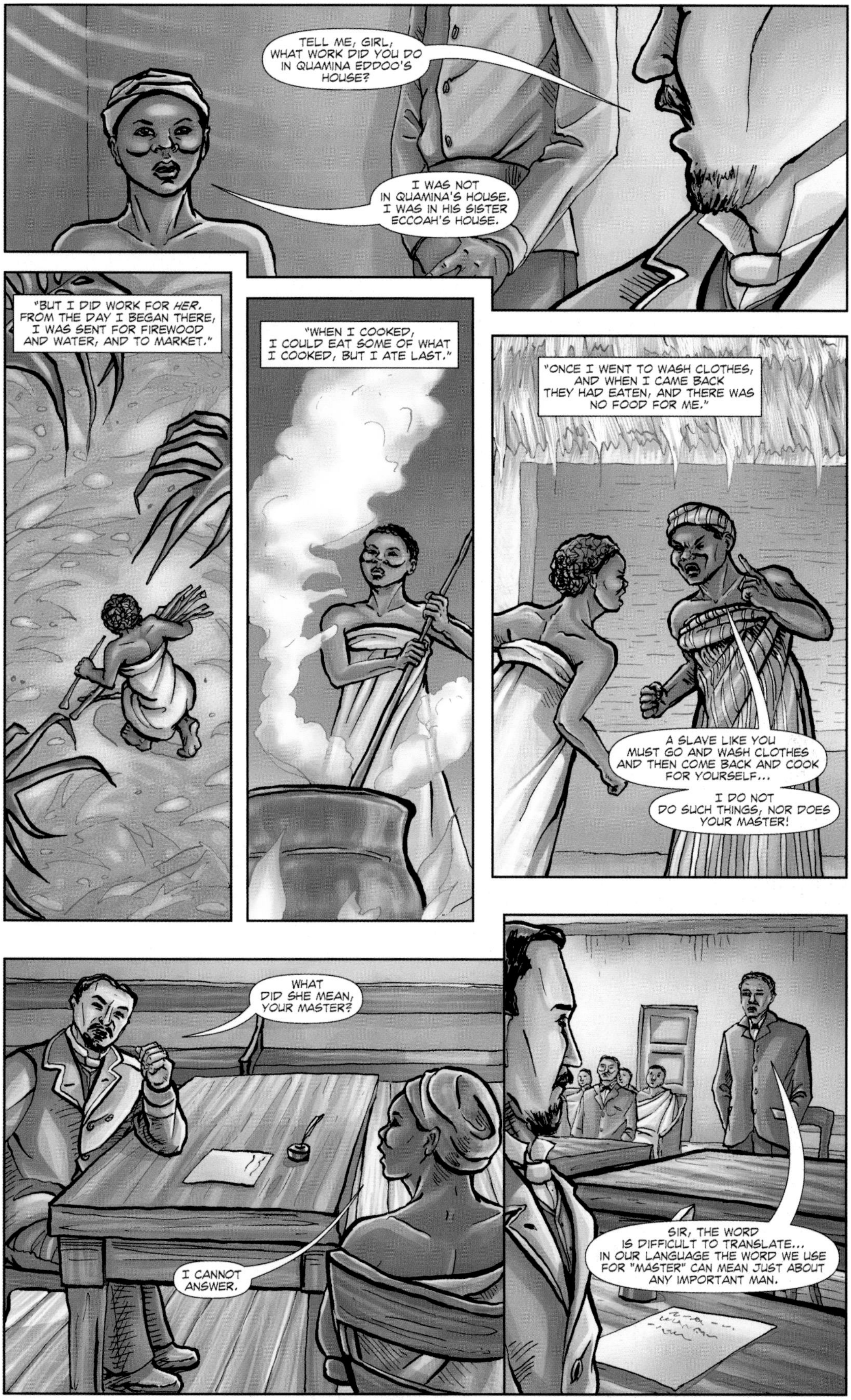
TELL ME, GIRL, WHAT WORK DID YOU DO IN QUAMINA EDDOO'S HOUSE?
I WAS NOT IN QUAMINA'S HOUSE. I WAS IN HIS SISTER ECCOAH'S HOUSE.
"BUT I DID WORK FOR *HER*. FROM THE DAY I BEGAN THERE, I WAS SENT FOR FIREWOOD AND WATER, AND TO MARKET."
"WHEN I COOKED, I COULD EAT SOME OF WHAT I COOKED, BUT I ATE LAST."
"ONCE I WENT TO WASH CLOTHES, AND WHEN I CAME BACK THEY HAD EATEN, AND THERE WAS NO FOOD FOR ME."
A SLAVE LIKE YOU MUST GO AND WASH CLOTHES AND THEN COME BACK AND COOK FOR YOURSELF...
I DO NOT DO SUCH THINGS, NOR DOES YOUR MASTER!
WHAT DID SHE MEAN, YOUR MASTER?
I CANNOT ANSWER.
SIR, THE WORD IS DIFFICULT TO TRANSLATE... IN OUR LANGUAGE THE WORD WE USE FOR "MASTER" CAN MEAN JUST ABOUT ANY IMPORTANT MAN.

ALL RIGHT, BUT DURING THESE TIMES YOU WERE WITH ECCOAH AND QUAMINA EDDOO, WERE YOU COMPELLED TO WORK AGAINST YOUR WILL?

WHAT DOES IT MEAN, AGAINST YOUR WILL?

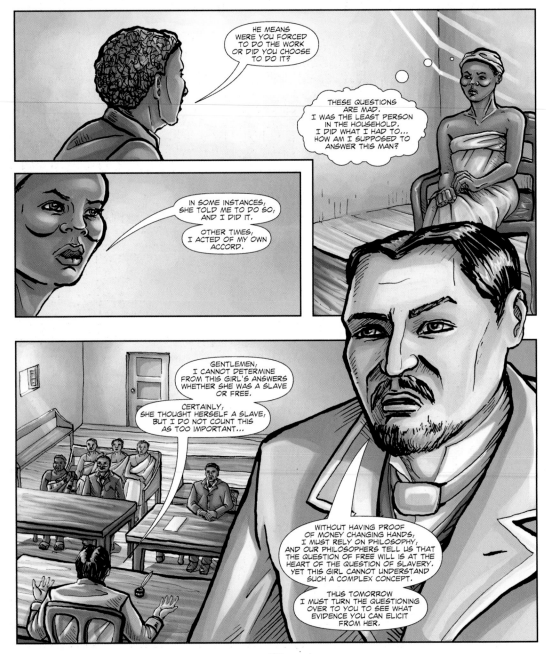

HE MEANS WERE YOU FORCED TO DO THE WORK OR DID YOU CHOOSE TO DO IT?

THESE QUESTIONS ARE MAD. I WAS THE LEAST PERSON IN THE HOUSEHOLD. I DID WHAT I HAD TO... HOW AM I SUPPOSED TO ANSWER THIS MAN?

IN SOME INSTANCES, SHE TOLD ME TO DO SO, AND I DID IT.

OTHER TIMES, I ACTED OF MY OWN ACCORD.

GENTLEMEN, I CANNOT DETERMINE FROM THIS GIRL'S ANSWERS WHETHER SHE WAS A SLAVE OR FREE.

CERTAINLY, SHE THOUGHT HERSELF A SLAVE, BUT I DO NOT COUNT THIS AS TOO IMPORTANT...

WITHOUT HAVING PROOF OF MONEY CHANGING HANDS, I MUST RELY ON PHILOSOPHY, AND OUR PHILOSOPHERS TELL US THAT THE QUESTION OF FREE WILL IS AT THE HEART OF THE QUESTION OF SLAVERY. YET THIS GIRL CANNOT UNDERSTAND SUCH A COMPLEX CONCEPT.

THUS TOMORROW I MUST TURN THE QUESTIONING OVER TO YOU TO SEE WHAT EVIDENCE YOU CAN ELICIT FROM HER.

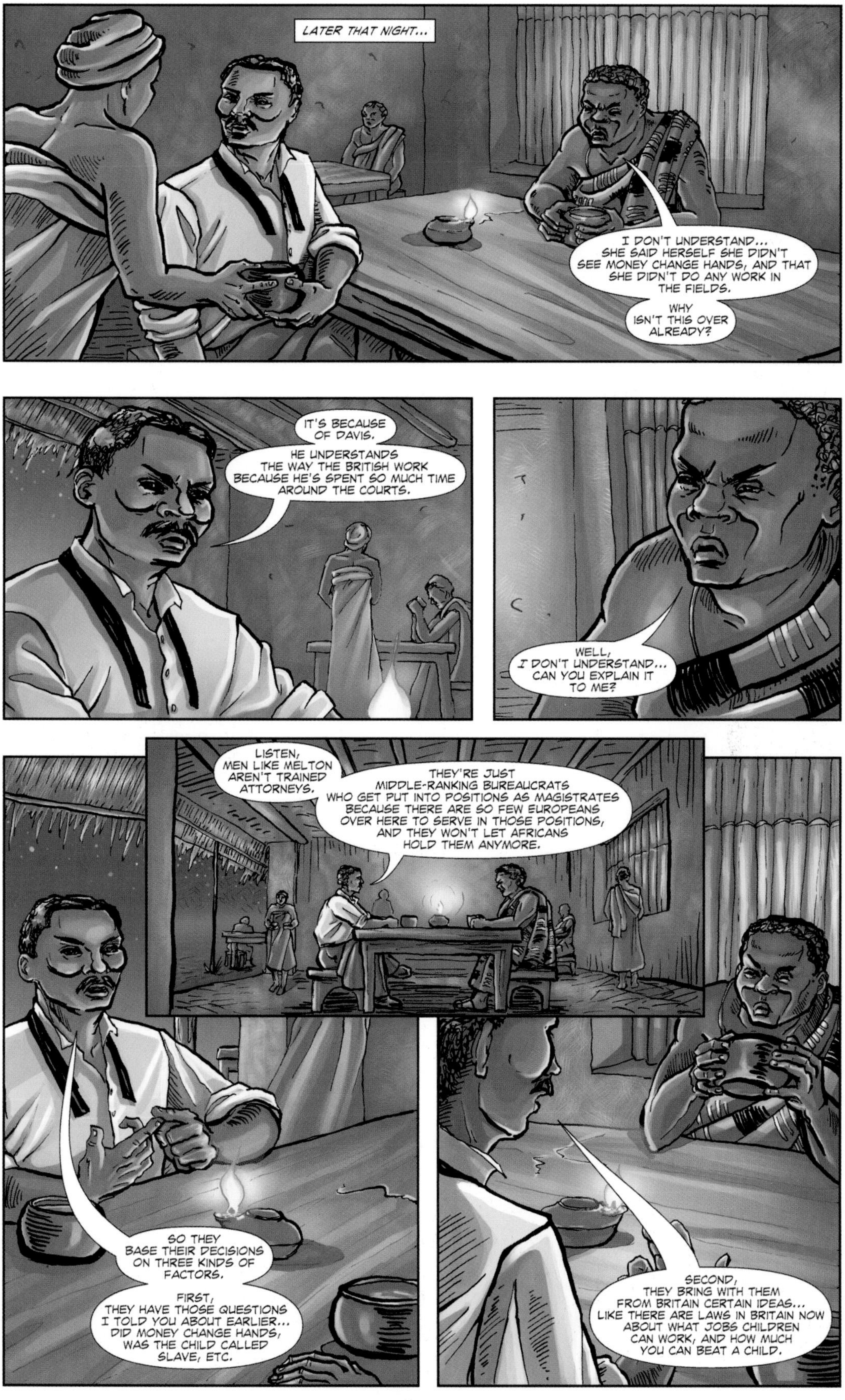
LATER THAT NIGHT...
I DON'T UNDERSTAND... SHE SAID HERSELF SHE DIDN'T SEE MONEY CHANGE HANDS, AND THAT SHE DIDN'T DO ANY WORK IN THE FIELDS.
WHY ISN'T THIS OVER ALREADY?
IT'S BECAUSE OF DAVIS.
HE UNDERSTANDS THE WAY THE BRITISH WORK BECAUSE HE'S SPENT SO MUCH TIME AROUND THE COURTS.
WELL, I DON'T UNDERSTAND... CAN YOU EXPLAIN IT TO ME?
LISTEN, MEN LIKE MELTON AREN'T TRAINED ATTORNEYS.
THEY'RE JUST MIDDLE-RANKING BUREAUCRATS WHO GET PUT INTO POSITIONS AS MAGISTRATES BECAUSE THERE ARE SO FEW EUROPEANS OVER HERE TO SERVE IN THOSE POSITIONS, AND THEY WON'T LET AFRICANS HOLD THEM ANYMORE.
SO THEY BASE THEIR DECISIONS ON THREE KINDS OF FACTORS.
FIRST, THEY HAVE THOSE QUESTIONS I TOLD YOU ABOUT EARLIER... DID MONEY CHANGE HANDS, WAS THE CHILD CALLED SLAVE, ETC.
SECOND, THEY BRING WITH THEM FROM BRITAIN CERTAIN IDEAS... LIKE THERE ARE LAWS IN BRITAIN NOW ABOUT WHAT JOBS CHILDREN CAN WORK, AND HOW MUCH YOU CAN BEAT A CHILD.

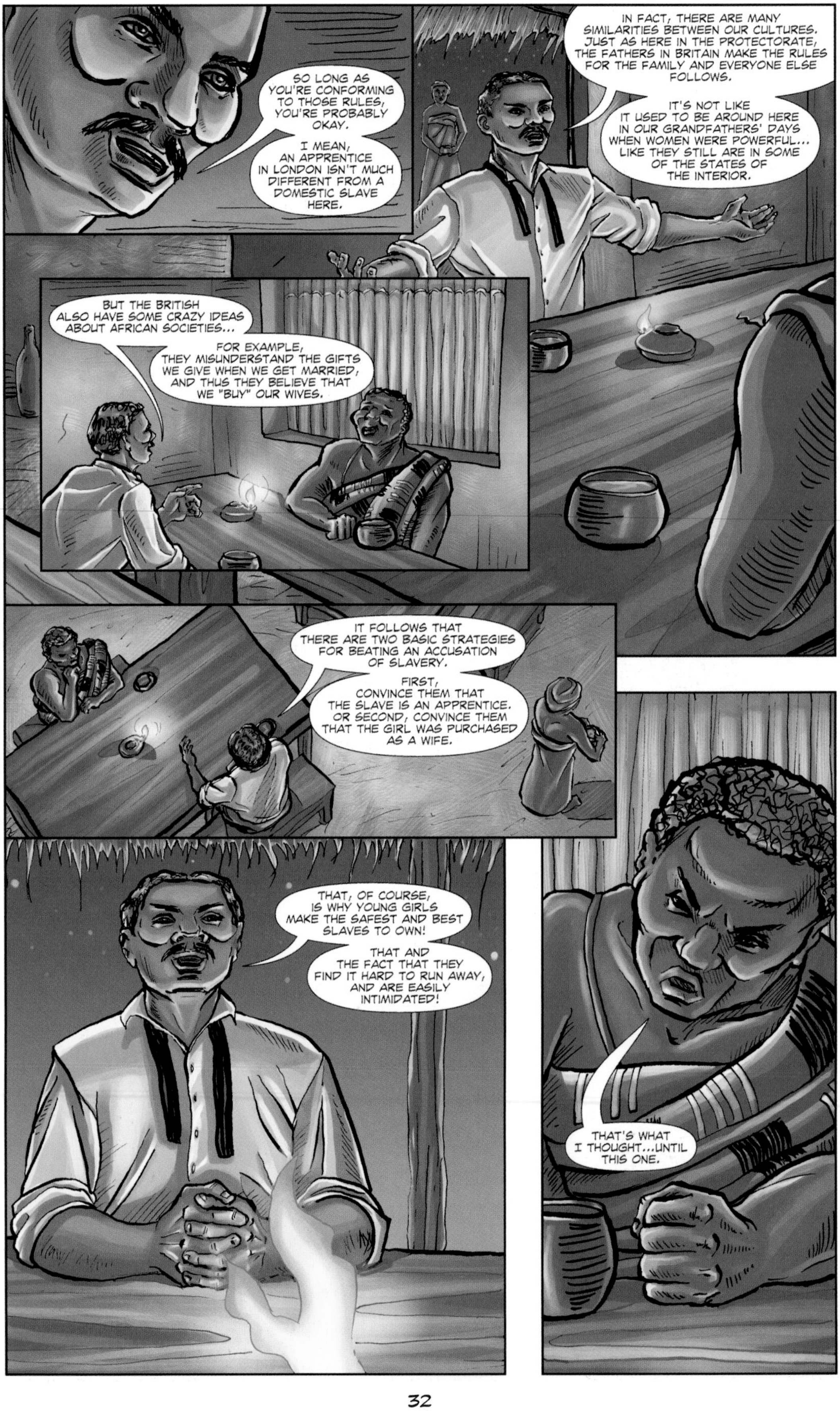
SO LONG AS YOU'RE CONFORMING TO THOSE RULES, YOU'RE PROBABLY OKAY.
I MEAN, AN APPRENTICE IN LONDON ISN'T MUCH DIFFERENT FROM A DOMESTIC SLAVE HERE.
IN FACT, THERE ARE MANY SIMILARITIES BETWEEN OUR CULTURES. JUST AS HERE IN THE PROTECTORATE, THE FATHERS IN BRITAIN MAKE THE RULES FOR THE FAMILY AND EVERYONE ELSE FOLLOWS.
IT'S NOT LIKE IT USED TO BE AROUND HERE IN OUR GRANDFATHERS' DAYS WHEN WOMEN WERE POWERFUL... LIKE THEY STILL ARE IN SOME OF THE STATES OF THE INTERIOR.
BUT THE BRITISH ALSO HAVE SOME CRAZY IDEAS ABOUT AFRICAN SOCIETIES...
FOR EXAMPLE, THEY MISUNDERSTAND THE GIFTS WE GIVE WHEN WE GET MARRIED, AND THUS THEY BELIEVE THAT WE "BUY" OUR WIVES.
IT FOLLOWS THAT THERE ARE TWO BASIC STRATEGIES FOR BEATING AN ACCUSATION OF SLAVERY.
FIRST, CONVINCE THEM THAT THE SLAVE IS AN APPRENTICE. OR SECOND, CONVINCE THEM THAT THE GIRL WAS PURCHASED AS A WIFE.
THAT, OF COURSE, IS WHY YOUNG GIRLS MAKE THE SAFEST AND BEST SLAVES TO OWN!
THAT AND THE FACT THAT THEY FIND IT HARD TO RUN AWAY, AND ARE EASILY INTIMIDATED!
THAT'S WHAT I THOUGHT...UNTIL THIS ONE.

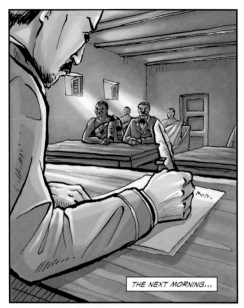

THE NEXT MORNING...

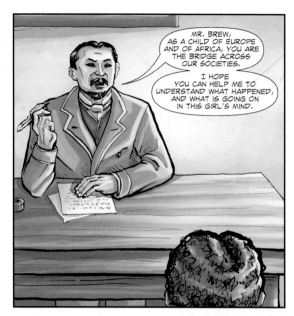

MR. BREW, AS A CHILD OF EUROPE AND OF AFRICA, YOU ARE THE BRIDGE ACROSS OUR SOCIETIES.

I HOPE YOU CAN HELP ME TO UNDERSTAND WHAT HAPPENED, AND WHAT IS GOING ON IN THIS GIRL'S MIND.

I SURELY WILL, SIR.

GIRL, I WILL NOW ASK YOU QUESTIONS AND YOU MUST ANSWER ME TRUTHFULLY...

WHY MUST I ANSWER YOUR QUESTIONS?

ARE YOU A JUDGE LIKE THE WHITE MAN IN THE SEAT? WHY ARE YOU ALWAYS SITTING WITH MY FORMER MASTER?

YOU MUST ANSWER WHAT I ASK TRUTHFULLY BECAUSE IT IS THE LAW. THAT'S ALL YOU NEED TO KNOW.

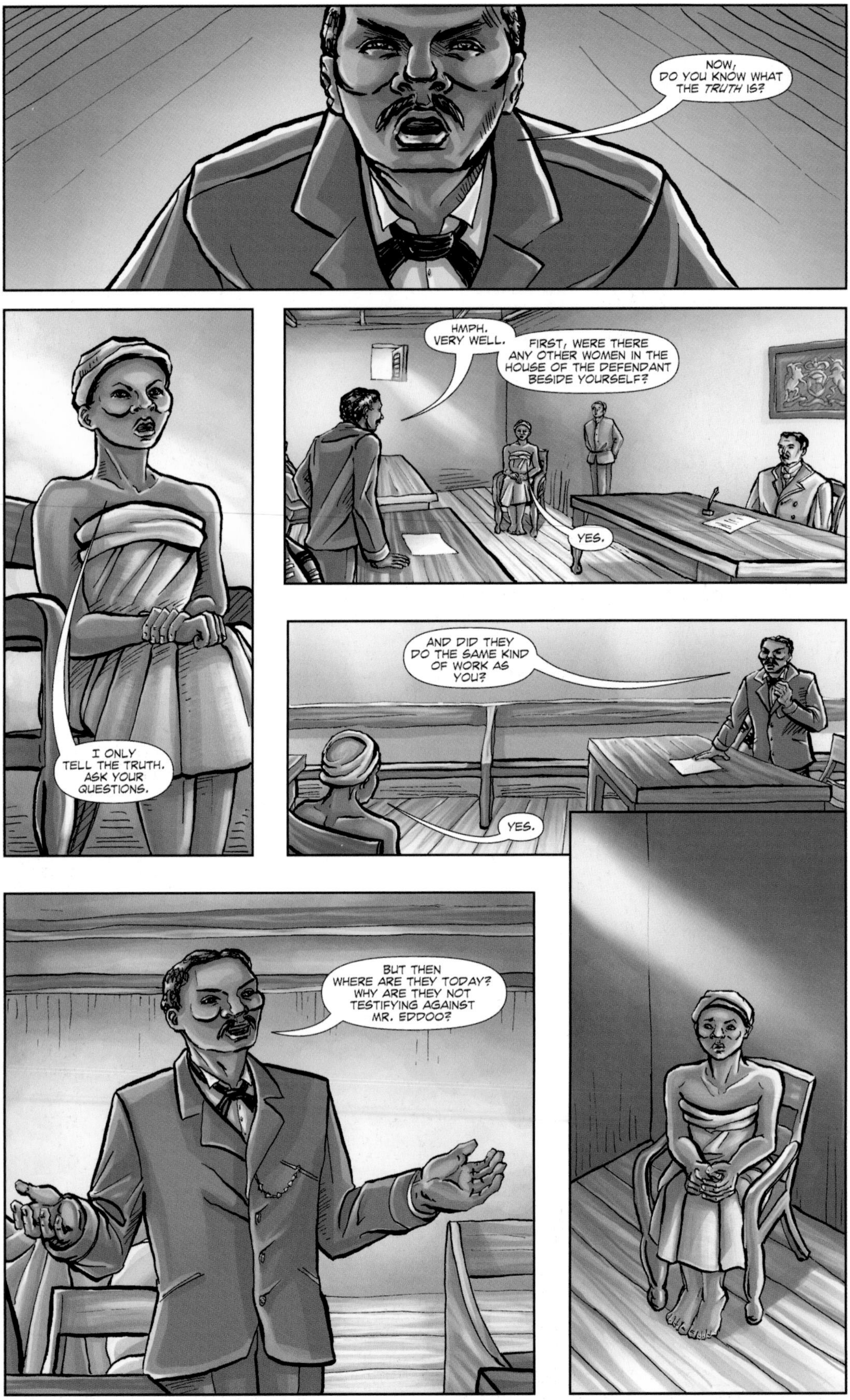

NOW, DO YOU KNOW WHAT THE *TRUTH* IS?
I ONLY TELL THE TRUTH. ASK YOUR QUESTIONS.
HMPH. VERY WELL.
FIRST, WERE THERE ANY OTHER WOMEN IN THE HOUSE OF THE DEFENDANT BESIDE YOURSELF?
YES.
AND DID THEY DO THE SAME KIND OF WORK AS YOU?
YES.
BUT THEN WHERE ARE THEY TODAY? WHY ARE THEY NOT TESTIFYING AGAINST MR. EDDOO?

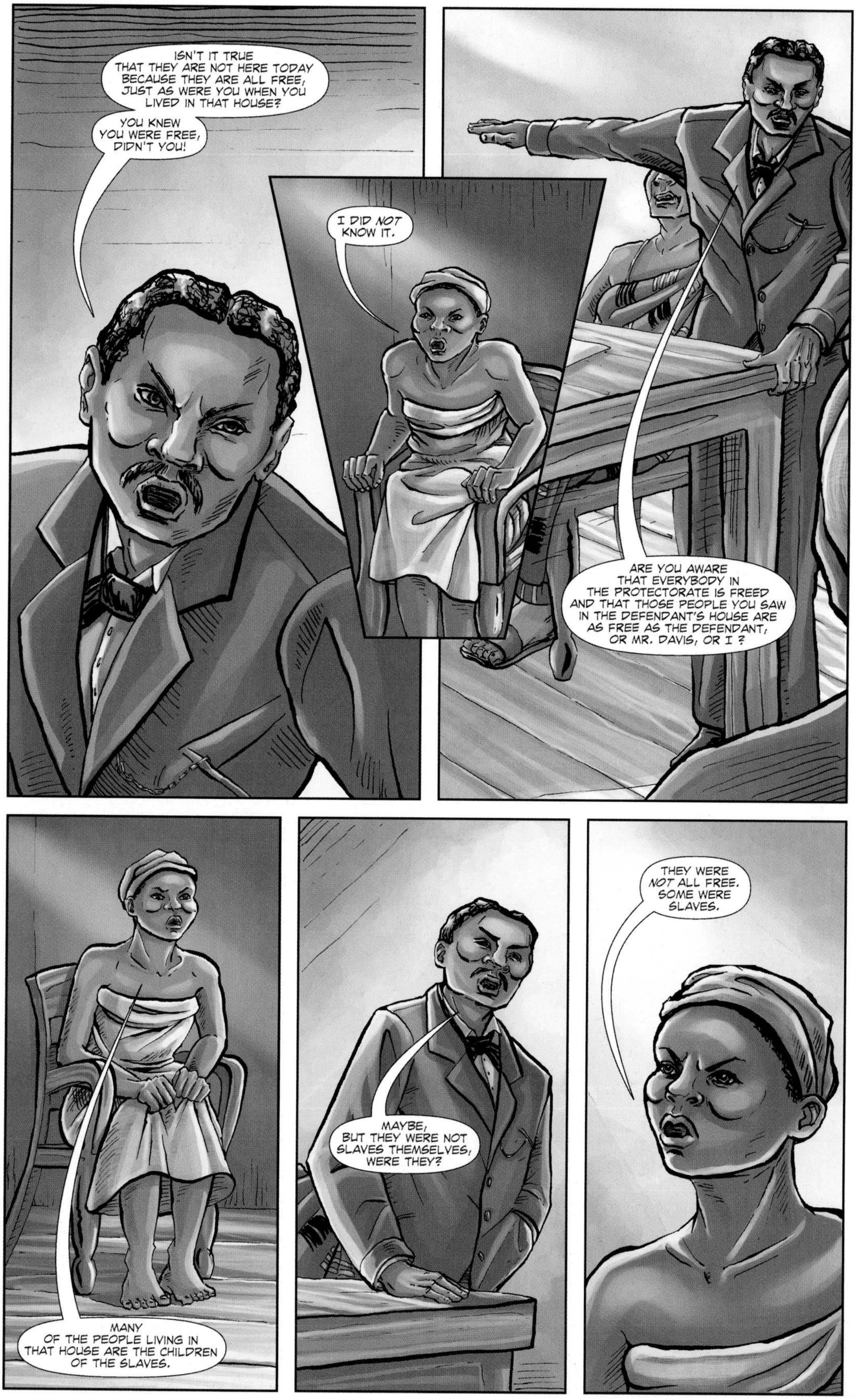
ISN'T IT TRUE THAT THEY ARE NOT HERE TODAY BECAUSE THEY ARE ALL FREE, JUST AS WERE YOU WHEN YOU LIVED IN THAT HOUSE?
YOU KNEW YOU WERE FREE, DIDN'T YOU!
I DID *NOT* KNOW IT.
ARE YOU AWARE THAT EVERYBODY IN THE PROTECTORATE IS FREED AND THAT THOSE PEOPLE YOU SAW IN THE DEFENDANT'S HOUSE ARE AS FREE AS THE DEFENDANT, OR MR. DAVIS, OR I ?
MANY OF THE PEOPLE LIVING IN THAT HOUSE ARE THE CHILDREN OF THE SLAVES.
MAYBE, BUT THEY WERE NOT SLAVES THEMSELVES, WERE THEY?
THEY WERE *NOT* ALL FREE. SOME WERE SLAVES.

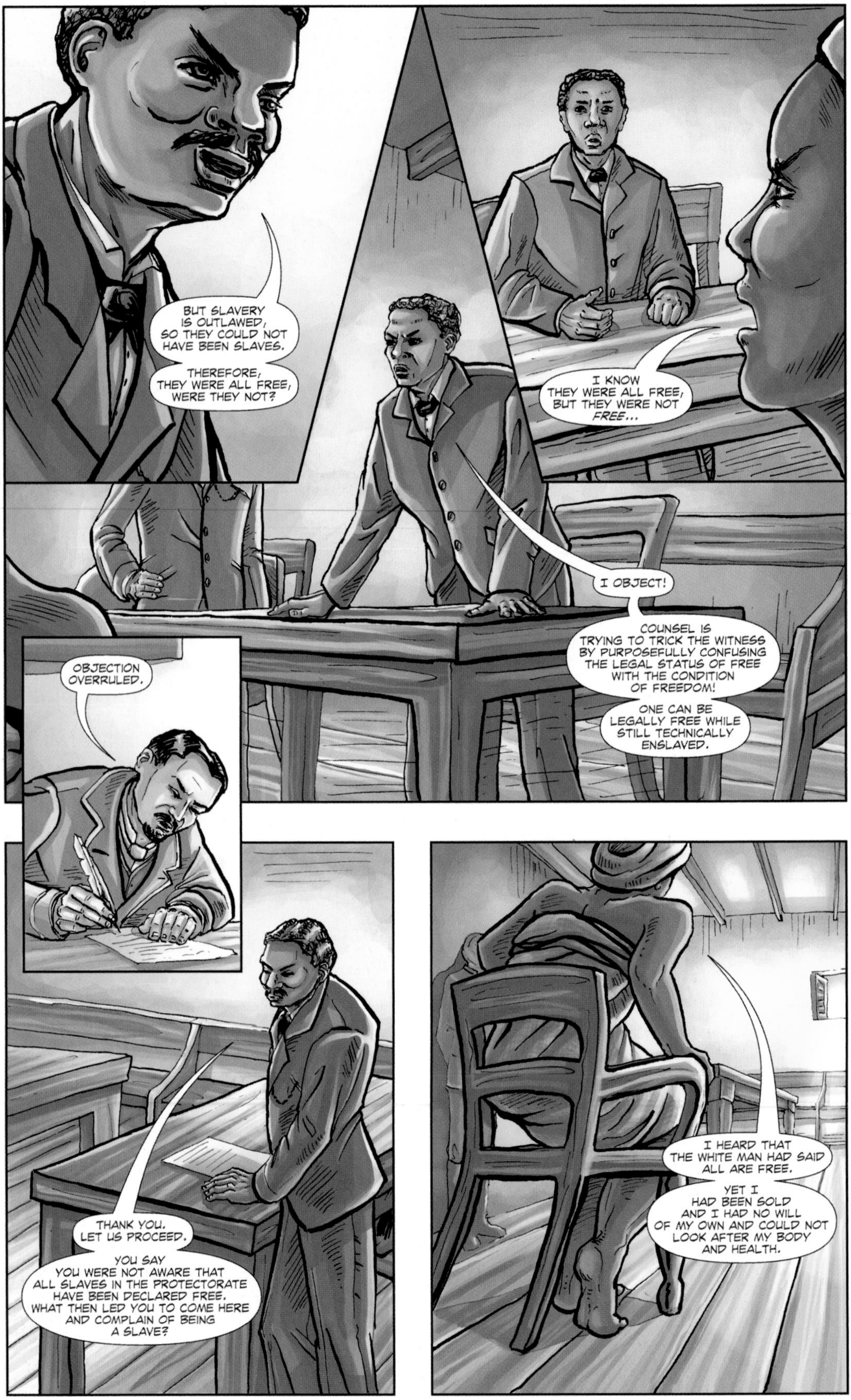
BUT SLAVERY IS OUTLAWED, SO THEY COULD NOT HAVE BEEN SLAVES.
THEREFORE, THEY WERE ALL FREE, WERE THEY NOT?
I KNOW THEY WERE ALL FREE, BUT THEY WERE NOT *FREE*...
I OBJECT!
COUNSEL IS TRYING TO TRICK THE WITNESS BY PURPOSEFULLY CONFUSING THE LEGAL STATUS OF FREE WITH THE CONDITION OF FREEDOM!
ONE CAN BE LEGALLY FREE WHILE STILL TECHNICALLY ENSLAVED.
OBJECTION OVERRULED.
THANK YOU. LET US PROCEED.
YOU SAY YOU WERE NOT AWARE THAT ALL SLAVES IN THE PROTECTORATE HAVE BEEN DECLARED FREE. WHAT THEN LED YOU TO COME HERE AND COMPLAIN OF BEING A SLAVE?
I HEARD THAT THE WHITE MAN HAD SAID ALL ARE FREE.
YET I HAD BEEN SOLD AND I HAD NO WILL OF MY OWN AND COULD NOT LOOK AFTER MY BODY AND HEALTH.

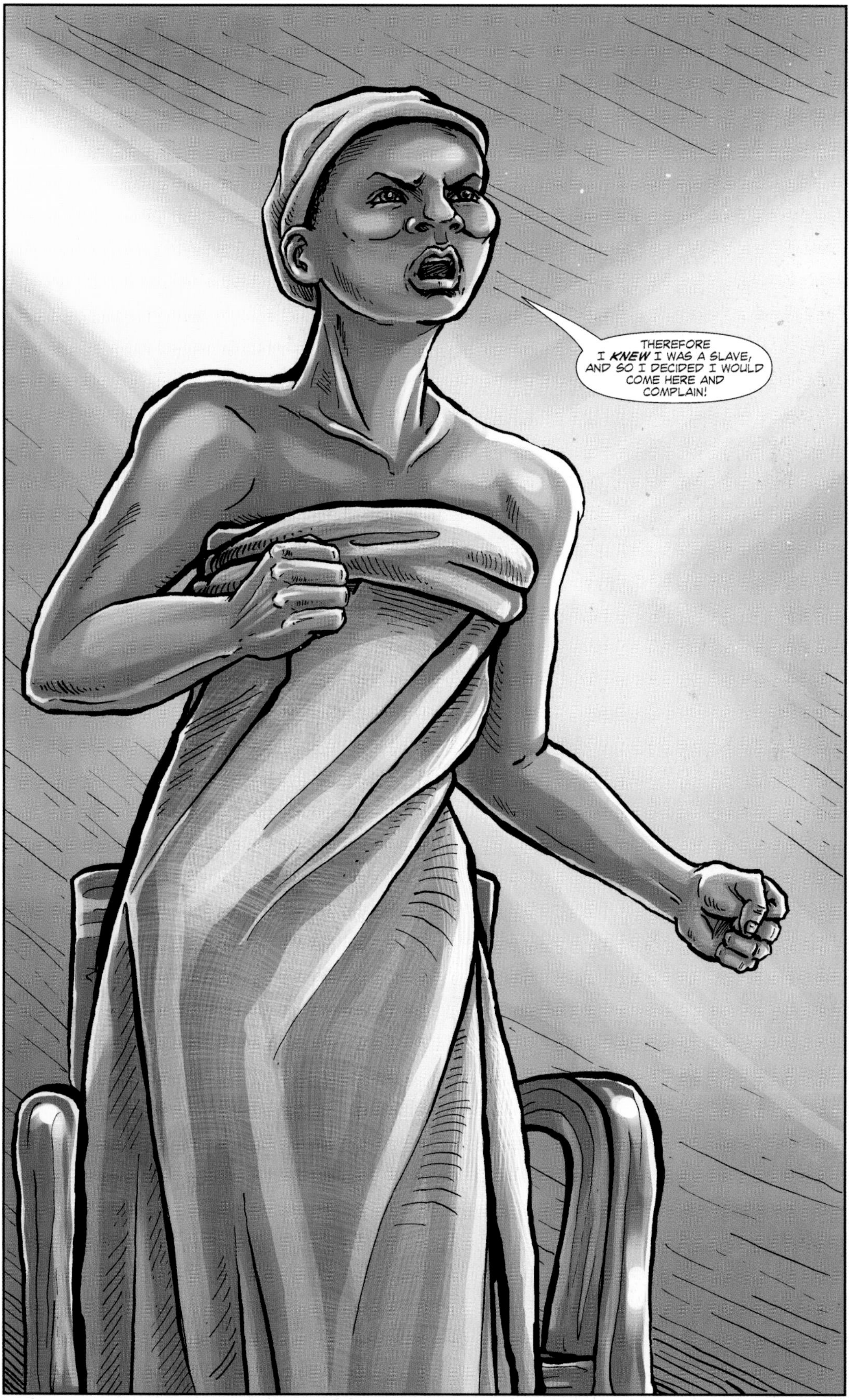
THEREFORE I KNEW I WAS A SLAVE, AND SO I DECIDED I WOULD COME HERE AND COMPLAIN!

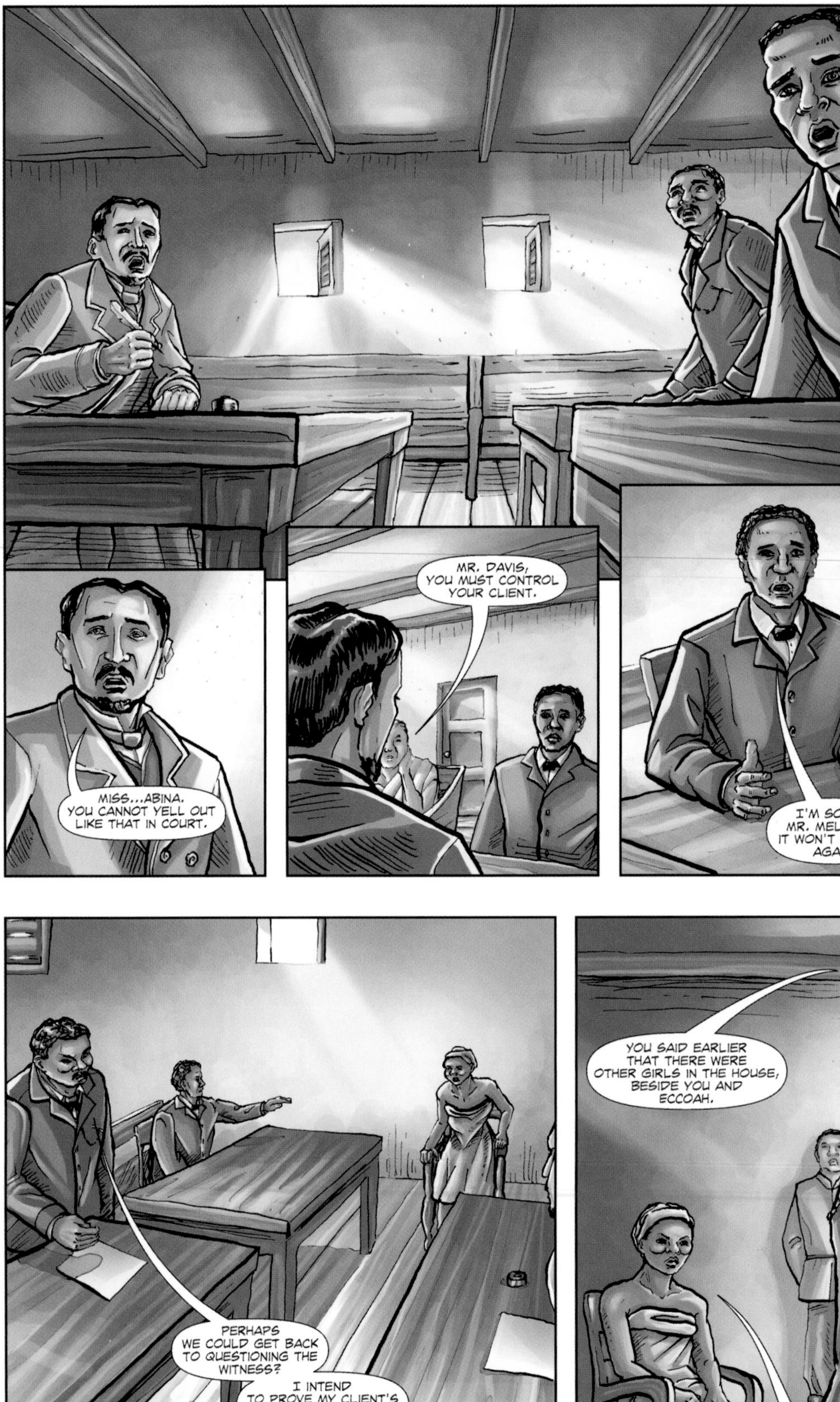
MISS...ABINA. YOU CANNOT YELL OUT LIKE THAT IN COURT.
MR. DAVIS, YOU MUST CONTROL YOUR CLIENT.
I'M SORRY, MR. MELTON... IT WON'T HAPPEN AGAIN.
PERHAPS WE COULD GET BACK TO QUESTIONING THE WITNESS?
I INTEND TO PROVE MY CLIENT'S INNOCENCE BY THE END OF THE DAY.
YOU SAID EARLIER THAT THERE WERE OTHER GIRLS IN THE HOUSE, BESIDE YOU AND ECCOAH.
YES...

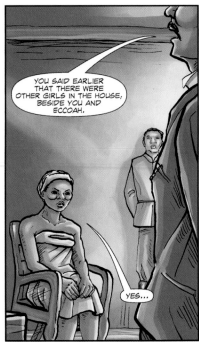

CHAPTER 4

LIFE AT QUAMINA EDDOO'S HOUSE

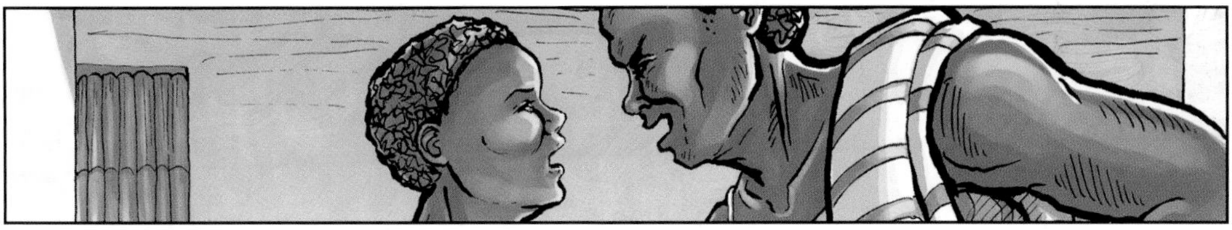

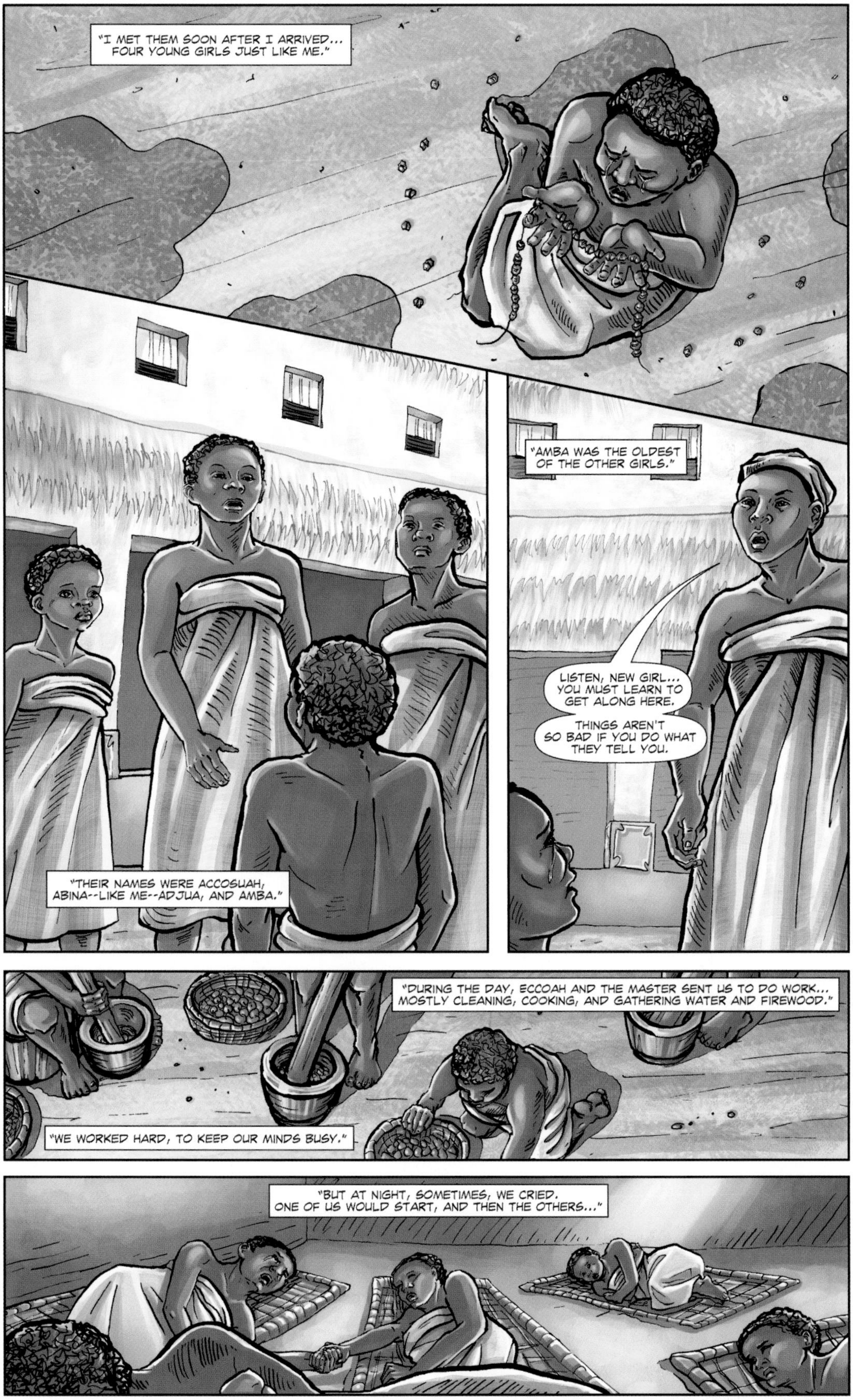
"I MET THEM SOON AFTER I ARRIVED... FOUR YOUNG GIRLS JUST LIKE ME."
"THEIR NAMES WERE ACCOSUAH, ABINA--LIKE ME--ADJUA, AND AMBA."
"AMBA WAS THE OLDEST OF THE OTHER GIRLS."
LISTEN, NEW GIRL... YOU MUST LEARN TO GET ALONG HERE.
THINGS AREN'T SO BAD IF YOU DO WHAT THEY TELL YOU.
"DURING THE DAY, ECCOAH AND THE MASTER SENT US TO DO WORK... MOSTLY CLEANING, COOKING, AND GATHERING WATER AND FIREWOOD."
"WE WORKED HARD, TO KEEP OUR MINDS BUSY."
"BUT AT NIGHT, SOMETIMES, WE CRIED. ONE OF US WOULD START, AND THEN THE OTHERS..."

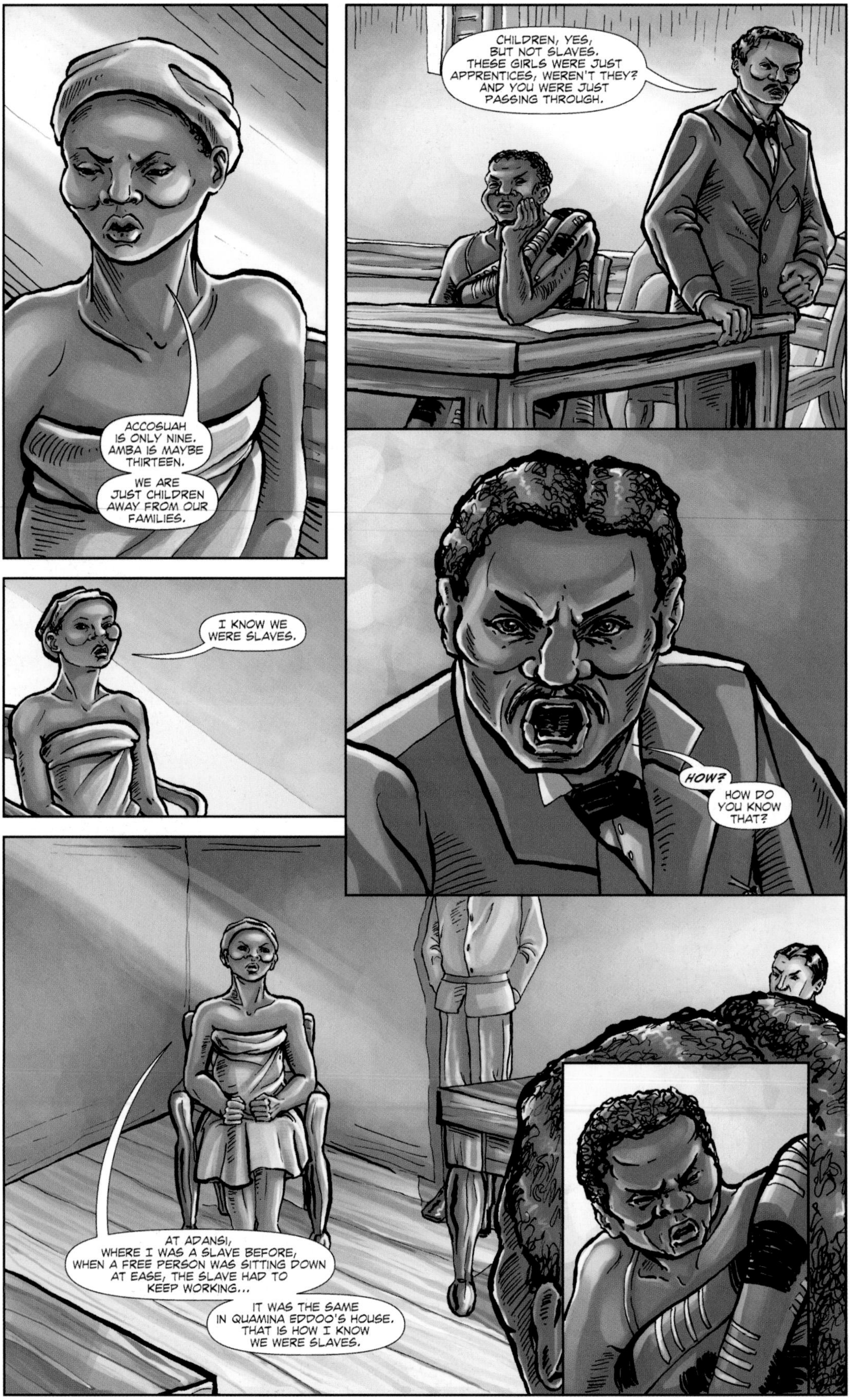
ACCOSUAH IS ONLY NINE. AMBA IS MAYBE THIRTEEN.
WE ARE JUST CHILDREN AWAY FROM OUR FAMILIES.
CHILDREN, YES, BUT NOT SLAVES. THESE GIRLS WERE JUST APPRENTICES, WEREN'T THEY? AND YOU WERE JUST PASSING THROUGH.
I KNOW WE WERE SLAVES.
HOW? HOW DO YOU KNOW THAT?
AT ADANSI, WHERE I WAS A SLAVE BEFORE, WHEN A FREE PERSON WAS SITTING DOWN AT EASE, THE SLAVE HAD TO KEEP WORKING...
IT WAS THE SAME IN QUAMINA EDDOO'S HOUSE. THAT IS HOW I KNOW WE WERE SLAVES.

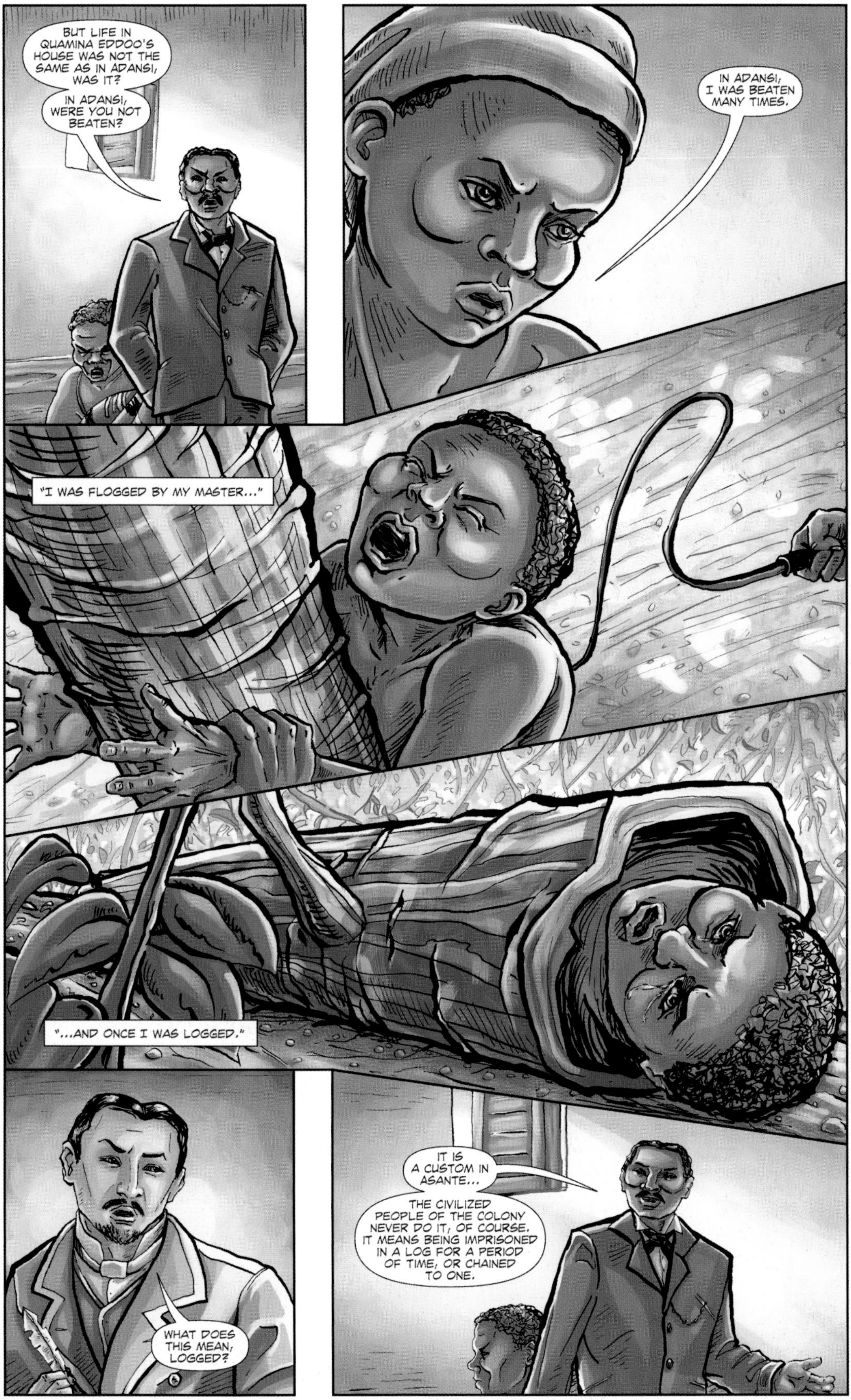
BUT LIFE IN QUAMINA EDDOO'S HOUSE WAS NOT THE SAME AS IN ADANSI, WAS IT?
IN ADANSI, WERE YOU NOT BEATEN?
IN ADANSI, I WAS BEATEN MANY TIMES.
"I WAS FLOGGED BY MY MASTER..."
"...AND ONCE I WAS LOGGED."
WHAT DOES THIS MEAN, LOGGED?
IT IS A CUSTOM IN ASANTE...
THE CIVILIZED PEOPLE OF THE COLONY NEVER DO IT, OF COURSE. IT MEANS BEING IMPRISONED IN A LOG FOR A PERIOD OF TIME, OR CHAINED TO ONE.

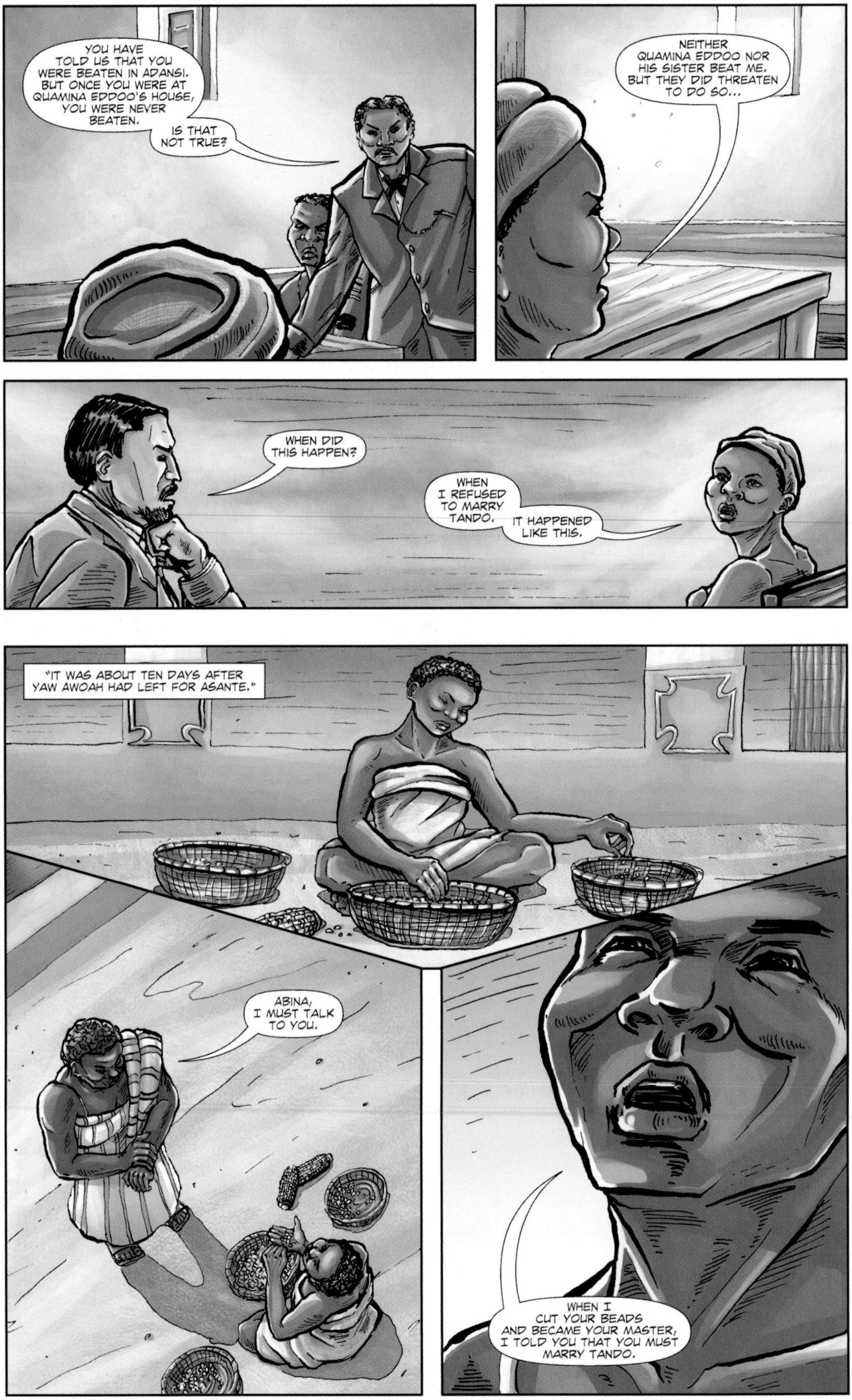

YOU HAVE TOLD US THAT YOU WERE BEATEN IN ADANSI. BUT ONCE YOU WERE AT QUAMINA EDDOO'S HOUSE, YOU WERE NEVER BEATEN.
IS THAT NOT TRUE?
NEITHER QUAMINA EDDOO NOR HIS SISTER BEAT ME. BUT THEY DID THREATEN TO DO SO...
WHEN DID THIS HAPPEN?
WHEN I REFUSED TO MARRY TANDO.
IT HAPPENED LIKE THIS.
"IT WAS ABOUT TEN DAYS AFTER YAW AWOAH HAD LEFT FOR ASANTE."
ABINA, I MUST TALK TO YOU.
WHEN I CUT YOUR BEADS AND BECAME YOUR MASTER, I TOLD YOU THAT YOU MUST MARRY TANDO.

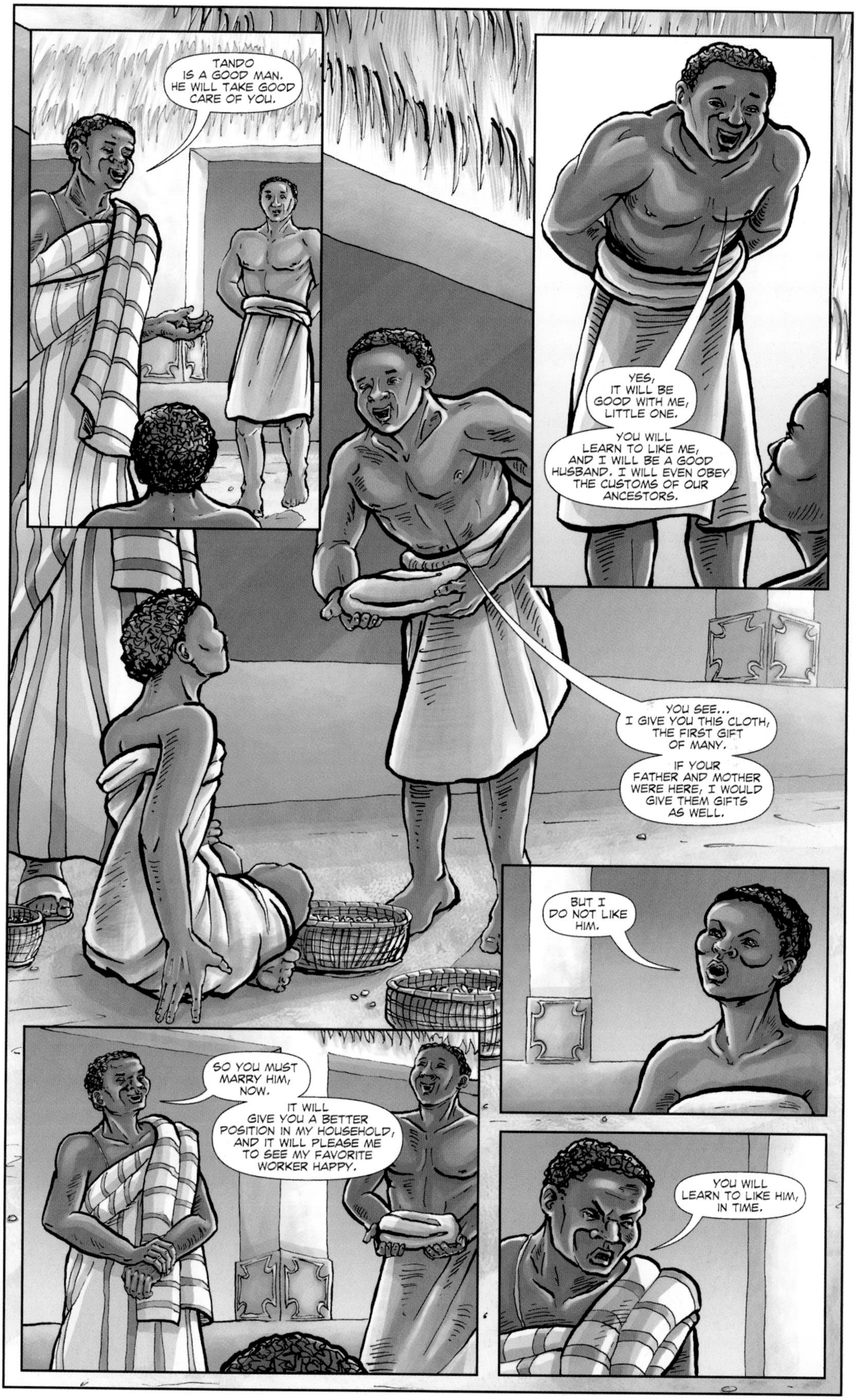
TANDO IS A GOOD MAN. HE WILL TAKE GOOD CARE OF YOU.
YES, IT WILL BE GOOD WITH ME, LITTLE ONE.
YOU WILL LEARN TO LIKE ME, AND I WILL BE A GOOD HUSBAND. I WILL EVEN OBEY THE CUSTOMS OF OUR ANCESTORS.
YOU SEE... I GIVE YOU THIS CLOTH, THE FIRST GIFT OF MANY.
IF YOUR FATHER AND MOTHER WERE HERE, I WOULD GIVE THEM GIFTS AS WELL.
BUT I DO NOT LIKE HIM.
SO YOU MUST MARRY HIM, NOW.
IT WILL GIVE YOU A BETTER POSITION IN MY HOUSEHOLD, AND IT WILL PLEASE ME TO SEE MY FAVORITE WORKER HAPPY.
YOU WILL LEARN TO LIKE HIM, IN TIME.

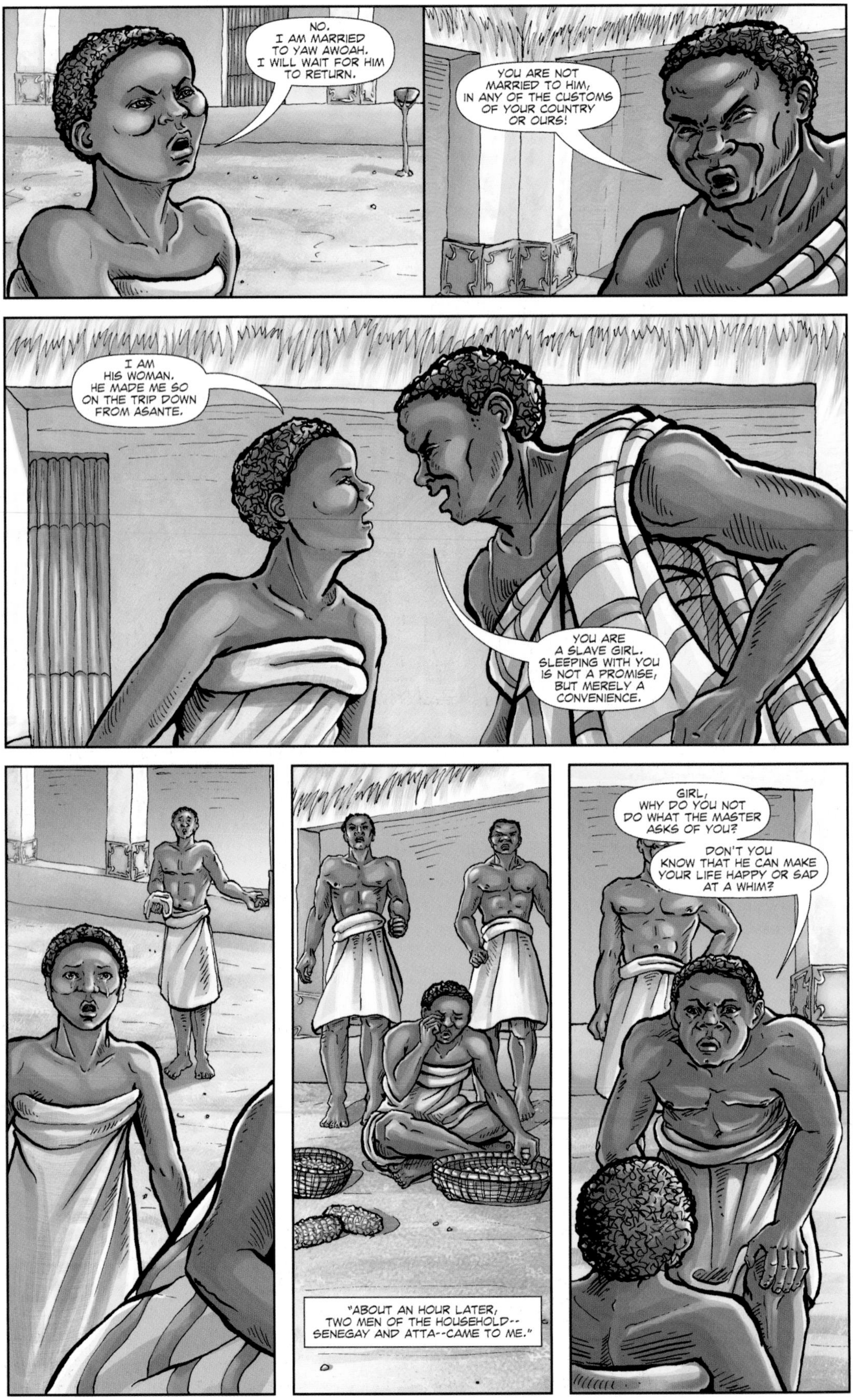
NO. I AM MARRIED TO YAW AWOAH. I WILL WAIT FOR HIM TO RETURN.
YOU ARE NOT MARRIED TO HIM, IN ANY OF THE CUSTOMS OF YOUR COUNTRY OR OURS!
I AM HIS WOMAN. HE MADE ME SO ON THE TRIP DOWN FROM ASANTE.
YOU ARE A SLAVE GIRL. SLEEPING WITH YOU IS NOT A PROMISE, BUT MERELY A CONVENIENCE.
"ABOUT AN HOUR LATER, TWO MEN OF THE HOUSEHOLD-- SENEGAY AND ATTA--CAME TO ME."
GIRL, WHY DO YOU NOT DO WHAT THE MASTER ASKS OF YOU?
DON'T YOU KNOW THAT HE CAN MAKE YOUR LIFE HAPPY OR SAD AT A WHIM?

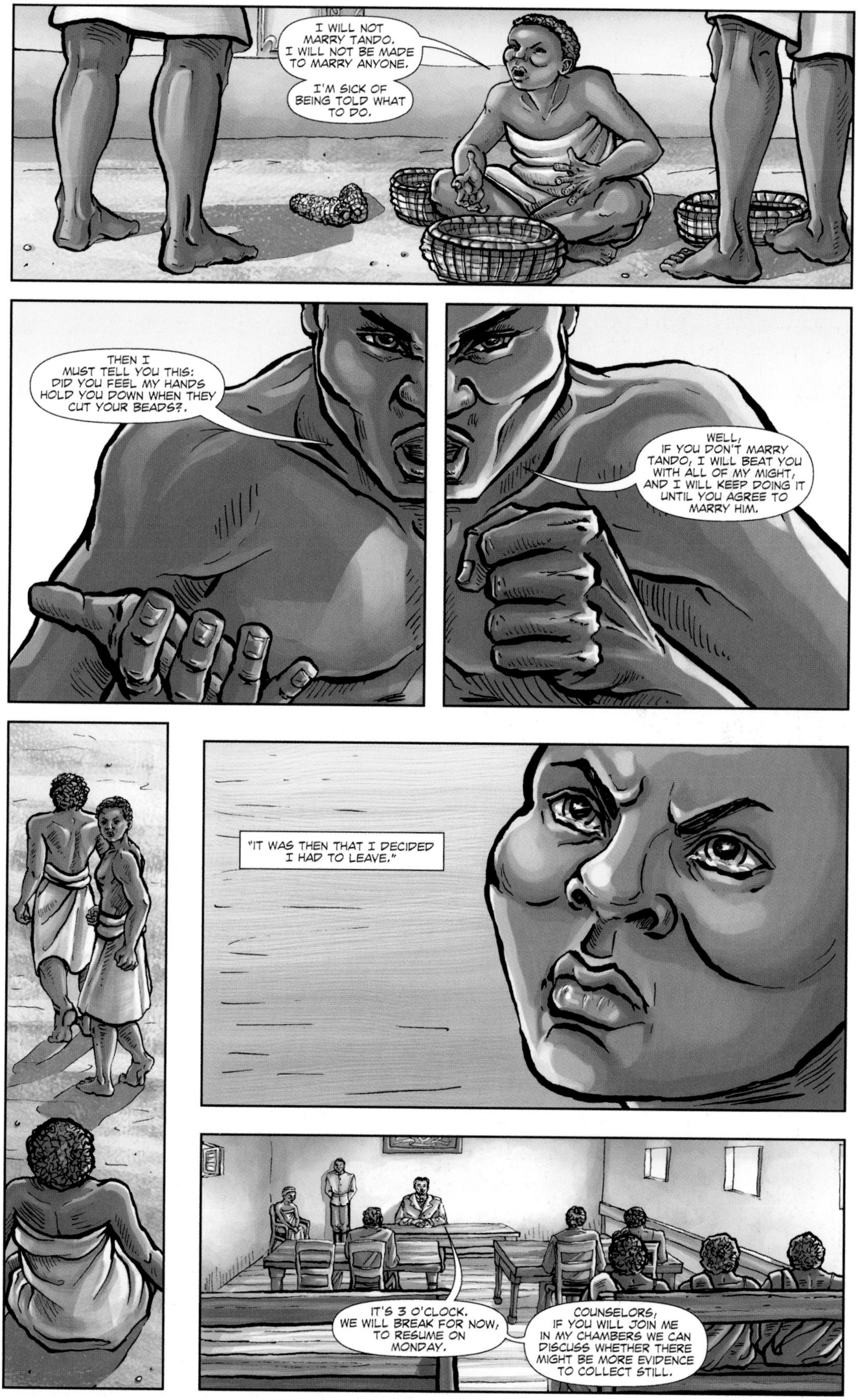
I WILL NOT MARRY TANDO. I WILL NOT BE MADE TO MARRY ANYONE.
I'M SICK OF BEING TOLD WHAT TO DO.
THEN I MUST TELL YOU THIS: DID YOU FEEL MY HANDS HOLD YOU DOWN WHEN THEY CUT YOUR BEADS?.
WELL, IF YOU DON'T MARRY TANDO, I WILL BEAT YOU WITH ALL OF MY MIGHT, AND I WILL KEEP DOING IT UNTIL YOU AGREE TO MARRY HIM.
"IT WAS THEN THAT I DECIDED I HAD TO LEAVE."
IT'S 3 O'CLOCK. WE WILL BREAK FOR NOW, TO RESUME ON MONDAY.
COUNSELORS, IF YOU WILL JOIN ME IN MY CHAMBERS WE CAN DISCUSS WHETHER THERE MIGHT BE MORE EVIDENCE TO COLLECT STILL.

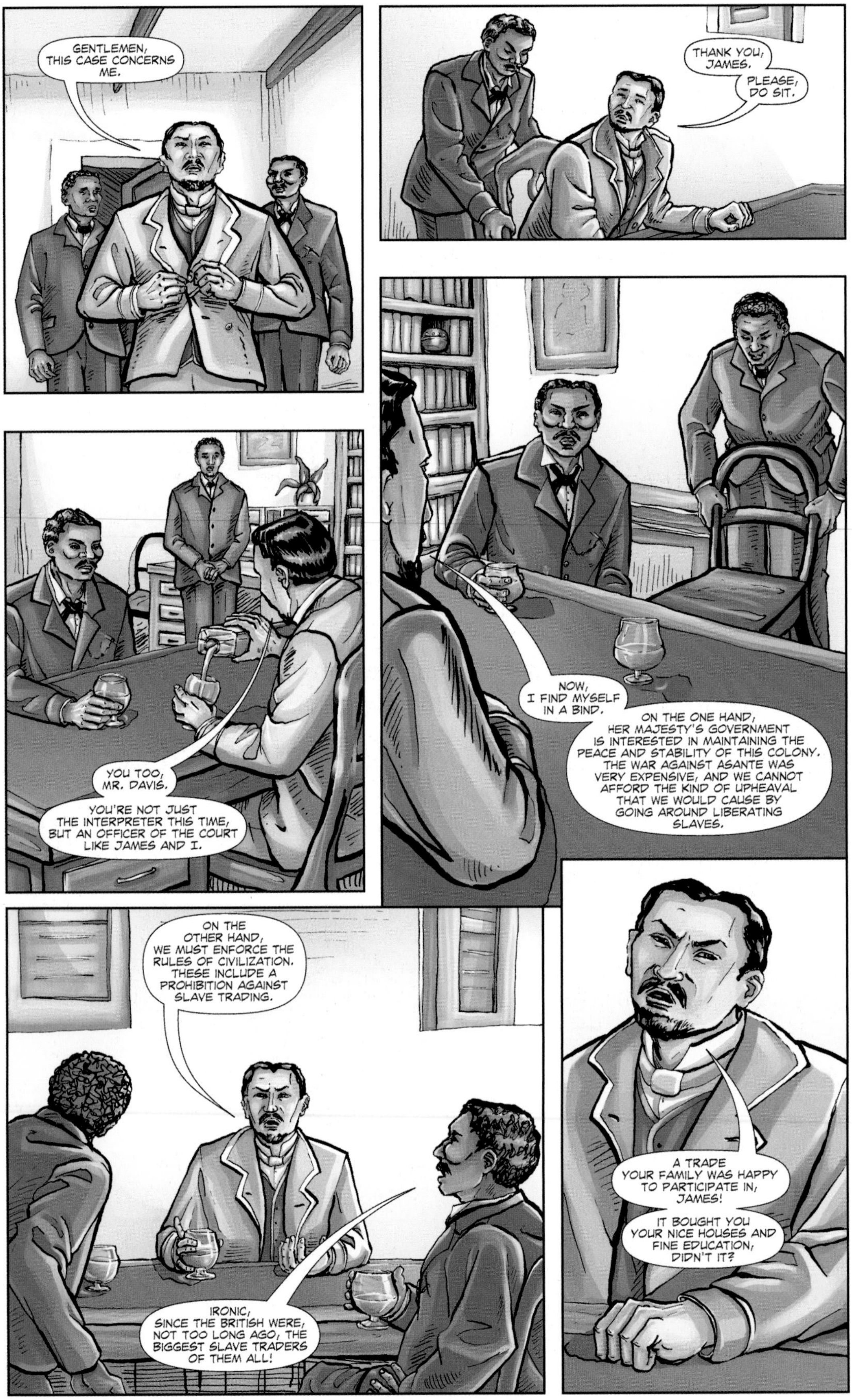
GENTLEMEN, THIS CASE CONCERNS ME.
THANK YOU, JAMES.
PLEASE, DO SIT.
YOU TOO, MR. DAVIS.
YOU'RE NOT JUST THE INTERPRETER THIS TIME, BUT AN OFFICER OF THE COURT LIKE JAMES AND I.
NOW, I FIND MYSELF IN A BIND.
ON THE ONE HAND, HER MAJESTY'S GOVERNMENT IS INTERESTED IN MAINTAINING THE PEACE AND STABILITY OF THIS COLONY. THE WAR AGAINST ASANTE WAS VERY EXPENSIVE, AND WE CANNOT AFFORD THE KIND OF UPHEAVAL THAT WE WOULD CAUSE BY GOING AROUND LIBERATING SLAVES.
ON THE OTHER HAND, WE MUST ENFORCE THE RULES OF CIVILIZATION. THESE INCLUDE A PROHIBITION AGAINST SLAVE TRADING.
IRONIC, SINCE THE BRITISH WERE, NOT TOO LONG AGO, THE BIGGEST SLAVE TRADERS OF THEM ALL!
A TRADE YOUR FAMILY WAS HAPPY TO PARTICIPATE IN, JAMES!
IT BOUGHT YOU YOUR NICE HOUSES AND FINE EDUCATION, DIDN'T IT?

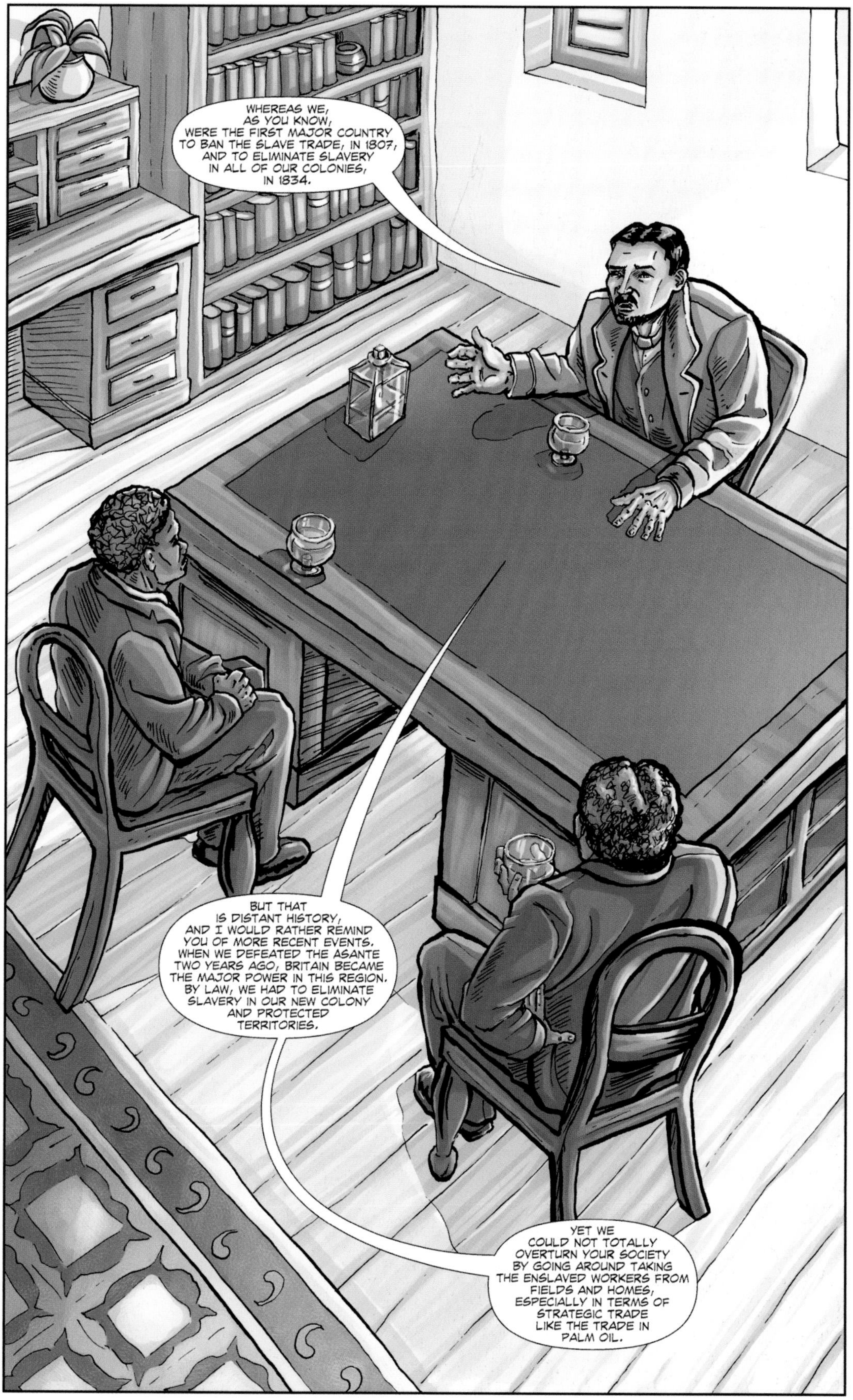
WHEREAS WE, AS YOU KNOW, WERE THE FIRST MAJOR COUNTRY TO BAN THE SLAVE TRADE, IN 1807, AND TO ELIMINATE SLAVERY IN ALL OF OUR COLONIES, IN 1834.
BUT THAT IS DISTANT HISTORY, AND I WOULD RATHER REMIND YOU OF MORE RECENT EVENTS. WHEN WE DEFEATED THE ASANTE TWO YEARS AGO, BRITAIN BECAME THE MAJOR POWER IN THIS REGION. BY LAW, WE HAD TO ELIMINATE SLAVERY IN OUR NEW COLONY AND PROTECTED TERRITORIES.
YET WE COULD NOT TOTALLY OVERTURN YOUR SOCIETY BY GOING AROUND TAKING THE ENSLAVED WORKERS FROM FIELDS AND HOMES, ESPECIALLY IN TERMS OF STRATEGIC TRADE LIKE THE TRADE IN PALM OIL.

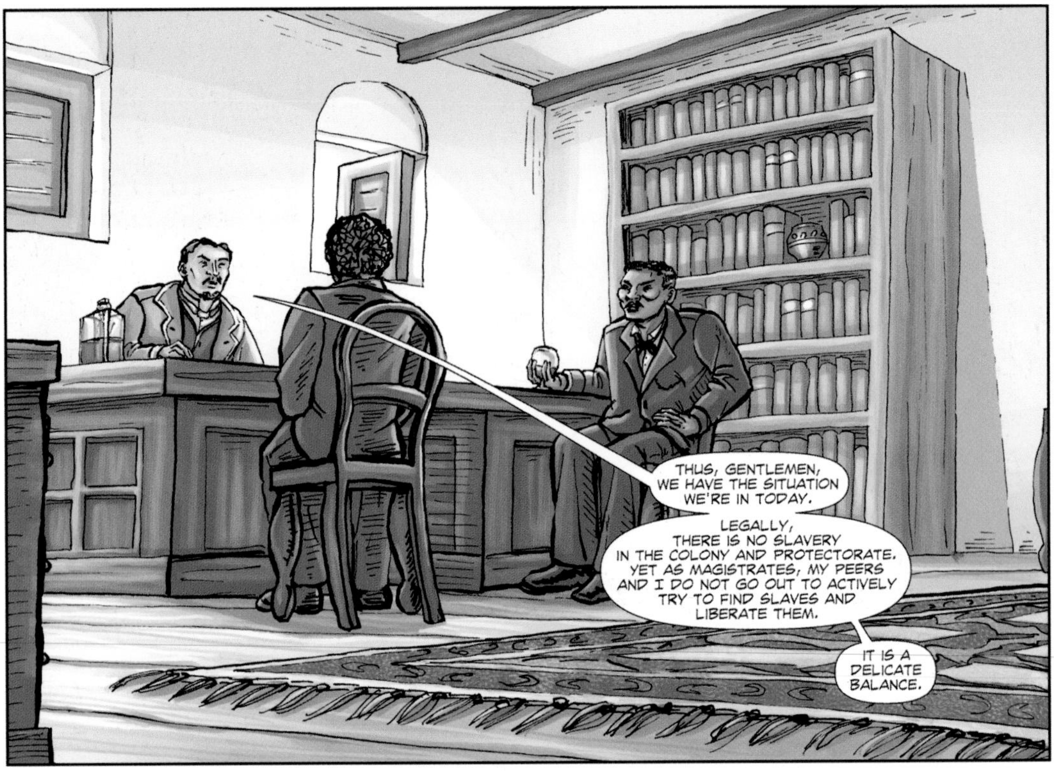
THUS, GENTLEMEN, WE HAVE THE SITUATION WE'RE IN TODAY.
LEGALLY, THERE IS NO SLAVERY IN THE COLONY AND PROTECTORATE. YET AS MAGISTRATES, MY PEERS AND I DO NOT GO OUT TO ACTIVELY TRY TO FIND SLAVES AND LIBERATE THEM.
IT IS A DELICATE BALANCE.

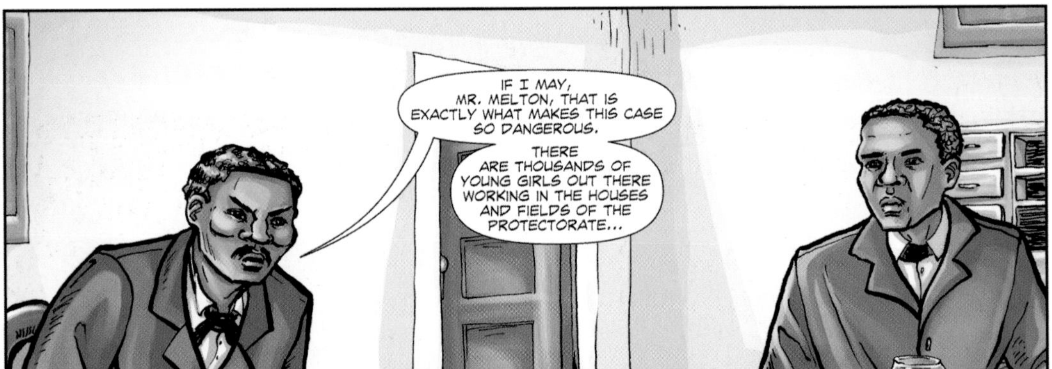
IF I MAY, MR. MELTON, THAT IS EXACTLY WHAT MAKES THIS CASE SO DANGEROUS.
THERE ARE THOUSANDS OF YOUNG GIRLS OUT THERE WORKING IN THE HOUSES AND FIELDS OF THE PROTECTORATE...

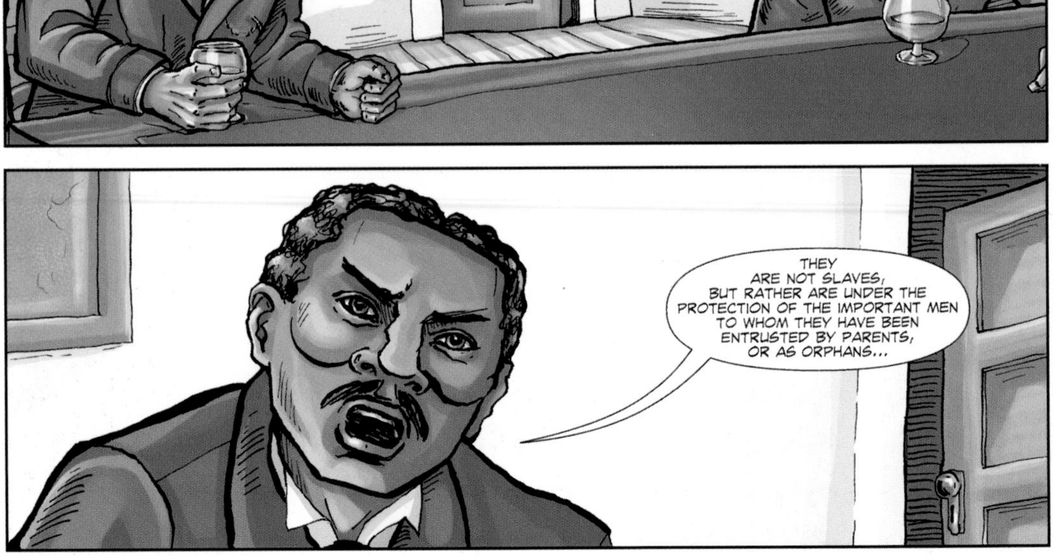
THEY ARE NOT SLAVES, BUT RATHER ARE UNDER THE PROTECTION OF THE IMPORTANT MEN TO WHOM THEY HAVE BEEN ENTRUSTED BY PARENTS, OR AS ORPHANS...

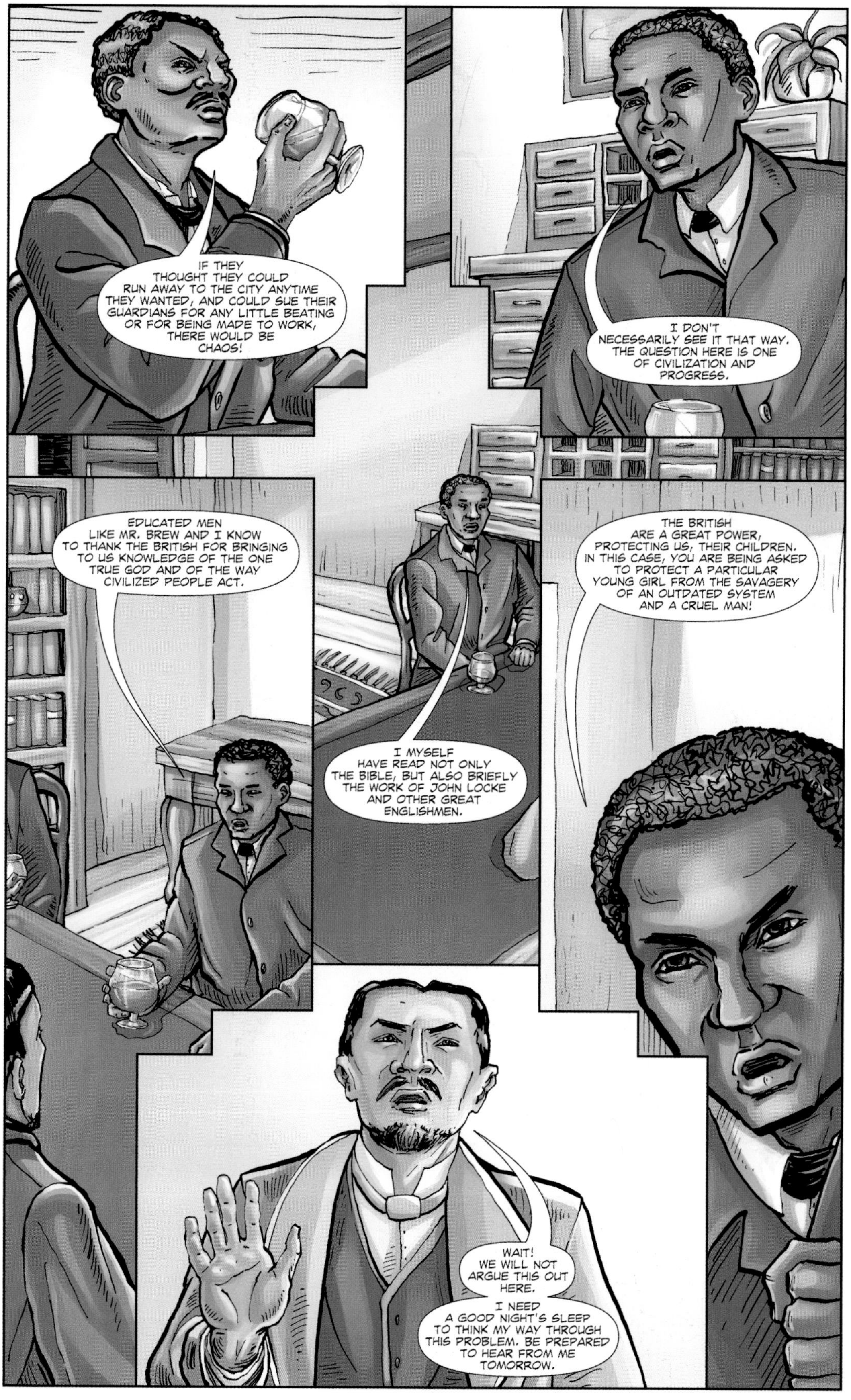
IF THEY THOUGHT THEY COULD RUN AWAY TO THE CITY ANYTIME THEY WANTED, AND COULD SUE THEIR GUARDIANS FOR ANY LITTLE BEATING OR FOR BEING MADE TO WORK, THERE WOULD BE CHAOS!
I DON'T NECESSARILY SEE IT THAT WAY. THE QUESTION HERE IS ONE OF CIVILIZATION AND PROGRESS.
EDUCATED MEN LIKE MR. BREW AND I KNOW TO THANK THE BRITISH FOR BRINGING TO US KNOWLEDGE OF THE ONE TRUE GOD AND OF THE WAY CIVILIZED PEOPLE ACT.
I MYSELF HAVE READ NOT ONLY THE BIBLE, BUT ALSO BRIEFLY THE WORK OF JOHN LOCKE AND OTHER GREAT ENGLISHMEN.
THE BRITISH ARE A GREAT POWER, PROTECTING US, THEIR CHILDREN. IN THIS CASE, YOU ARE BEING ASKED TO PROTECT A PARTICULAR YOUNG GIRL FROM THE SAVAGERY OF AN OUTDATED SYSTEM AND A CRUEL MAN!
WAIT! WE WILL NOT ARGUE THIS OUT HERE.
I NEED A GOOD NIGHT'S SLEEP TO THINK MY WAY THROUGH THIS PROBLEM. BE PREPARED TO HEAR FROM ME TOMORROW.

CHAPTER 5

HE DID NOTHING GOOD FOR ME

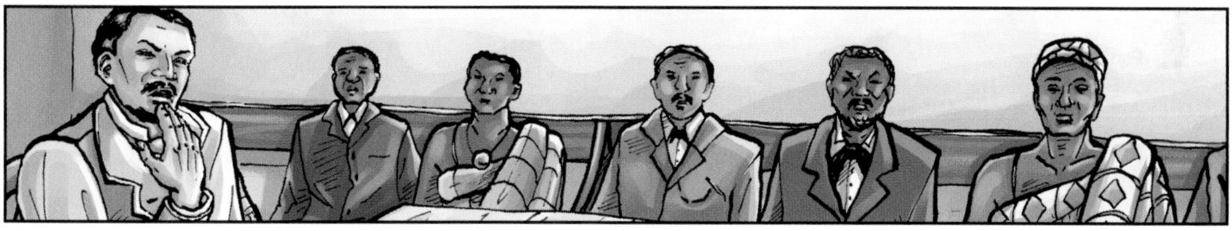

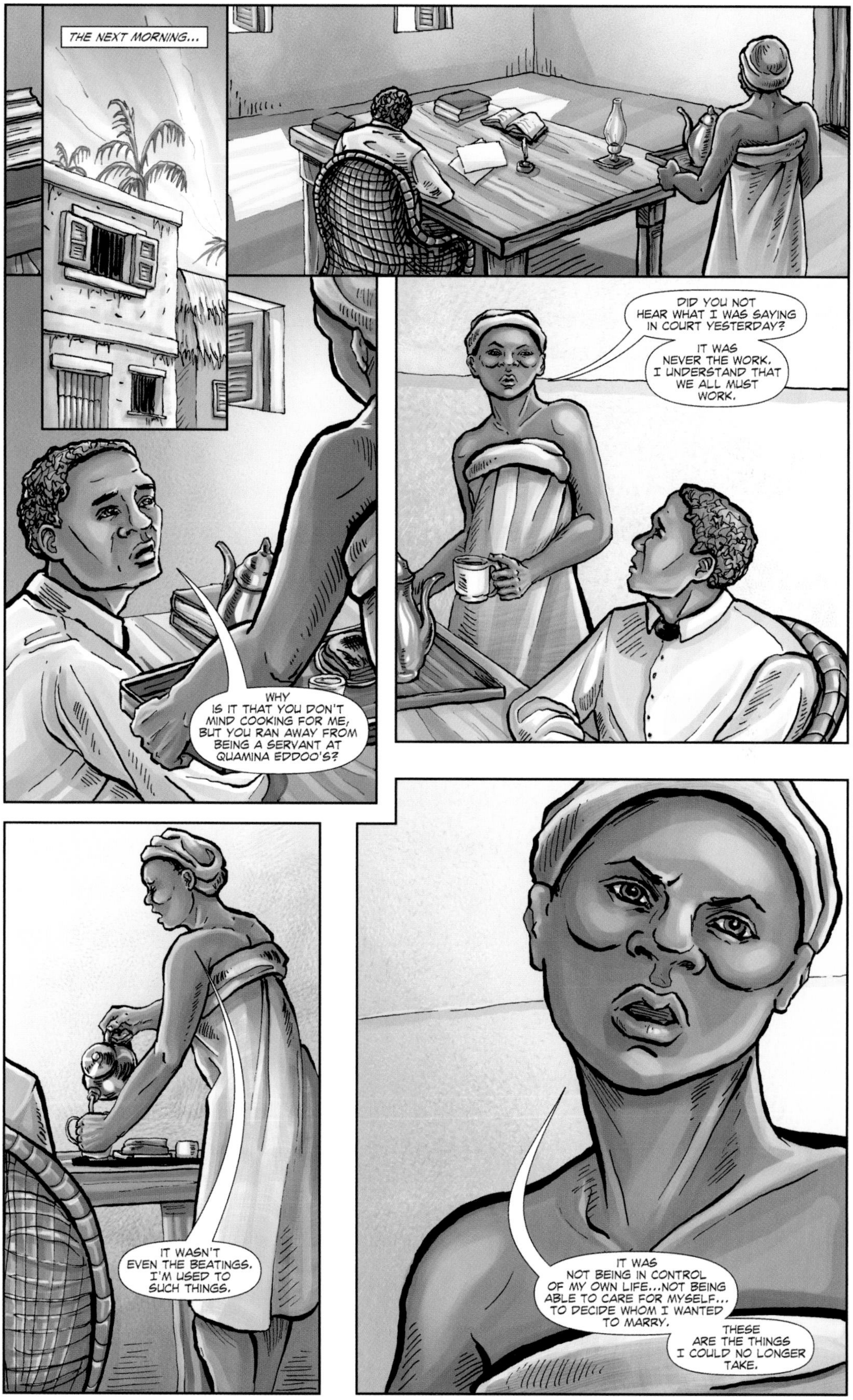
THE NEXT MORNING...
WHY IS IT THAT YOU DON'T MIND COOKING FOR ME, BUT YOU RAN AWAY FROM BEING A SERVANT AT QUAMINA EDDOO'S?
DID YOU NOT HEAR WHAT I WAS SAYING IN COURT YESTERDAY?
IT WAS NEVER THE WORK. I UNDERSTAND THAT WE ALL MUST WORK.
IT WASN'T EVEN THE BEATINGS. I'M USED TO SUCH THINGS.
IT WAS NOT BEING IN CONTROL OF MY OWN LIFE...NOT BEING ABLE TO CARE FOR MYSELF... TO DECIDE WHOM I WANTED TO MARRY.
THESE ARE THE THINGS I COULD NO LONGER TAKE.

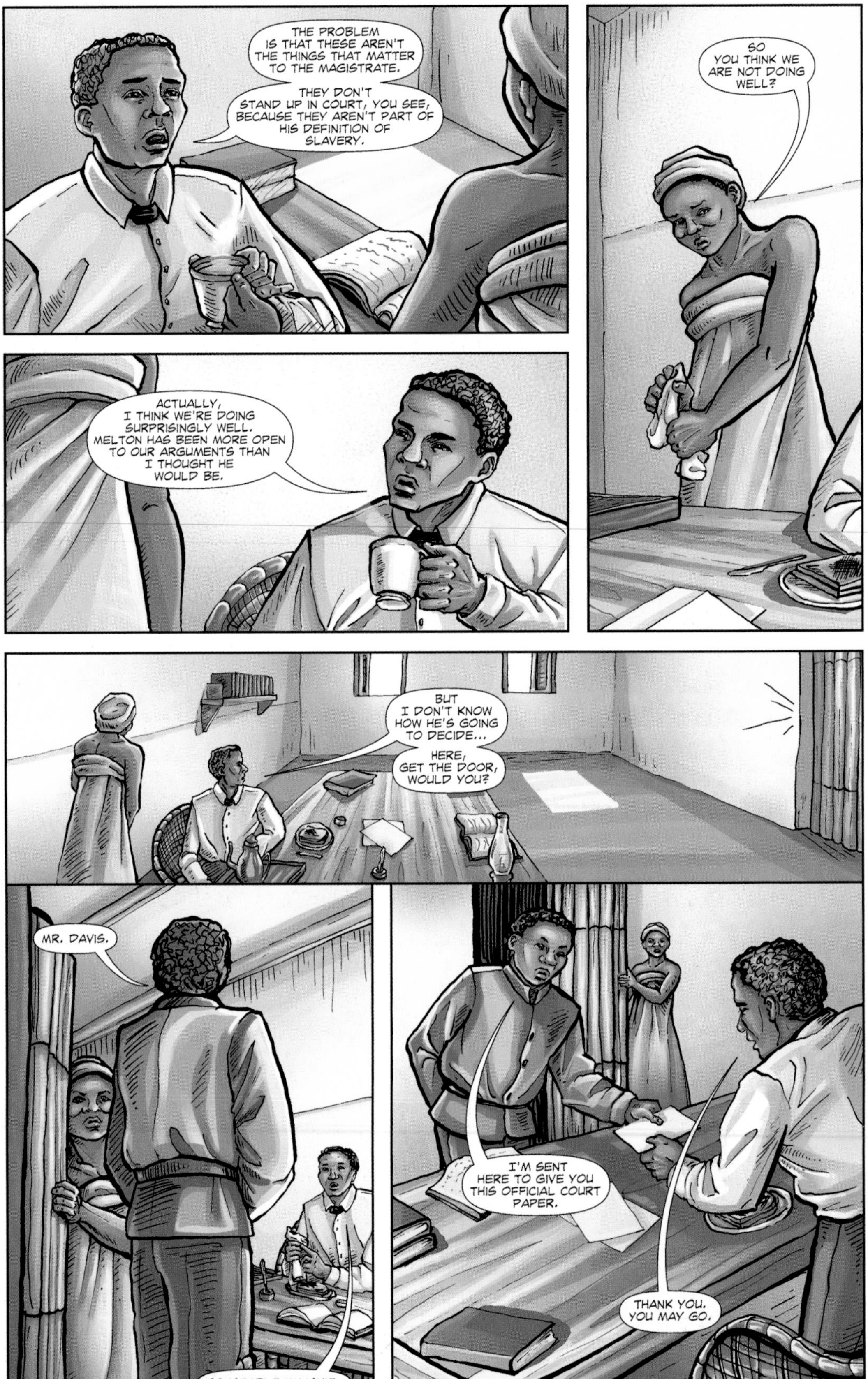
THE PROBLEM IS THAT THESE AREN'T THE THINGS THAT MATTER TO THE MAGISTRATE.
THEY DON'T STAND UP IN COURT, YOU SEE, BECAUSE THEY AREN'T PART OF HIS DEFINITION OF SLAVERY.
SO YOU THINK WE ARE NOT DOING WELL?
ACTUALLY, I THINK WE'RE DOING SURPRISINGLY WELL. MELTON HAS BEEN MORE OPEN TO OUR ARGUMENTS THAN I THOUGHT HE WOULD BE.
BUT I DON'T KNOW HOW HE'S GOING TO DECIDE...
HERE, GET THE DOOR, WOULD YOU?
MR. DAVIS.
CONSTABLE MUNSHIE.
I'M SENT HERE TO GIVE YOU THIS OFFICIAL COURT PAPER.
THANK YOU. YOU MAY GO.

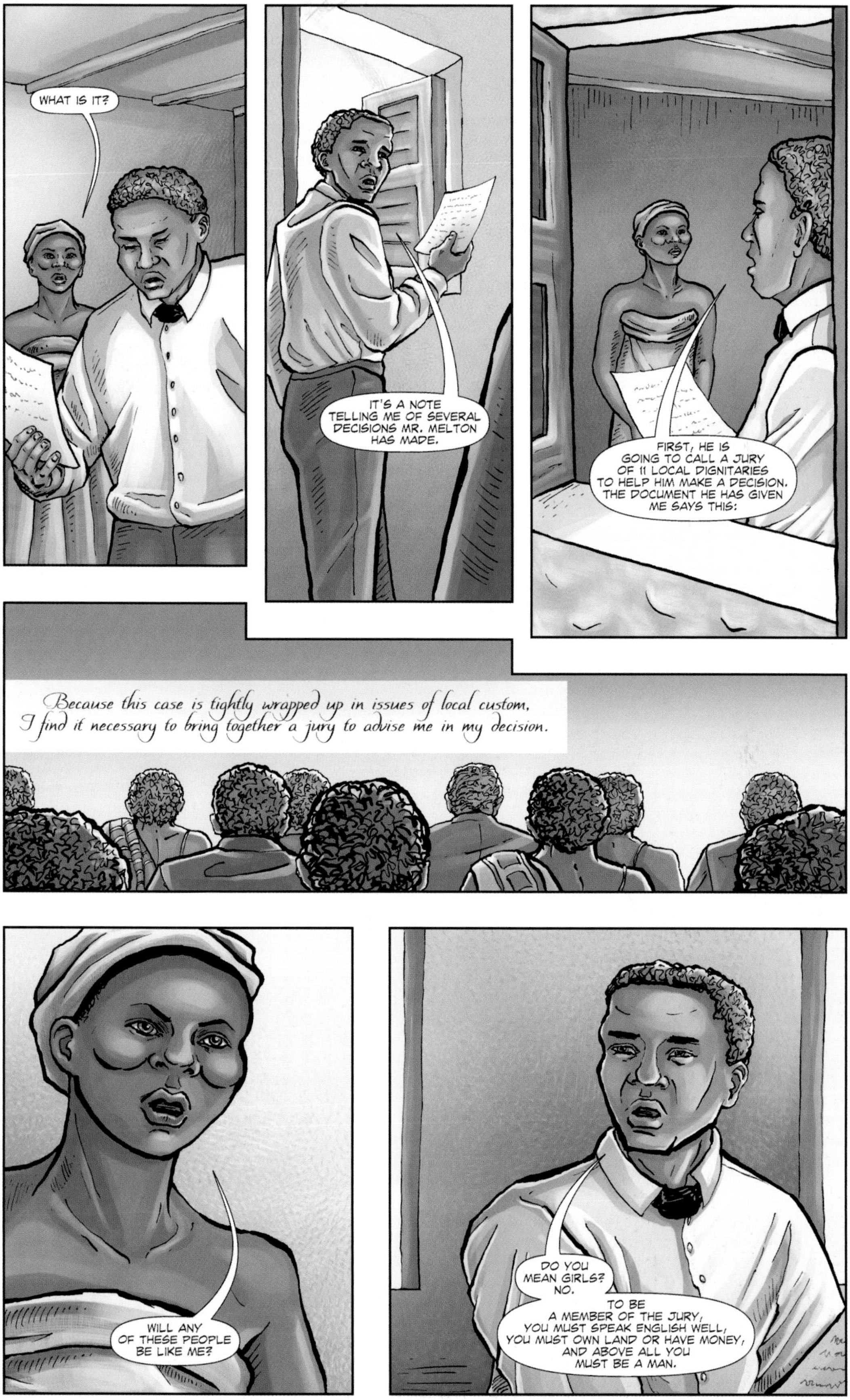
WHAT IS IT?
IT'S A NOTE TELLING ME OF SEVERAL DECISIONS MR. MELTON HAS MADE.
FIRST, HE IS GOING TO CALL A JURY OF 11 LOCAL DIGNITARIES TO HELP HIM MAKE A DECISION. THE DOCUMENT HE HAS GIVEN ME SAYS THIS:
Because this case is tightly wrapped up in issues of local custom, I find it necessary to bring together a jury to advise me in my decision.
WILL ANY OF THESE PEOPLE BE LIKE ME?
DO YOU MEAN GIRLS? NO.
TO BE A MEMBER OF THE JURY, YOU MUST SPEAK ENGLISH WELL, YOU MUST OWN LAND OR HAVE MONEY, AND ABOVE ALL YOU MUST BE A MAN.

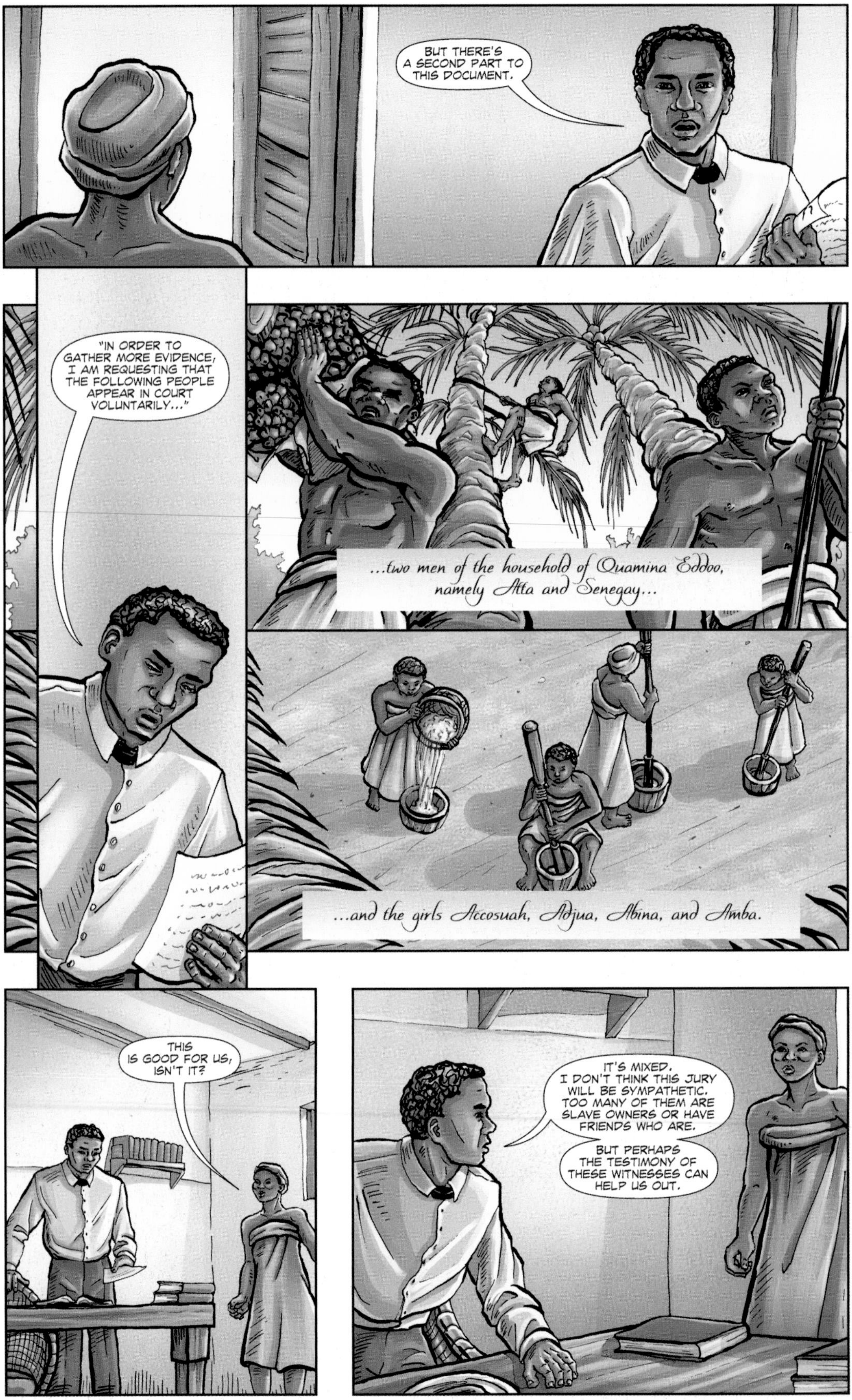
BUT THERE'S A SECOND PART TO THIS DOCUMENT.
"IN ORDER TO GATHER MORE EVIDENCE, I AM REQUESTING THAT THE FOLLOWING PEOPLE APPEAR IN COURT VOLUNTARILY..."
...two men of the household of Quamina Eddoo, namely Atta and Senegay...
...and the girls Accosuah, Adjua, Abina, and Amba.
THIS IS GOOD FOR US, ISN'T IT?
IT'S MIXED. I DON'T THINK THIS JURY WILL BE SYMPATHETIC. TOO MANY OF THEM ARE SLAVE OWNERS OR HAVE FRIENDS WHO ARE.
BUT PERHAPS THE TESTIMONY OF THESE WITNESSES CAN HELP US OUT.

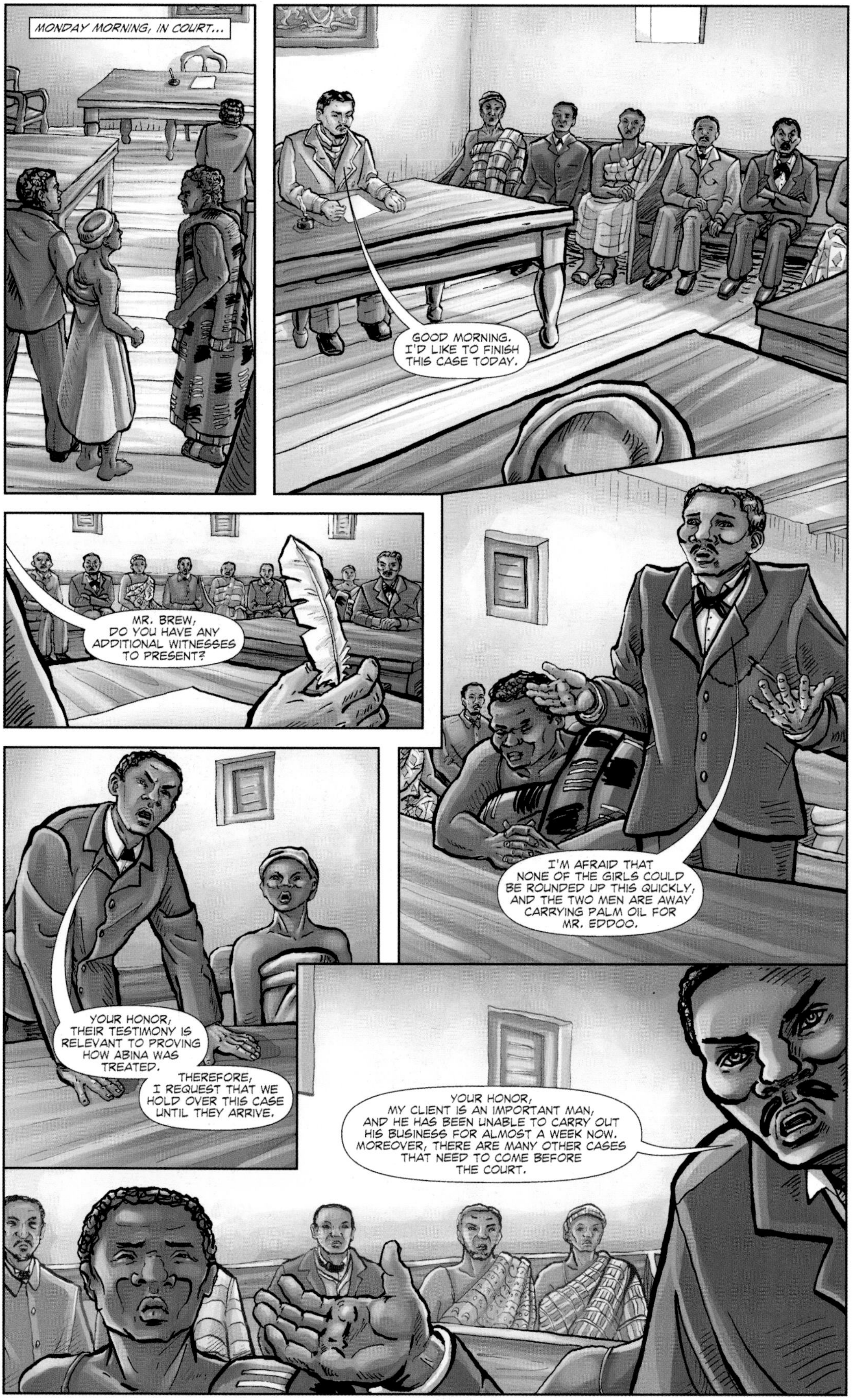
MONDAY MORNING, IN COURT...
GOOD MORNING. I'D LIKE TO FINISH THIS CASE TODAY.
MR. BREW, DO YOU HAVE ANY ADDITIONAL WITNESSES TO PRESENT?
I'M AFRAID THAT NONE OF THE GIRLS COULD BE ROUNDED UP THIS QUICKLY, AND THE TWO MEN ARE AWAY CARRYING PALM OIL FOR MR. EDDOO.
YOUR HONOR, THEIR TESTIMONY IS RELEVANT TO PROVING HOW ABINA WAS TREATED.
THEREFORE, I REQUEST THAT WE HOLD OVER THIS CASE UNTIL THEY ARRIVE.
YOUR HONOR, MY CLIENT IS AN IMPORTANT MAN, AND HE HAS BEEN UNABLE TO CARRY OUT HIS BUSINESS FOR ALMOST A WEEK NOW. MOREOVER, THERE ARE MANY OTHER CASES THAT NEED TO COME BEFORE THE COURT.

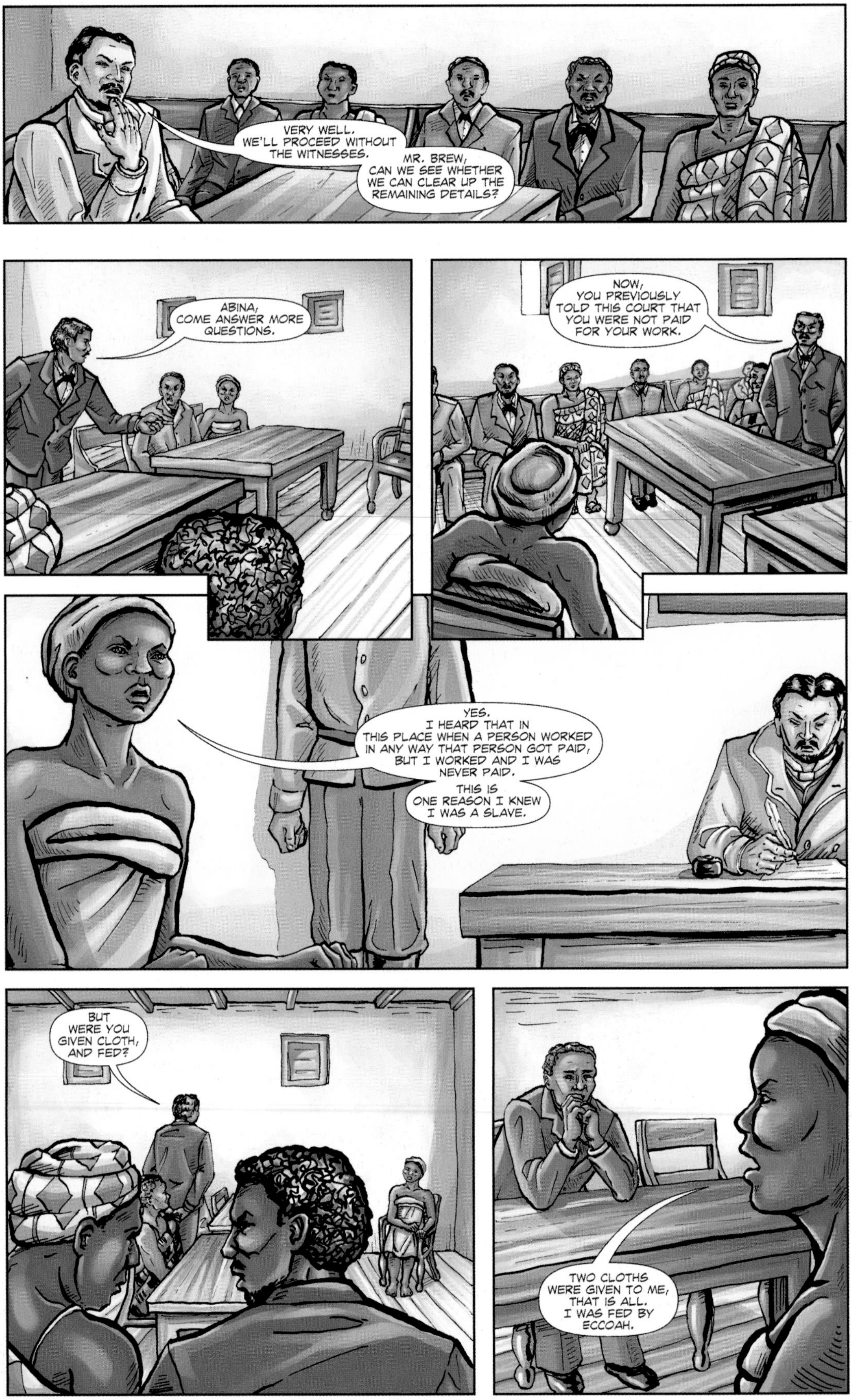
VERY WELL. WE'LL PROCEED WITHOUT THE WITNESSES.
MR. BREW, CAN WE SEE WHETHER WE CAN CLEAR UP THE REMAINING DETAILS?
ABINA, COME ANSWER MORE QUESTIONS.
NOW, YOU PREVIOUSLY TOLD THIS COURT THAT YOU WERE NOT PAID FOR YOUR WORK.
YES. I HEARD THAT IN THIS PLACE WHEN A PERSON WORKED IN ANY WAY THAT PERSON GOT PAID, BUT I WORKED AND I WAS NEVER PAID.
THIS IS ONE REASON I KNEW I WAS A SLAVE.
BUT WERE YOU GIVEN CLOTH, AND FED?
TWO CLOTHS WERE GIVEN TO ME, THAT IS ALL. I WAS FED BY ECCOAH.

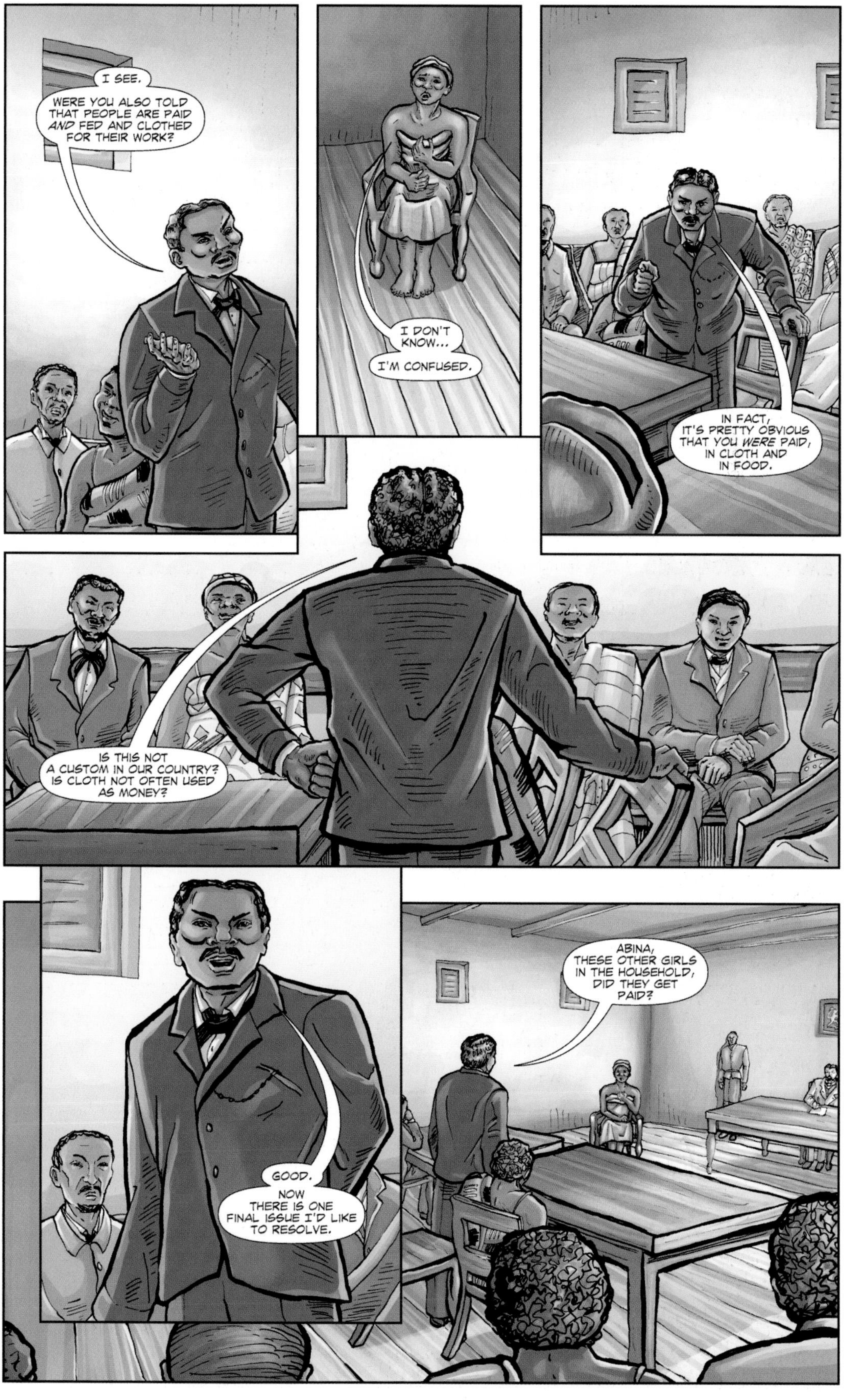
I SEE.
WERE YOU ALSO TOLD THAT PEOPLE ARE PAID *AND* FED AND CLOTHED FOR THEIR WORK?
I DON'T KNOW...
I'M CONFUSED.
IN FACT, IT'S PRETTY OBVIOUS THAT YOU *WERE* PAID, IN CLOTH AND IN FOOD.
IS THIS NOT A CUSTOM IN OUR COUNTRY? IS CLOTH NOT OFTEN USED AS MONEY?
GOOD.
NOW THERE IS ONE FINAL ISSUE I'D LIKE TO RESOLVE.
ABINA, THESE OTHER GIRLS IN THE HOUSEHOLD, DID THEY GET PAID?

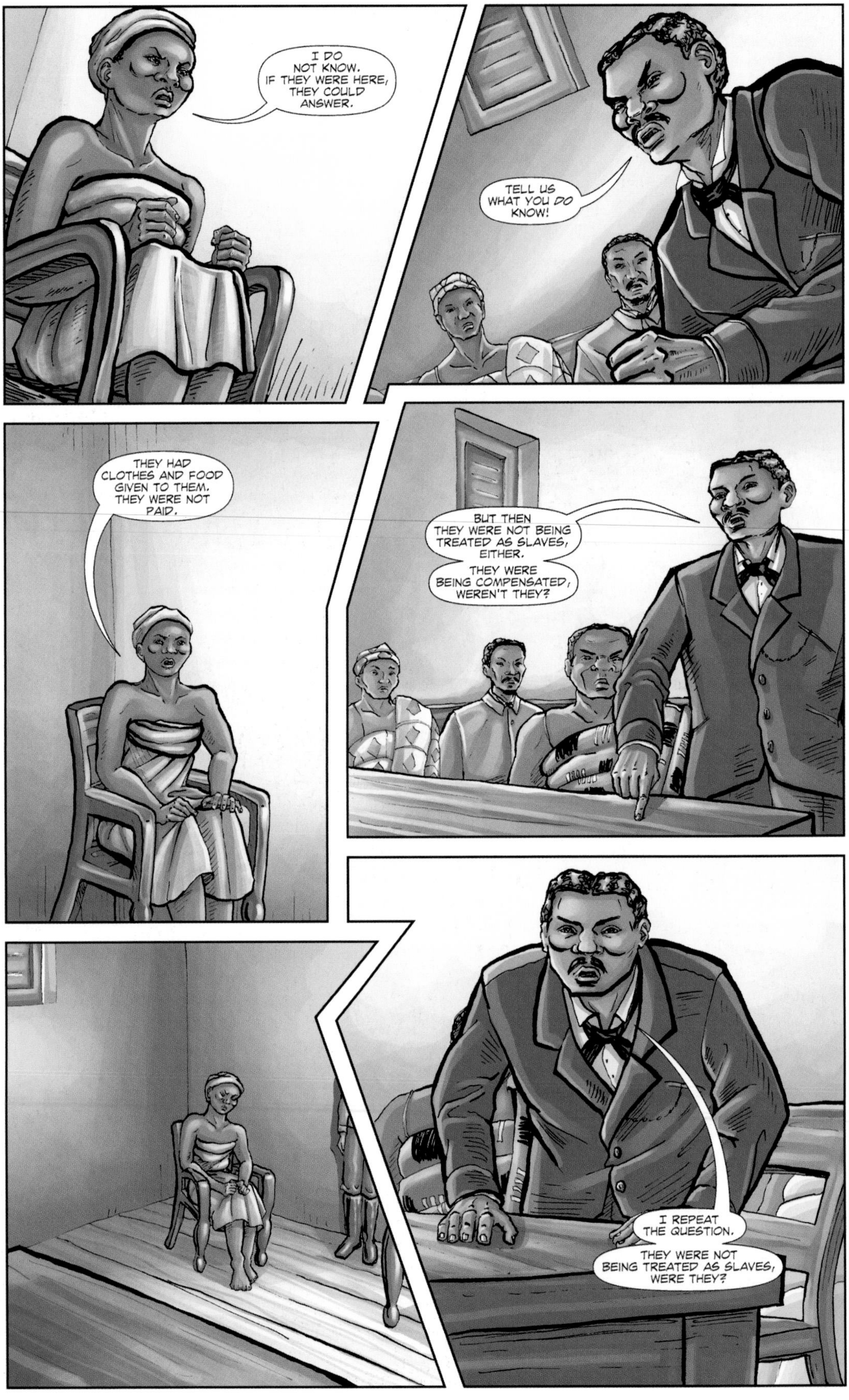
I DO NOT KNOW. IF THEY WERE HERE, THEY COULD ANSWER.
TELL US WHAT YOU *DO* KNOW!
THEY HAD CLOTHES AND FOOD GIVEN TO THEM. THEY WERE NOT PAID.
BUT THEN THEY WERE NOT BEING TREATED AS SLAVES, EITHER.
THEY WERE BEING COMPENSATED, WEREN'T THEY?
I REPEAT THE QUESTION.
THEY WERE NOT BEING TREATED AS SLAVES, WERE THEY?

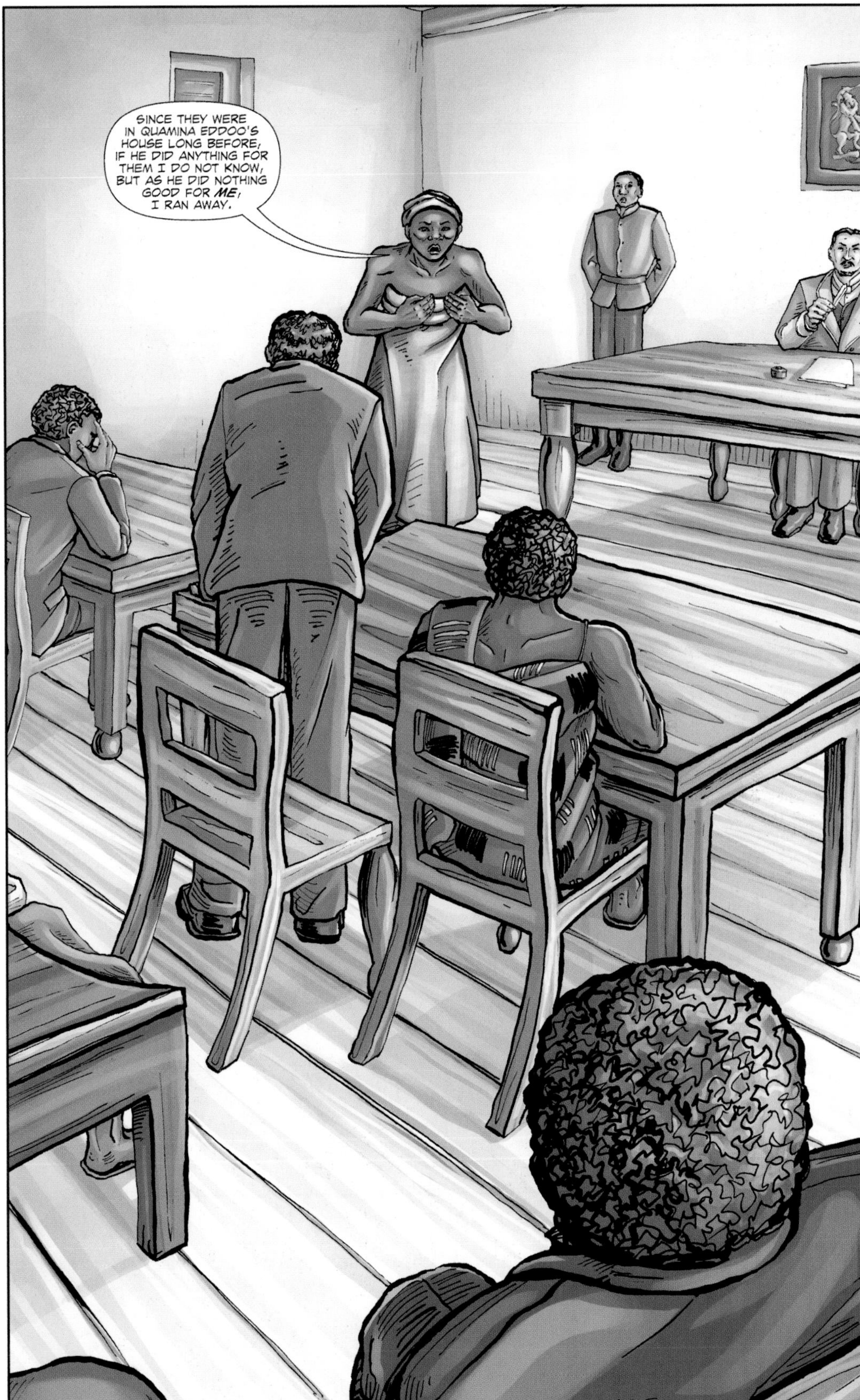
SINCE THEY WERE IN QUAMINA EDDOO'S HOUSE LONG BEFORE; IF HE DID ANYTHING FOR THEM I DO NOT KNOW; BUT AS HE DID NOTHING GOOD FOR *ME*, I RAN AWAY.

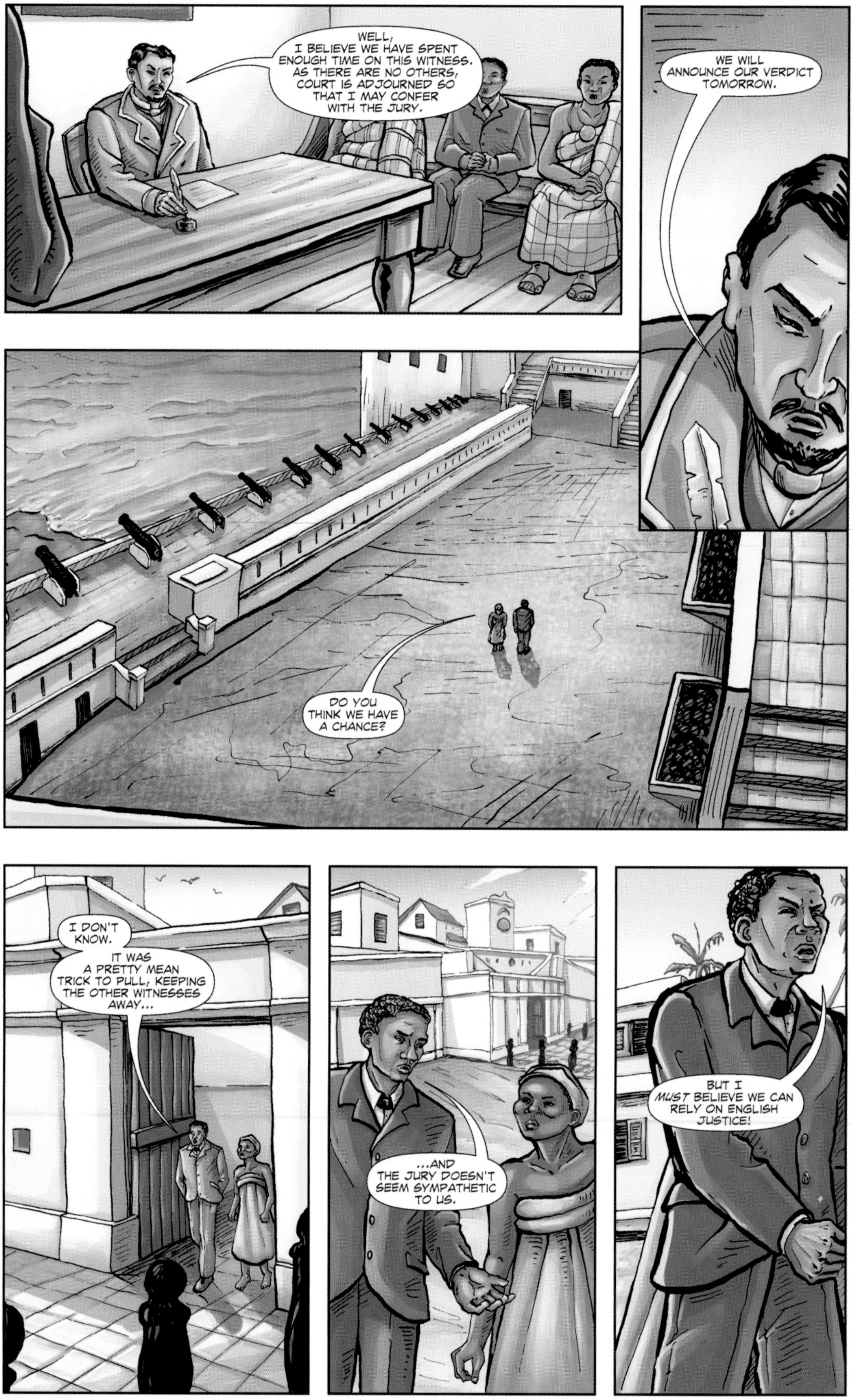

WELL, I BELIEVE WE HAVE SPENT ENOUGH TIME ON THIS WITNESS. AS THERE ARE NO OTHERS, COURT IS ADJOURNED SO THAT I MAY CONFER WITH THE JURY.
WE WILL ANNOUNCE OUR VERDICT TOMORROW.
DO YOU THINK WE HAVE A CHANCE?
I DON'T KNOW.
IT WAS A PRETTY MEAN TRICK TO PULL, KEEPING THE OTHER WITNESSES AWAY...
...AND THE JURY DOESN'T SEEM SYMPATHETIC TO US.
BUT I *MUST* BELIEVE WE CAN RELY ON ENGLISH JUSTICE!

CHAPTER 6
ABINA SILENCED, ABINA REDEEMED

ALL DAY, ALL OVER THE GOLD COAST COLONY AND PROTECTORATE, PEOPLE GO ABOUT THEIR BUSINESS.

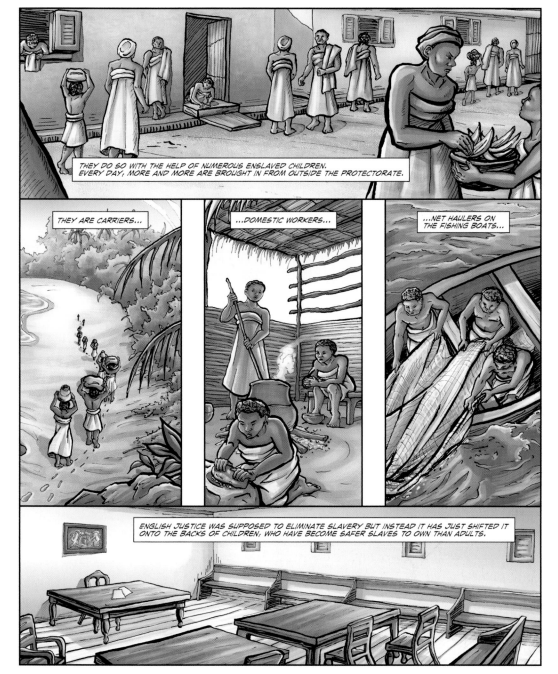

THEY DO SO WITH THE HELP OF NUMEROUS ENSLAVED CHILDREN. EVERY DAY, MORE AND MORE ARE BROUGHT IN FROM OUTSIDE THE PROTECTORATE.

THEY ARE CARRIERS...

...DOMESTIC WORKERS...

...NET HAULERS ON THE FISHING BOATS...

ENGLISH JUSTICE WAS SUPPOSED TO ELIMINATE SLAVERY BUT INSTEAD IT HAS JUST SHIFTED IT ONTO THE BACKS OF CHILDREN, WHO HAVE BECOME SAFER SLAVES TO OWN THAN ADULTS.

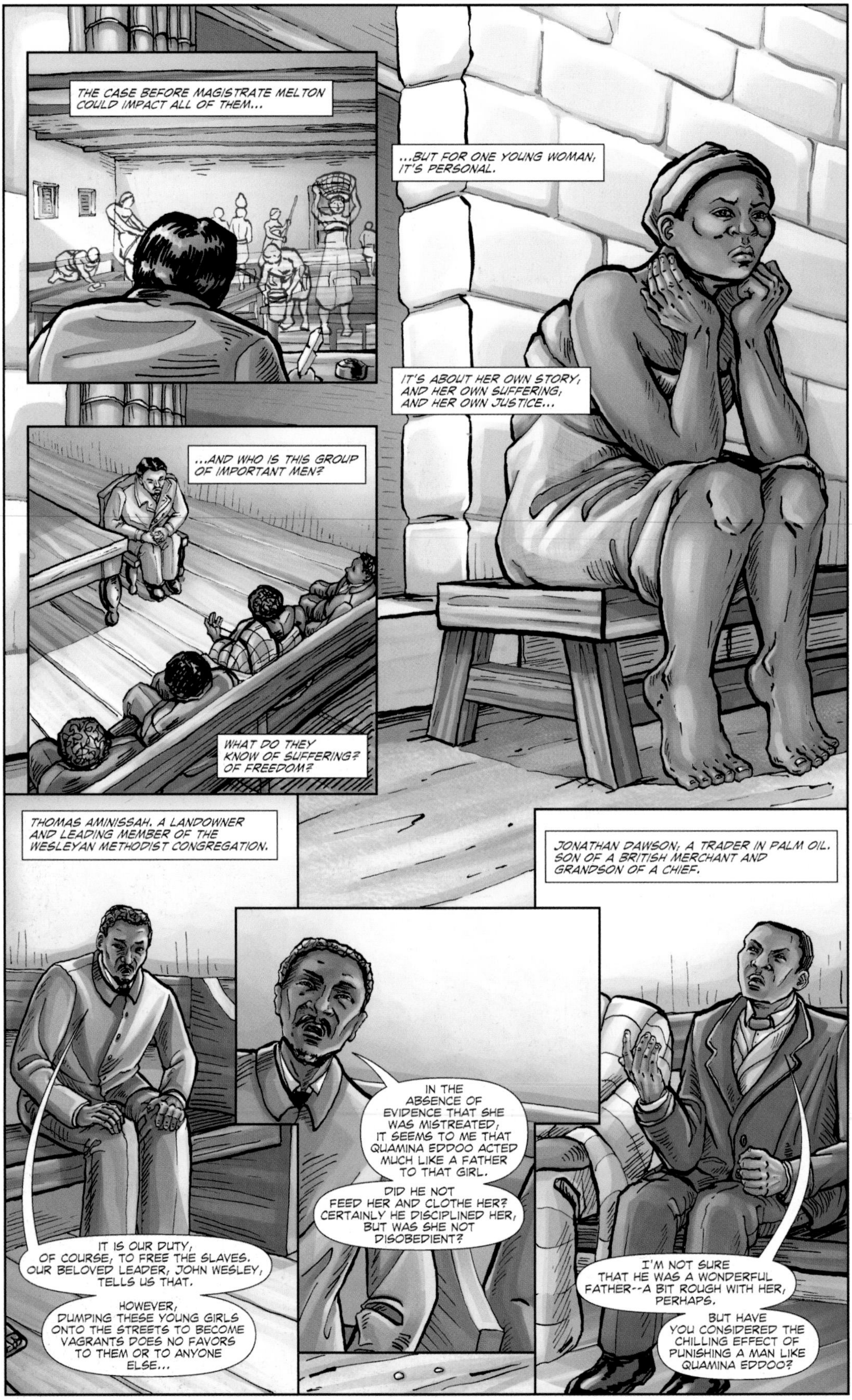
THE CASE BEFORE MAGISTRATE MELTON COULD IMPACT ALL OF THEM...
...BUT FOR ONE YOUNG WOMAN, IT'S PERSONAL.
IT'S ABOUT HER OWN STORY, AND HER OWN SUFFERING, AND HER OWN JUSTICE...
...AND WHO IS THIS GROUP OF IMPORTANT MEN?
WHAT DO THEY KNOW OF SUFFERING? OF FREEDOM?
THOMAS AMINISSAH. A LANDOWNER AND LEADING MEMBER OF THE WESLEYAN METHODIST CONGREGATION.
IT IS OUR DUTY, OF COURSE, TO FREE THE SLAVES. OUR BELOVED LEADER, JOHN WESLEY, TELLS US THAT.
HOWEVER, DUMPING THESE YOUNG GIRLS ONTO THE STREETS TO BECOME VAGRANTS DOES NO FAVORS TO THEM OR TO ANYONE ELSE...
IN THE ABSENCE OF EVIDENCE THAT SHE WAS MISTREATED, IT SEEMS TO ME THAT QUAMINA EDDOO ACTED MUCH LIKE A FATHER TO THAT GIRL.
DID HE NOT FEED HER AND CLOTHE HER? CERTAINLY HE DISCIPLINED HER, BUT WAS SHE NOT DISOBEDIENT?
JONATHAN DAWSON; A TRADER IN PALM OIL. SON OF A BRITISH MERCHANT AND GRANDSON OF A CHIEF.
I'M NOT SURE THAT HE WAS A WONDERFUL FATHER--A BIT ROUGH WITH HER, PERHAPS.
BUT HAVE YOU CONSIDERED THE CHILLING EFFECT OF PUNISHING A MAN LIKE QUAMINA EDDOO?

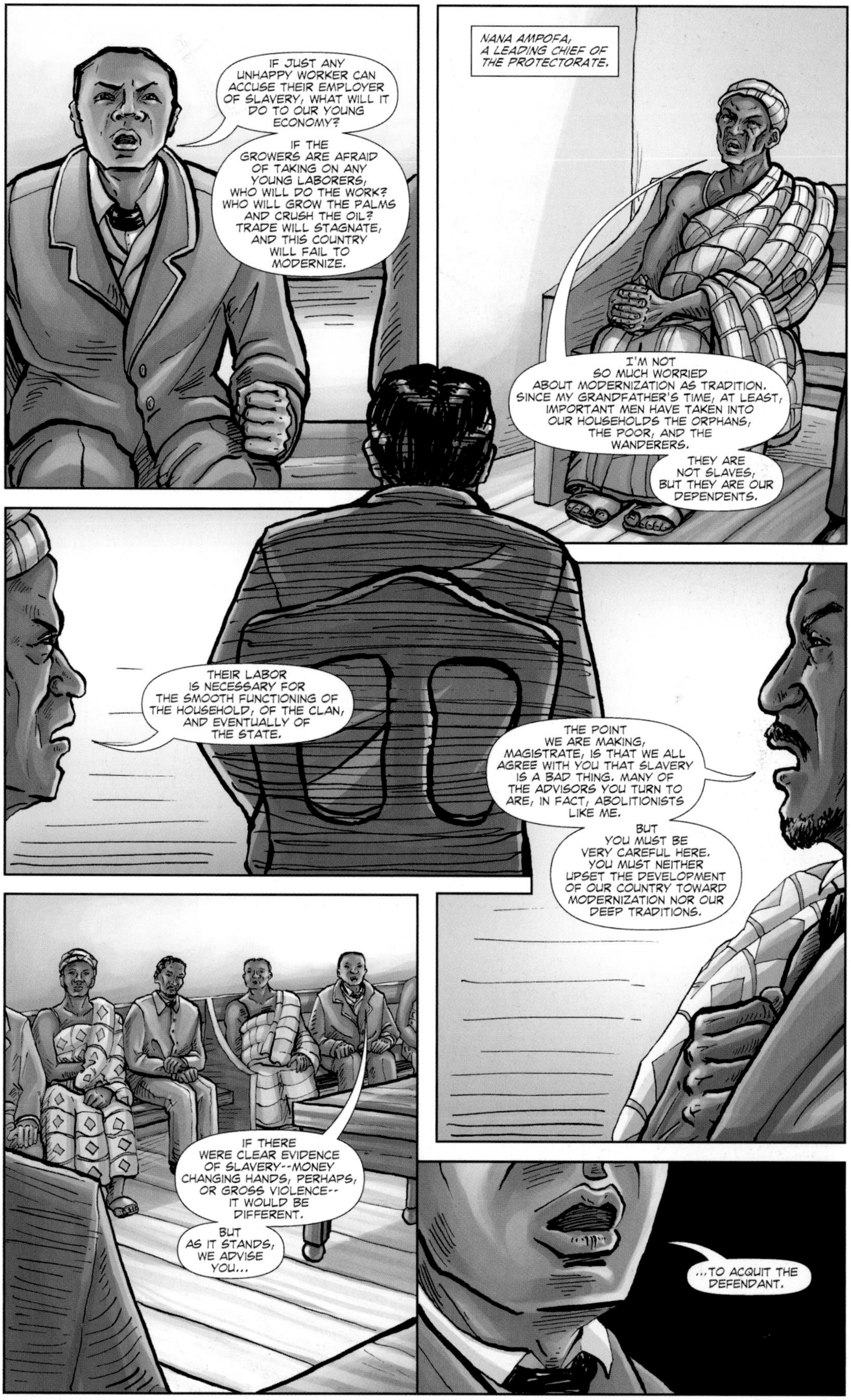
IF JUST ANY UNHAPPY WORKER CAN ACCUSE THEIR EMPLOYER OF SLAVERY, WHAT WILL IT DO TO OUR YOUNG ECONOMY?
IF THE GROWERS ARE AFRAID OF TAKING ON ANY YOUNG LABORERS, WHO WILL DO THE WORK? WHO WILL GROW THE PALMS AND CRUSH THE OIL? TRADE WILL STAGNATE, AND THIS COUNTRY WILL FAIL TO MODERNIZE.
NANA AMPOFA, A LEADING CHIEF OF THE PROTECTORATE.
I'M NOT SO MUCH WORRIED ABOUT MODERNIZATION AS TRADITION. SINCE MY GRANDFATHER'S TIME, AT LEAST, IMPORTANT MEN HAVE TAKEN INTO OUR HOUSEHOLDS THE ORPHANS, THE POOR, AND THE WANDERERS.
THEY ARE NOT SLAVES, BUT THEY ARE OUR DEPENDENTS.
THEIR LABOR IS NECESSARY FOR THE SMOOTH FUNCTIONING OF THE HOUSEHOLD, OF THE CLAN, AND EVENTUALLY OF THE STATE.
THE POINT WE ARE MAKING, MAGISTRATE, IS THAT WE ALL AGREE WITH YOU THAT SLAVERY IS A BAD THING. MANY OF THE ADVISORS YOU TURN TO ARE, IN FACT, ABOLITIONISTS LIKE ME.
BUT YOU MUST BE VERY CAREFUL HERE. YOU MUST NEITHER UPSET THE DEVELOPMENT OF OUR COUNTRY TOWARD MODERNIZATION NOR OUR DEEP TRADITIONS.
IF THERE WERE CLEAR EVIDENCE OF SLAVERY--MONEY CHANGING HANDS, PERHAPS, OR GROSS VIOLENCE--IT WOULD BE DIFFERENT.
BUT AS IT STANDS, WE ADVISE YOU...
...TO ACQUIT THE DEFENDANT.

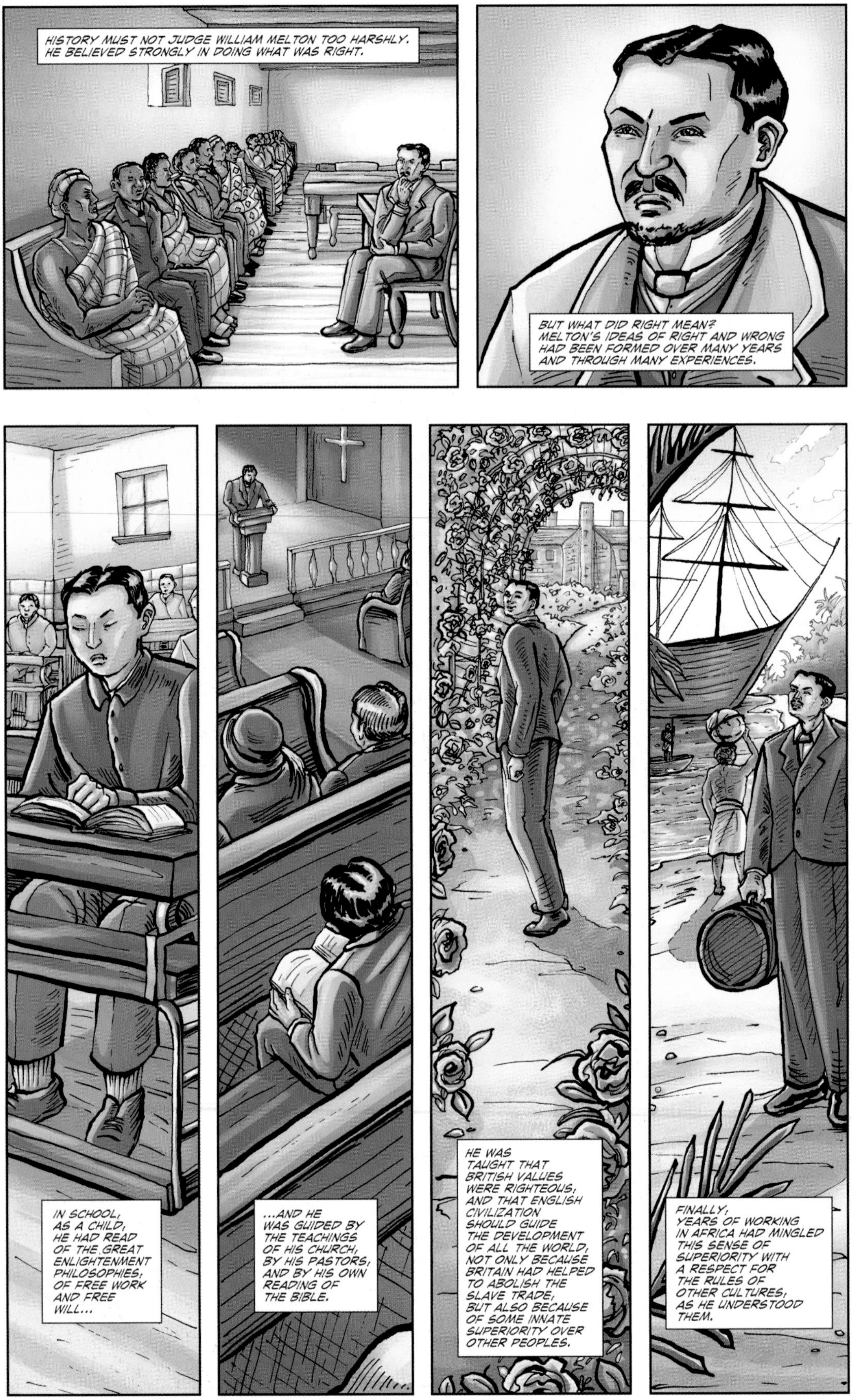
HISTORY MUST NOT JUDGE WILLIAM MELTON TOO HARSHLY. HE BELIEVED STRONGLY IN DOING WHAT WAS RIGHT.
BUT WHAT DID RIGHT MEAN? MELTON'S IDEAS OF RIGHT AND WRONG HAD BEEN FORMED OVER MANY YEARS AND THROUGH MANY EXPERIENCES.
IN SCHOOL, AS A CHILD, HE HAD READ OF THE GREAT ENLIGHTENMENT PHILOSOPHIES, OF FREE WORK AND FREE WILL...
...AND HE WAS GUIDED BY THE TEACHINGS OF HIS CHURCH, BY HIS PASTORS, AND BY HIS OWN READING OF THE BIBLE.
HE WAS TAUGHT THAT BRITISH VALUES WERE RIGHTEOUS, AND THAT ENGLISH CIVILIZATION SHOULD GUIDE THE DEVELOPMENT OF ALL THE WORLD, NOT ONLY BECAUSE BRITAIN HAD HELPED TO ABOLISH THE SLAVE TRADE, BUT ALSO BECAUSE OF SOME INNATE SUPERIORITY OVER OTHER PEOPLES.
FINALLY, YEARS OF WORKING IN AFRICA HAD MINGLED THIS SENSE OF SUPERIORITY WITH A RESPECT FOR THE RULES OF OTHER CULTURES, AS HE UNDERSTOOD THEM.

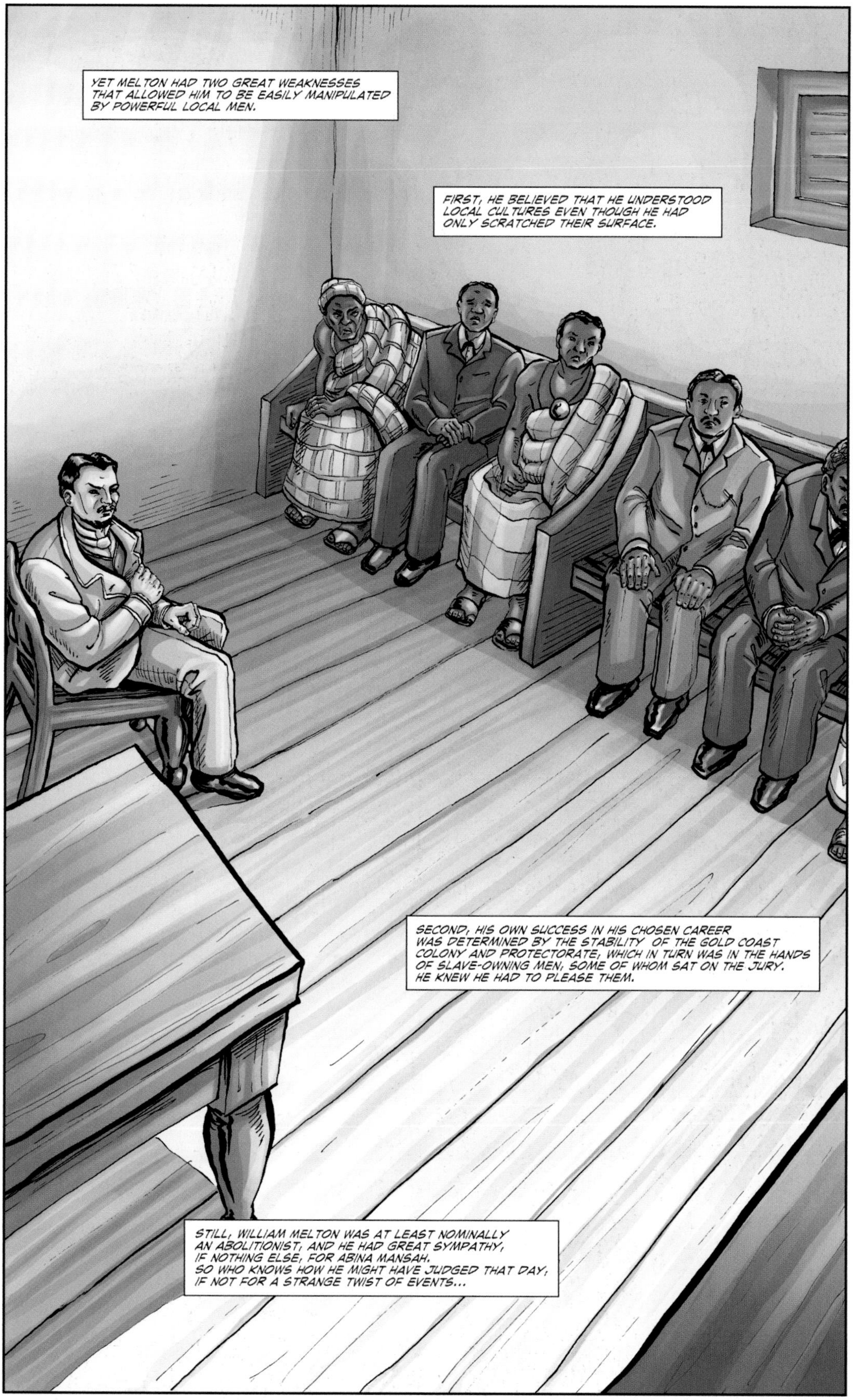
YET MELTON HAD TWO GREAT WEAKNESSES THAT ALLOWED HIM TO BE EASILY MANIPULATED BY POWERFUL LOCAL MEN.
FIRST, HE BELIEVED THAT HE UNDERSTOOD LOCAL CULTURES EVEN THOUGH HE HAD ONLY SCRATCHED THEIR SURFACE.
SECOND, HIS OWN SUCCESS IN HIS CHOSEN CAREER WAS DETERMINED BY THE STABILITY OF THE GOLD COAST COLONY AND PROTECTORATE, WHICH IN TURN WAS IN THE HANDS OF SLAVE-OWNING MEN; SOME OF WHOM SAT ON THE JURY. HE KNEW HE HAD TO PLEASE THEM.
STILL, WILLIAM MELTON WAS AT LEAST NOMINALLY AN ABOLITIONIST, AND HE HAD GREAT SYMPATHY, IF NOTHING ELSE, FOR ABINA MANSAH. SO WHO KNOWS HOW HE MIGHT HAVE JUDGED THAT DAY, IF NOT FOR A STRANGE TWIST OF EVENTS...

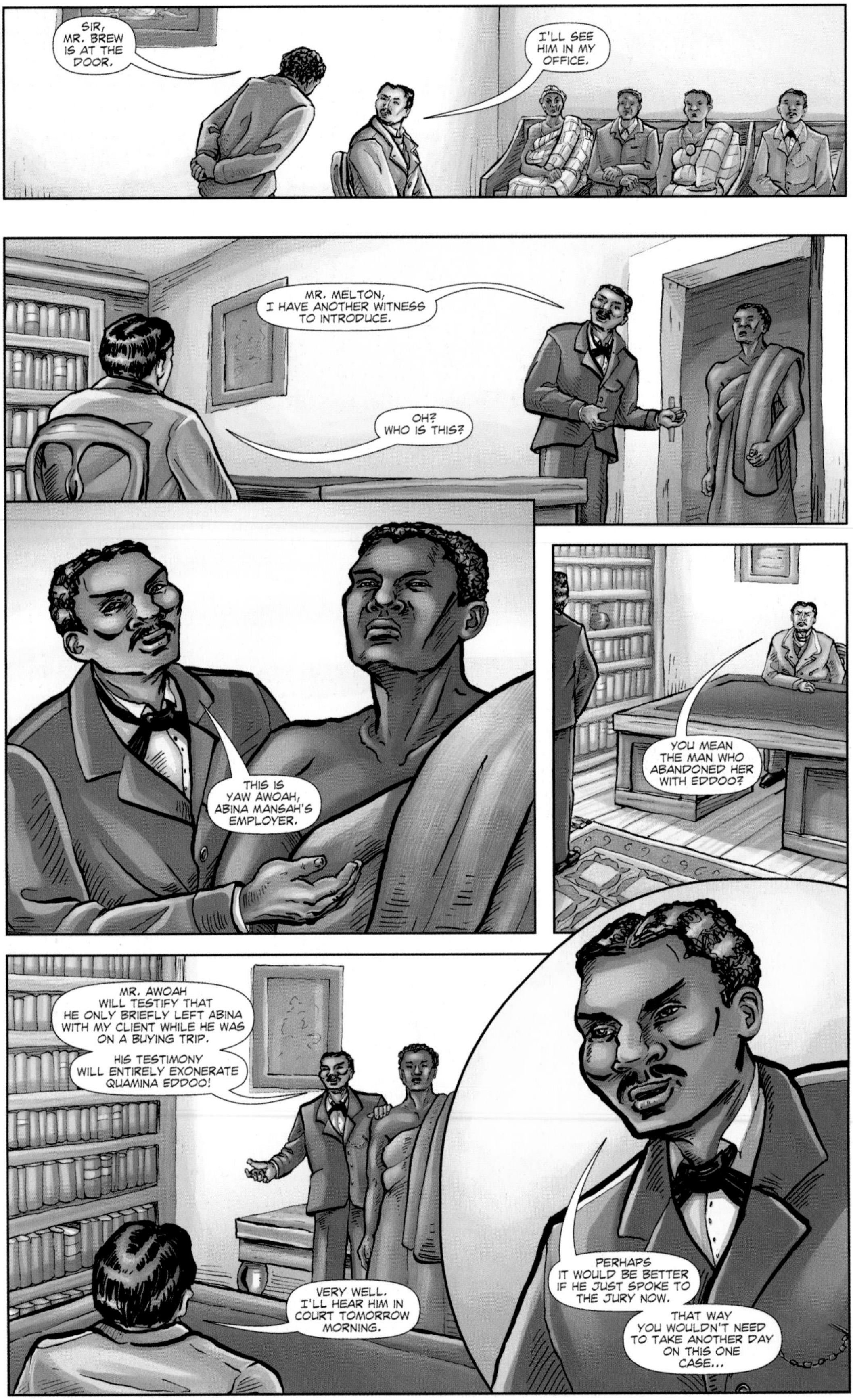
SIR, MR. BREW IS AT THE DOOR.
I'LL SEE HIM IN MY OFFICE.
MR. MELTON, I HAVE ANOTHER WITNESS TO INTRODUCE.
OH? WHO IS THIS?
THIS IS YAW AWOAH, ABINA MANSAH'S EMPLOYER.
YOU MEAN THE MAN WHO ABANDONED HER WITH EDDOO?
MR. AWOAH WILL TESTIFY THAT HE ONLY BRIEFLY LEFT ABINA WITH MY CLIENT WHILE HE WAS ON A BUYING TRIP.
HIS TESTIMONY WILL ENTIRELY EXONERATE QUAMINA EDDOO!
VERY WELL. I'LL HEAR HIM IN COURT TOMORROW MORNING.
PERHAPS IT WOULD BE BETTER IF HE JUST SPOKE TO THE JURY NOW.
THAT WAY YOU WOULDN'T NEED TO TAKE ANOTHER DAY ON THIS ONE CASE...

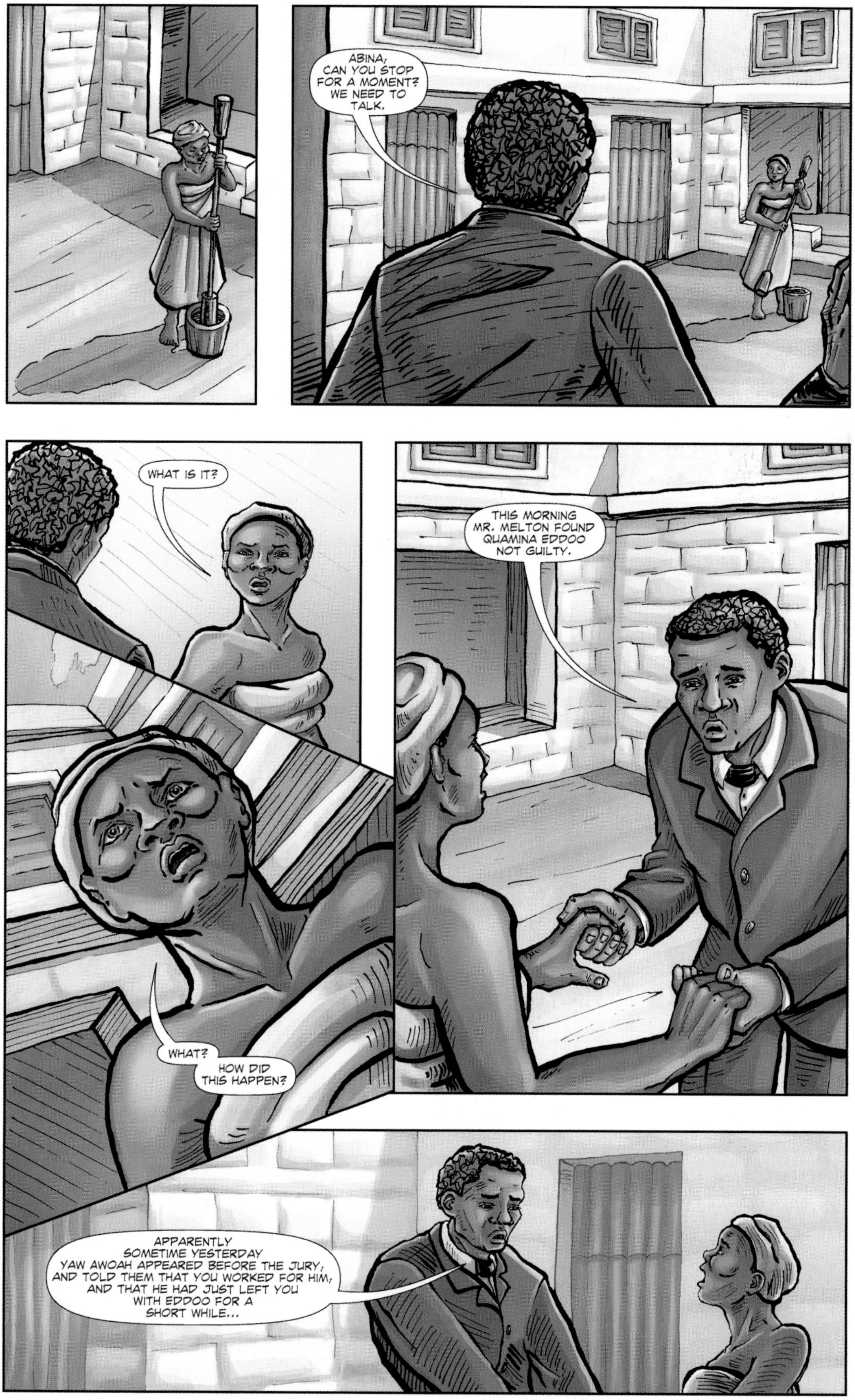
ABINA, CAN YOU STOP FOR A MOMENT? WE NEED TO TALK.
WHAT IS IT?
THIS MORNING MR. MELTON FOUND QUAMINA EDDOO NOT GUILTY.
WHAT?
HOW DID THIS HAPPEN?
APPARENTLY SOMETIME YESTERDAY YAW AWOAH APPEARED BEFORE THE JURY, AND TOLD THEM THAT YOU WORKED FOR HIM, AND THAT HE HAD JUST LEFT YOU WITH EDDOO FOR A SHORT WHILE...

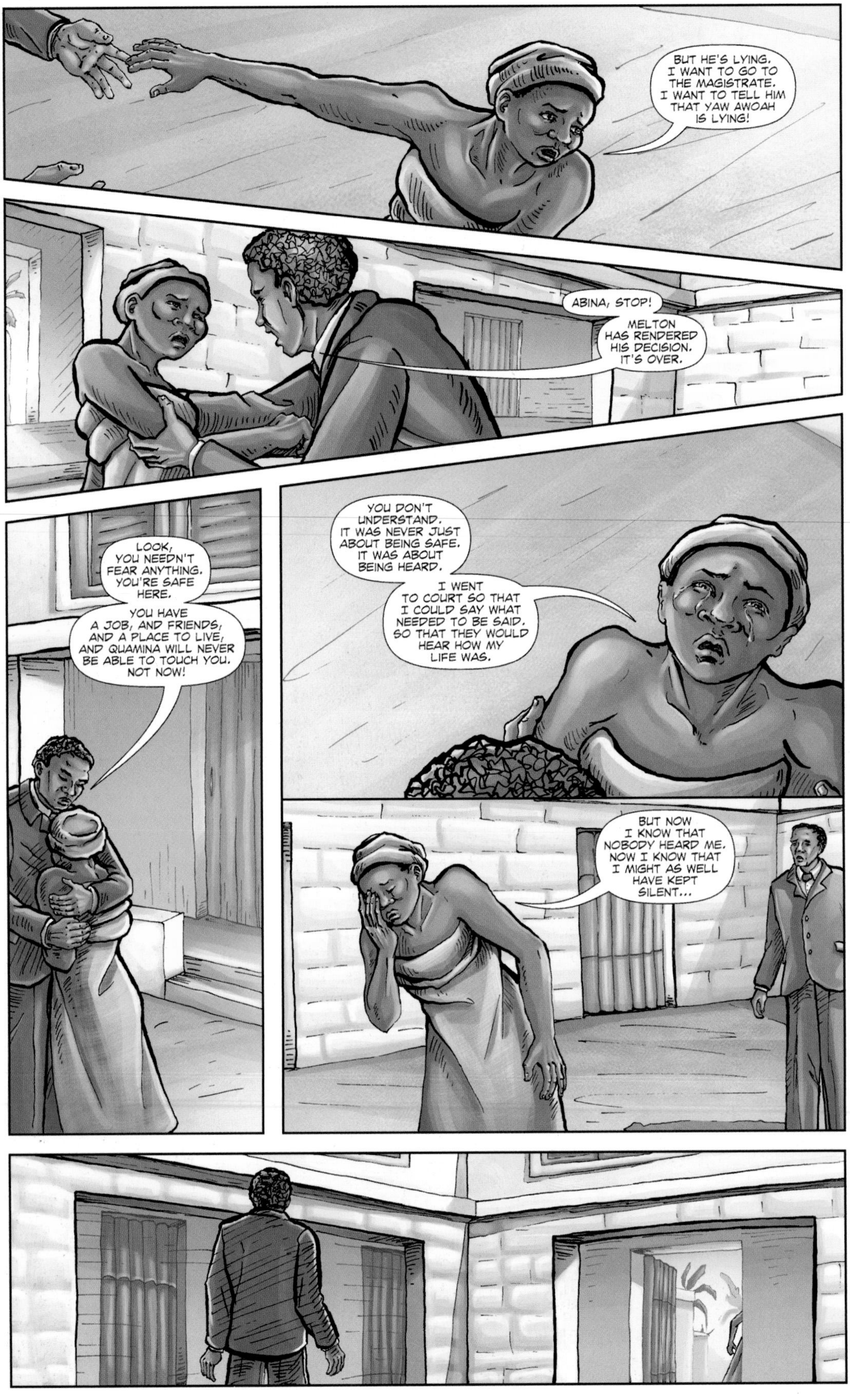

BUT HE'S LYING. I WANT TO GO TO THE MAGISTRATE. I WANT TO TELL HIM THAT YAW AWOAH IS LYING!
ABINA, STOP!
MELTON HAS RENDERED HIS DECISION. IT'S OVER.
LOOK, YOU NEEDN'T FEAR ANYTHING. YOU'RE SAFE HERE.
YOU HAVE A JOB, AND FRIENDS, AND A PLACE TO LIVE, AND QUAMINA WILL NEVER BE ABLE TO TOUCH YOU. NOT NOW!
YOU DON'T UNDERSTAND. IT WAS NEVER JUST ABOUT BEING SAFE. IT WAS ABOUT BEING HEARD.
I WENT TO COURT SO THAT I COULD SAY WHAT NEEDED TO BE SAID, SO THAT THEY WOULD HEAR HOW MY LIFE WAS.
BUT NOW I KNOW THAT NOBODY HEARD ME. NOW I KNOW THAT I MIGHT AS WELL HAVE KEPT SILENT...

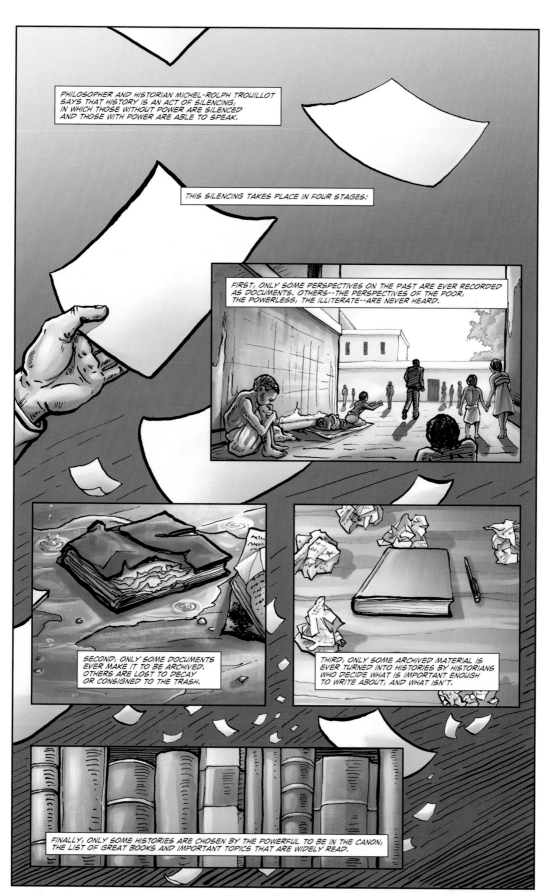

PHILOSOPHER AND HISTORIAN MICHEL-ROLPH TROUILLOT SAYS THAT HISTORY IS AN ACT OF SILENCING, IN WHICH THOSE WITHOUT POWER ARE SILENCED AND THOSE WITH POWER ARE ABLE TO SPEAK.

THIS SILENCING TAKES PLACE IN FOUR STAGES:

FIRST, ONLY SOME PERSPECTIVES ON THE PAST ARE EVER RECORDED AS DOCUMENTS. OTHERS--THE PERSPECTIVES OF THE POOR, THE POWERLESS, THE ILLITERATE--ARE NEVER HEARD.

SECOND, ONLY SOME DOCUMENTS EVER MAKE IT TO BE ARCHIVED. OTHERS ARE LOST TO DECAY OR CONSIGNED TO THE TRASH.

THIRD, ONLY SOME ARCHIVED MATERIAL IS EVER TURNED INTO HISTORIES BY HISTORIANS WHO DECIDE WHAT IS IMPORTANT ENOUGH TO WRITE ABOUT, AND WHAT ISN'T.

FINALLY, ONLY SOME HISTORIES ARE CHOSEN BY THE POWERFUL TO BE IN THE CANON, THE LIST OF GREAT BOOKS AND IMPORTANT TOPICS THAT ARE WIDELY READ.

FOLLOWING HER TESTIMONY, THE BOOK WAS CLOSED ON THE STORY OF ABINA MANSAH FOR 125 YEARS. SHE WAS INDEED SILENCED BY HISTORY... AS IF NOBODY HAD HEARD HER AT ALL.

QUAMINA EDDOO APPEARS ONLY INTERMITTENTLY IN THE HISTORICAL RECORDS OF THE TIME; BUT...

...THERE ARE PLENTY OF DOCUMENTS FROM HIS LAWYER JAMES HUTTON BREW, AND EVEN ARTICLES AND BOOKS ABOUT HIM. THE SAME IS TRUE OF WILLIAM MELTON.

MUCH OF THE HISTORY OF THE GOLD COAST IS WRITTEN ABOUT (AND BY) MEN LIKE BREW, AND DAVIS, AND MELTON; FOR THEY ARE IMPORTANT MEN.

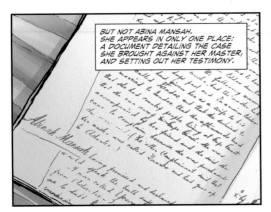

BUT NOT ABINA MANSAH. SHE APPEARS IN ONLY ONE PLACE: A DOCUMENT DETAILING THE CASE SHE BROUGHT AGAINST HER MASTER, AND SETTING OUT HER TESTIMONY.

FOR 125 YEARS, HER TESTIMONY WAS HIDDEN ON A SHELF, AND HER VOICE WAS SILENT.

BUT A VOICE LIKE HERS CANNOT BE SILENCED FOREVER, AND ONE DAY, NOT TOO LONG AGO...

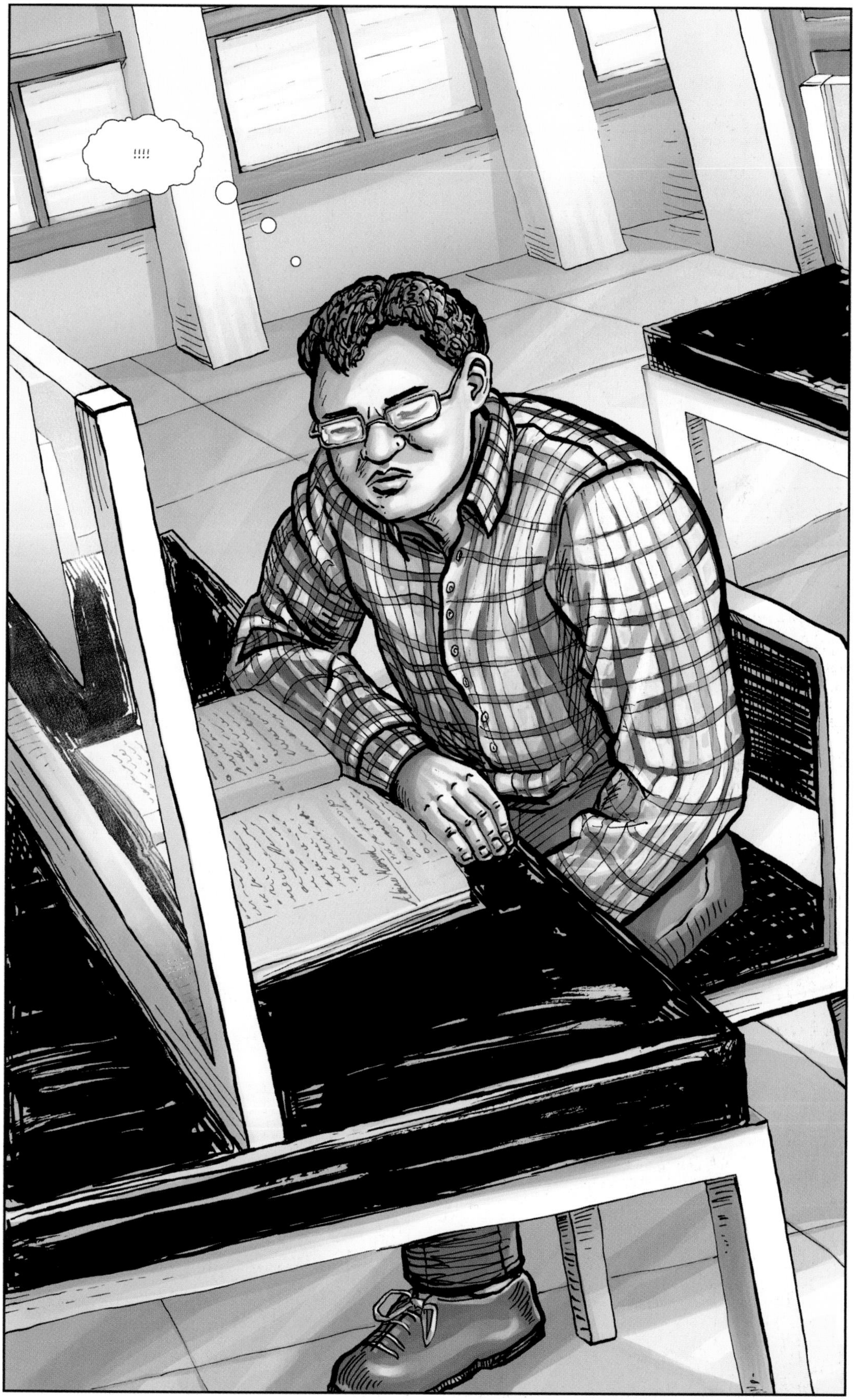
!!!!

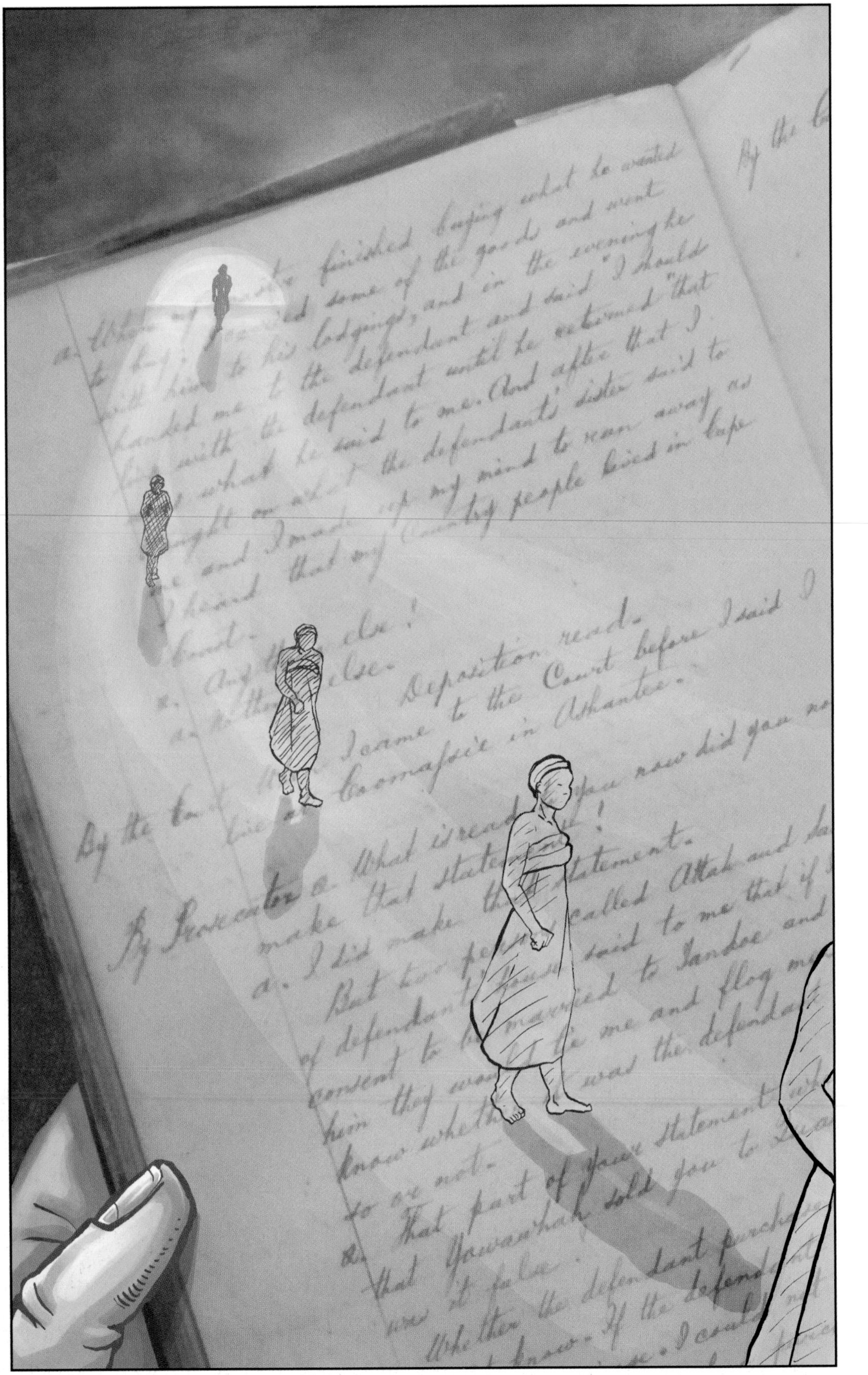
finished buying what he wanted
some of the goods and went
to his lodgings, and in the evening he
to the defendant and said "I should
defendant until he returned" that
he said to me. And after that I
the defendant's sister said to
my mind to run away as
that my country people lived in Cape
Coast.
Anything else!
Nothing else.
Deposition read.
I came to the Court before I said I
Coomassie in Ashantee.
What is read you now did you
make that statement!
I did make that statement.
called Attah and
said to me that if
consent to be married to Sandoe and
me and flog me
was the defendant
or not.
That part of your statement
that Yowarrhah sold you to
was it false
Whether the defendant purchased

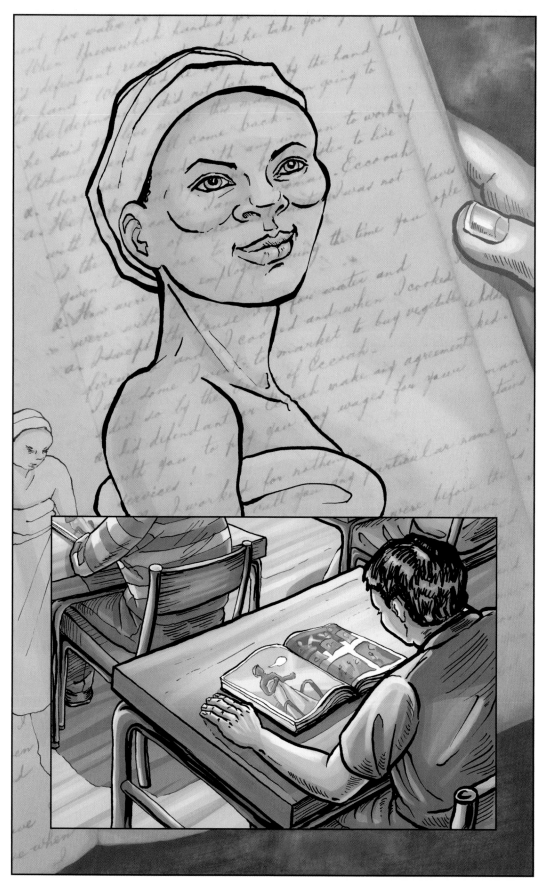

PART II
THE TRANSCRIPT

HYE WON HYE
"THAT WHICH DOES NOT BURN"

SCT 5-4-19 *REGINA V. QUAMINA EDDOO*, 10 NOV 1876

ACTING JUDICIAL ASSESSOR WILLIAM MELTON PRESIDING

Abinah Mansah, having been promised and declared that she would speak the truth says:

ABINA MANSAH A man called Yowawhah brought me from Ashantee. I was his wife. He brought me to Salt Pond. Yowawhah went on purchasing goods. On the same day as he finished, he handed me over to defendant to be with him, and said that he was going back and would return.

About ten days after the defendant gave me two cloths and told me that he had given me in marriage to one of his house people, and I remonstrated with defendant. I asked him how it was (that when I had been left by Yowawhah to live with him, and that he would return), that he had given me in marriage to one of his people. On this I thought that I had been sold and I ran away. At the time the defendant said he had given me in marriage to Tandoe. And the defendant said that if I did not consent to be married to Tandoe he would tie me up and flog me. I heard I had country people living at Cape Coast, and for what the defendant said I ran away and came to Cape Coast.

The defendant's sister said to me "You have taken some cloths to go and wash for some person, but will you not cook for your mother." I thought on this that I had been purchased. That also induced me to run away.

PROSECUTOR DAVIS On the evening as your master took you to the defendant did he say to you "I shall not take away the cloths on your person because I have known your body, but I will cut my beads and did he not cut the beads?

The form of the question is objected to by Mr. Brew on behalf of the defendant.

PROSECUTOR DAVIS On the evening as your master took you to defendant what did he say to you?

ABINA MANSAH When my master finished buying what he wanted to buy; I carried some of the goods and went with him to his lodgings, and in the evening he handed me to the defendant and said "I should live with the defendant until he returned" that was what he said to me. And after that I thought on what the defendant's sister said to me and I made up my mind to run away as I heard that my country people lived in Cape Coast.

PROSECUTOR DAVIS Anything else?

ABINA MANSAH Nothing else.

ABINA MANSAH When I came to the Court before I said I live at Coomassie in Ashantee.

PROSECUTOR DAVIS What is read to you now did you not make that statement?

ABINA MANSAH I did make that statement. But two persons called Attah and Sanygar of defendant's house said to me that if I did not consent to be married to Tandoe and live with him they would tie me and flog me. I do not know whether it was the defendant that said so or not.

PROSECUTOR DAVIS That part of your statement where you say that Yawawhah would give you to Quamin Eddoo was it false?

ABINA MANSAH Whether the defendant purchased me or not I do not know. If the defendant had not given me in marriage, I could not have formed any idea that he had purchased me.

PROSECUTOR DAVIS Do you see then that you were a slave?

ABINA MANSAH Yes, I thought I was a slave, because when I went for water or firewood I was not paid.

AJA MELTON When Yawawhah handed you to defendant did defendant receive you? Did he take you by the hand? What did he say?

ABINA MANSAH He (defendant) did not take me by the hand. He [Yawawhah] said "Go live with this man. I am going to Ashantee [Asante] and will come back.

AJA MELTON Were you placed with any woman to work?

ABINA MANSAH He (defendant) gave me to his sister to live with her, because I am a woman. Eccoah is the name of defendant's sister. I was not given to anyone to work.

AJA MELTON How were you employed during the time you were with Eccoah?

ABINA MANSAH I swept the house. I go for water and firewood and I cooked and when I cooked I ate some. I went to market to buy vegetables. I did so by the order of Eccoah.

AJA MELTON Did defendant or Eccoah make any agreement with you to pay you any wages for your services?

ABINA MANSAH No I worked for nothing.

AJA MELTON Did Eccoah call you any particular name?

ABINA MANSAH No

AJA MELTON Did you not say when you were before the court before that she called you her slave?

ABINA MANSAH On the occasion when I went and washed some clothes and returned, defendant's sister said to me: "a person like you go out and wash cloths for other persons not for me nor your master," "did you expect other persons to cook for you to eat," "a slave like you."

AJA MELTON When Eccoah said "Your master" what did she mean?

ABINA MANSAH I cannot answer.

AJA MELTON During the time you were with Eccoah did she compel you to do these things against your will?

ABINA MANSAH In some instances, she said "do so" and "do that" others I did of my own accord.

AJA MELTON When you were a slave at Adansi what kind of work did you do there?

ABINA MANSAH I did the same work as defendant's sister told me.

AJA MELTON When Yowawhah left you with defendant did he take away your cloth?

ABINA MANSAH No only the beads below my knee in remembrance.

AJA MELTON You have been a slave in Adansi and know how slaves are treated did you experience the same kind of treatment whilst with defendant and his sister?

ABINA MANSAH Yes in the same way that I was treated at Adansi the same way I was treated at Salt Pond.

AJA MELTON Are free persons treated in the same way?

ABINA MANSAH No.

AJA MELTON Then not being treated as a free person what did you consider you were. What did you know that you were?

ABINA MANSAH A slave cannot be treated as a free person. [While] I was a slave at Adansi there is a word by which a person who is a domestic slave and another by which a slave is called which is "Amerperlay" or slave.

AJA MELTON Were you addressed by that name by Eccoah?

ABINA MANSAH On the day that I returned from washing the clothes she called me "Amerperlay" which in the Kreppee means slave.

AJA MELTON Had you a will of your own. Could you do as you pleased without the control of Eccoah?

ABINA MANSAH What came in my own I did it and what came in my own mind I did it.

AJA MELTON Altogether did Eccoah treat you as a free person or as a slave?

ABINA MANSAH She treated me as a slave and called me a slave.

AJA MELTON Did you when she so called and treated you believe that Yowahwah would return?

Here the witness who appears to understand Fantee speaks in that language

ABINA MANSAH I did not think he would return, because Eccoah scolded me and abused me. I thought then that Yowahwah had sold me and that he would not return.

JAMES HUTTON BREW From that time that defendant placed you in his sister's hand did she commence to treat you as a slave?

ABINA MANSAH Yes. When I was handed to Tandoe to be his wife he gave the Handkerchief I hold in my hand. Defendant said he was going to have plenty of cloths sewn for me by this. I thought that I had been sold.

JAMES HUTTON BREW Were you given to Tandoe to be his wife by the defendant without first asking you, without your consent and against your will?

ABINA MANSAH Defendant asked me if I liked him and I said I did not.

JAMES HUTTON BREW Were there any other women in the house of defendant besides yourself?

ABINA MANSAH Yes

JAMES HUTTON BREW Did they do any kind of work also?

ABINA MANSAH Yes

JAMES HUTTON BREW Did they also go for wood and water, marketing and do the same work as you did?

ABINA MANSAH Yes

JAMES HUTTON BREW Were you not aware that all the people in the house were free?

ABINA MANSAH I did not know.

JAMES HUTTON BREW Are you aware that everybody in the Protectorate is freed and that those people you saw in defendant's house are as free as defendant and others?

ABINA MANSAH I did not know that I was free.

JAMES HUTTON BREW As to the others you saw in defendant's house?

ABINA MANSAH I did not know this. They the persons whom I saw are all the children of slaves.

JAMES HUTTON BREW You say you are not aware that all slaves in the Protectorate have been declared free. What led you then to come and lodge this complaint?

ABINA MANSAH I heard that master (meaning white man) had said we were all free. Yet I had been sold and I had no will of my own and I could not look after my body and health: that I am a slave and I would therefore come and complain.

JAMES HUTTON BREW So then you were aware that all the people in defendant's house were free, as you state, with the exception of yourself?

ABINA MANSAH They were not all free, but some were slaves.

JAMES HUTTON BREW [Question repeated.]

ABINA MANSAH I know that all are free.

JAMES HUTTON BREW You said you performed certain work. Were you fed and clothed if so by whom?

ABINA MANSAH Two cloths were given to me that is all. I was fed by Eccoah.

JAMES HUTTON BREW Did you pay for these and the house you live in?

ABINA MANSAH No

JAMES HUTTON BREW Who put the notion into your head that because you were not paid for the services you rendered you were therefore a slave?

ABINA MANSAH I heard that in this place when a man worked in any way he was paid, but I worked and I was not paid. So I thought I am really purchased.

JAMES HUTTON BREW You heard also that people are fed and clothed for nothing and paid besides for nothing?

ABINA MANSAH I heard that also.

JAMES HUTTON BREW [Question repeated in a different form.]

ABINA MANSAH If one did not work he could not get cloth nor food to eat.

JAMES HUTTON BREW You heard that if you worked you would be fed and clothed and paid altogether?

ABINA MANSAH I heard that.

JAMES HUTTON BREW How long were you in defendant's house before you ran away?

ABINA MANSAH I did not count but I came away in the same month.

JAMES HUTTON BREW Whilst you were there did you see those of whom you have spoken were fed clothed and paid by defendant?

ABINA MANSAH They had clothes and food given to them. They were not paid.

JAMES HUTTON BREW Were you treated in any way differently from the others or were you all treated alike?

ABINA MANSAH As I was not in the house long I could not tell if he had given them anything before. I did not see him give them anything.

JAMES HUTTON BREW As to treatment.

ABINA MANSAH They were all clothed and fed, but not fed [sic . . . meant "paid," I think].

ABINA MANSAH When I came I had two cloths given to me. As they were in defendant's house long before if the defendant had done anything for them I could not tell but as for me he did nothing good for me not having been in the house long, and I ran away.

JAMES HUTTON BREW How were you treated by defendant or his sister that you were induced to run away? Harshly treated by your master the defendant were you chastised or merely scolded?

ABINA MANSAH I did not live in defendant's house as he gave me to his sister. I lived in his sister's house if defendant's sister told me to do this and that I got up and went and did it. When I did wrong his sister scolded me but never flogged me.

JAMES HUTTON BREW In going for firewood, water etc. were you compelled to go by any species of coercion or threats or told to do so in the ordinary manner, and you went and did it?

ABINA MANSAH If she says go for firewood, or water or to market I go. She forces me.

JAMES HUTTON BREW Do you mean requested, solicited, or how?

ABINA MANSAH I was asked.

JAMES HUTTON BREW Were you threatened with ill treatment or punishment if you refused to go?

ABINA MANSAH If she said to me "go for firewood" and I said "I won't go" She said if you don't you will be tied and flogged and I said "Now all are free. I also am free. I claim freedom." That was why I ran away.

JAMES HUTTON BREW How often were you threatened with punishment under such circumstances?

ABINA MANSAH About three times.

JAMES HUTTON BREW Was threat of punishment made in the presence of any one besides yourself?

ABINA MANSAH Some children but no elderly person belonging to the house of about from 9 to 13 year of age all girls vis: Accosuah, Abina, Adjuah, Ambah (the eldest of all).

JAMES HUTTON BREW In whose house were these girls living?

ABINA MANSAH In defendant's sisters house.

JAMES HUTTON BREW Is not defendant's sister's house a portion of the house in which defendant lives?

ABINA MANSAH They all lived in one house.

JAMES HUTTON BREW You stated how people were treated as slaves at Adansi. State how slaves and free people are there treated.

ABINA MANSAH At Adansi when a free person is sitting down at ease the slave is working that is what I know.

JAMES HUTTON BREW Did free person do no work in this household?

ABINA MANSAH On any day when the freeman liked he worked. I did the necessary work such as woman do if it was firewood or water or plantains I went and fetched it.

JAMES HUTTON BREW Were you not cuffed and beaten at times?

ABINA MANSAH I was not long at Adansi before I was brought to this place. When I did wrong I was scolded.

JAMES HUTTON BREW Were you a slave before you came to Adansi?

ABINA MANSAH I was a slave to Eddoo Buffo.

JAMES HUTTON BREW Were you never during that time beaten for misconduct or anything like that?

ABINA MANSAH When I was with Eddo Buffoe and did wrong I was flogged and sometimes I was logged.[1]

JAMES HUTTON BREW Did Eccoah treat you differently to what she did the other maidservants in the house?

ABINA MANSAH She did not treat me in the same manner as she treated those I met in the house. When she gave them cloths she gave me none that is all.

---

1   Chained to a log as punishment

JAMES HUTTON BREW You said that some one threatened to tie her [you?] up and flog her if she would not marry Tandoe. Who was it. Defendant or Seney Agay or Attah?

ABINA MANSAH Attah and Senegay.

JAMES HUTTON BREW You said you made a statement in court in which you declared to as a fact that Yaowahwah sold you to defendant. Do you still say so? Of your own knowledge?

ABINA MANSAH If when Yowahwah gave me to defendant to keep the defendant had not given me in marriage to Tandoe I would not have entertained such an idea that I had been sold. Because defendant gave me in marriage I knew that I had been sold.

JAMES HUTTON BREW In what way were you given in marriage?

ABINA MANSAH My master said that I should be married to Tandoe and that he would give me plenty of cloths, and I said I did not like him. Defendant was in earnest. Tandoe first gave me this handkerchief, but my master was vexed and asked Tandoe why he gave me this when he was going to give me plenty of cloths.

JAMES HUTTON BREW You said that only one occasion Eccoah called you a slave. Did she say "you are my slave" or that "Eddoo's slave" or simply that you are a slave?

ABINA MANSAH "You are your master's slave" when she said this I sat down and said I did not like this and I made up my mind to come away.

JAMES HUTTON BREW You are certain of this?

ABINA MANSAH Yes Ambah and Adjuah and Accosuah were present.

JAMES HUTTON BREW Do you know how much you were sold for?

ABINA MANSAH I do not know.

JAMES HUTTON BREW Do you know how slaves are sold and handed over?

ABINA MANSAH I know it.

JAMES HUTTON BREW Are any ceremonies observed on such occasions if so what?

ABINA MANSAH Yes

JAMES HUTTON BREW Were any of them gone through on your alleged sale to Edoo?

ABINA MANSAH There was no observance kept to show the sale of a slave the only thing which was done was the cutting of the beads at the time.

JAMES HUTTON BREW Is that one of the observances?

ABINA MANSAH It was one

PART III
HISTORICAL
CONTEXT

NKYIMU
"PRECISION IS NECESSARY"

In the previous two sections of this book, you have encountered a **primary source** and a **secondary source**. The primary source (Part II) is a document from the nineteenth century that purports to be an eyewitness description of what happened in the courtroom in which Abina Mansah appeared in 1876 and which contains an account of her life up to that point. The secondary source (Part I) is a graphic interpretation of that document jointly prepared by an historian and an artist. Like many others who interpret the past, we have strived to create a representation that is reasonably accurate, authentic to the experiences and perspectives of the individuals represented, and useful to our audience. How did we turn the short primary source into a longer interpretation that tried to meet these criteria? How can we know whether our account of the events surrounding Abina Mansah's day in court is a reasonably accurate and useful interpretation? How can you, the reader, trust the work we have produced?

In the next two parts of this book, we will attempt to answer those questions by sharing with you the process we went through in developing our interpretation. We will show you the information we used and discuss the questions we asked ourselves as we wrote and illustrated Abina's story. The first task in this process is to explain our understanding of the time and place in which Abina and the "important men" lived (Part III). Then, we will also share with you the philosophical, ethical, and theoretical questions that confronted us and our solutions for dealing with them (Part IV).

The act of setting an historical narrative in the context of the time and place in which it happened is called **historicization**. Most historians see their job as reconstructing past events. They seek to understand not only what happened but also how people experienced events and why these events happened. Like detectives, historians work with evidence—written documents, archaeological remains, spoken words—each of which provides only a small part of the story. Only by putting these small parts together can historians get a reasonable understanding of what happened, why it happened, and how people who lived in that time and place experienced it. For *Abinah and the Important Men*, that means gaining a better understanding of what life was like on the Gold Coast in 1876, of the institution of slavery and its abolition in the region, and finally, of the biographies of the main individuals in the story.

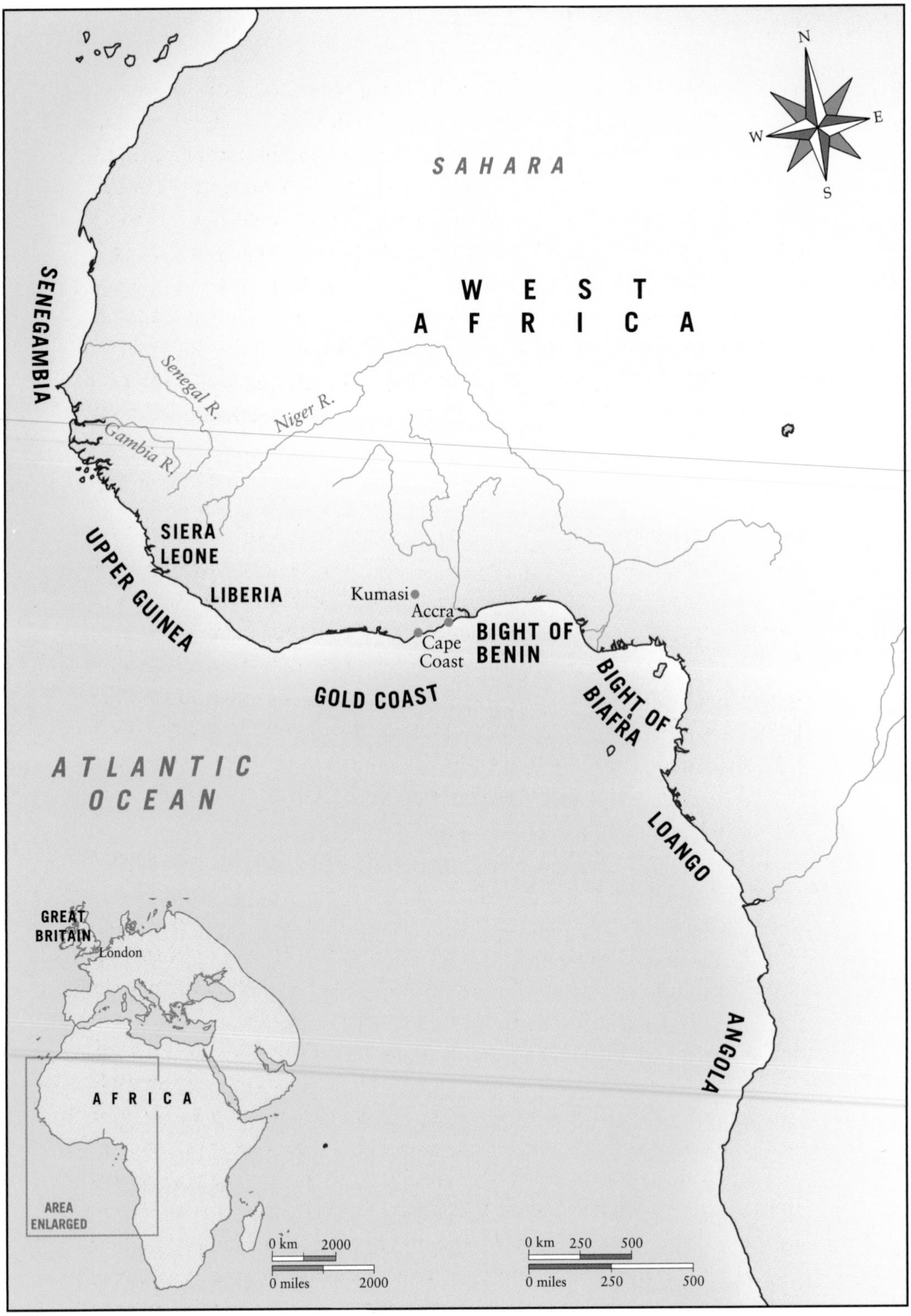
N
E
W
S
SAHARA
WEST AFRICA
SENEGAMBIA
Senegal R.
Niger R.
Gambia R.
SIERA LEONE
UPPER GUINEA
LIBERIA
Kumasi
Accra
Cape Coast
BIGHT OF BENIN
GOLD COAST
BIGHT OF BIAFRA
ATLANTIC OCEAN
LOANGO
ANGOLA
GREAT BRITAIN
London
AFRICA
AREA ENLARGED
0 km 2000
0 miles 2000
0 km 250 500
0 miles 250 500

MAP 1 West Africa and the Gold Coast

THE GOLD COAST, CA. 1876

The **Gold Coast** is a name bestowed by Europeans upon a stretch of West Africa roughly approximating the southern half of the modern-day state of Ghana (see Map 1). The name derives from the fact that from the eighth to the sixteenth centuries (and even today) the inhabitants of the region extracted a great deal of gold that entered the world economy, first by crossing the Sahara Desert into North Africa, and later, through trade with European merchants who visited the coast. In fact, gold was only one of many materials in this region's history produced by the hard work of its people and from its rich soil and desired by the outside world. Over the past millennium, foreigners have often come seeking their wealth from the soil and people of the Gold Coast, whether by trading in gold, kola nuts, palm oil, or cocoa.

EARLY HISTORY

The human presence in West Africa stretches back many thousands of years, but for most of that period the Gold Coast was populated by many small bands of hunter-gatherers. Traces of their language may survive in the Etsi or Guan languages still spoken by a few groups along the coast and in the mountains of the region today. However, recent research suggests that agriculture became prevalent in the savanna to the north as far back as ca. 1700 B.C.E., and over the next two millennia foraging slowly gave way to a more settled way of life in the forest zone of the Gold Coast, where first yams, and later cassava and plantains, became the staple foods of dense populations.

In the fifteenth century (ca. 1440 C.E.), the period from which emerge the oldest surviving written sources for the forest region that we know as the Gold Coast, large-scale, organized societies that subsisted on agriculture—and which produced enough of a surplus to support a specialized labor force—developed. The people in these societies spoke languages that later developed into the modern languages of southern Ghana—Ga-Adangbe, Ewe, and especially the **Akan** family of Twi languages (Fante, Akuapem, and **Asante**) (see Map 2). It was the Twi-speaking Akan people who came dominate the area discussed in this story. Like many of their neighbors, the Akan organized themselves over several centuries into a society that had several major institutions. The most important of these was and remains the *abusua*, or extended family (see Glossary). The abusua institution probably developed in order to organize shared family labor for big tasks like clearing forests to plant crops, and also in order to promote the fertility of the community. The asafo was a way for a large group to provide resources to members in need, especially child-bearing women and

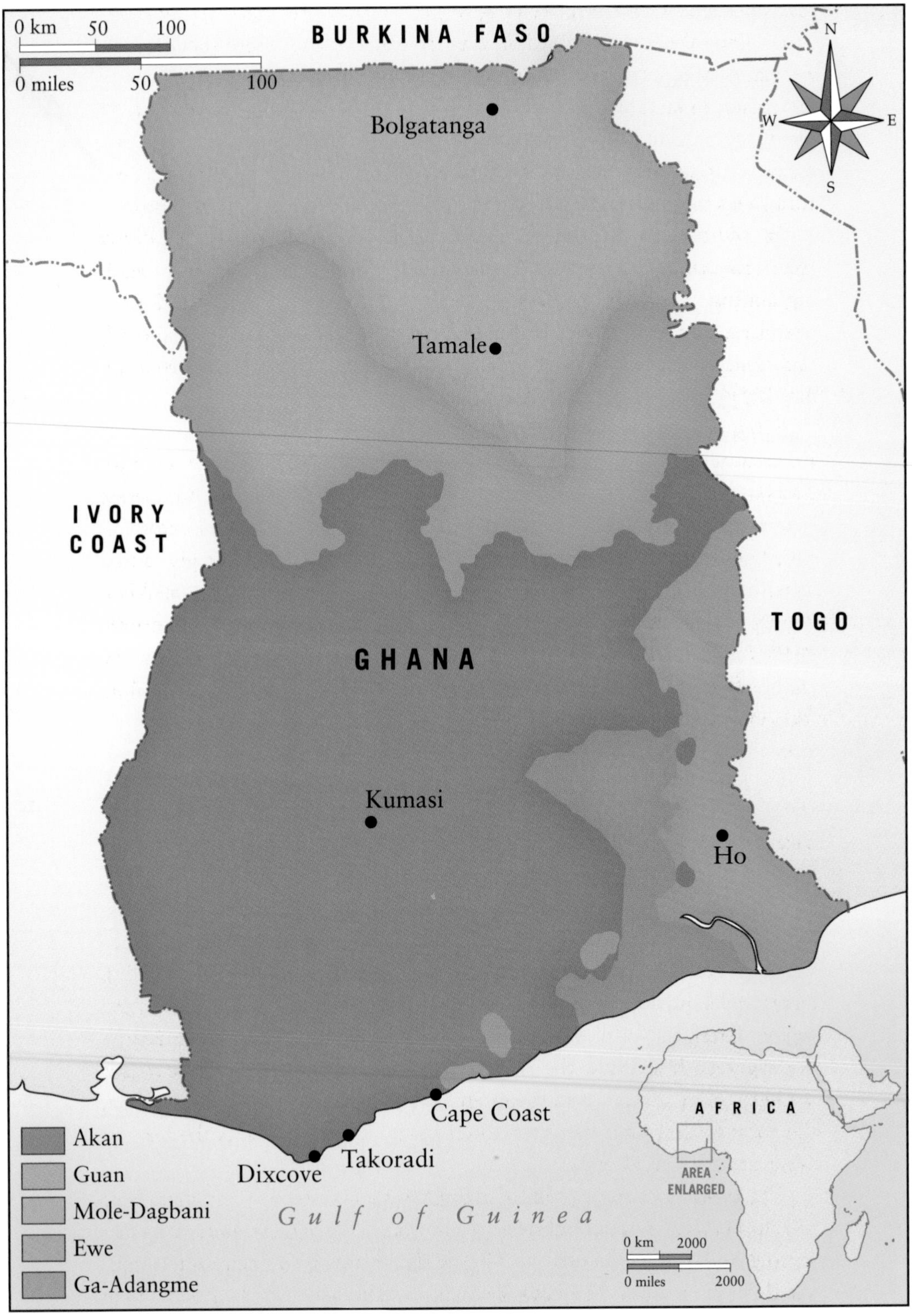
0 km 50 100
0 miles 50 100
BURKINA FASO
N
W
E
S
Bolgatanga
Tamale
IVORY COAST
GHANA
TOGO
Kumasi
Ho
Cape Coast
Takoradi
Dixcove
Gulf of Guinea
Akan
Guan
Mole-Dagbani
Ewe
Ga-Adangme
AFRICA
AREA ENLARGED
0 km 2000
0 miles 2000

MAP 2 Major Language Groups of Ghana

also children. These large-scale groups were (and remain) largely organized along the lines of **matrilineality**. In other words, every individual is a member of a particular abusua through his or her mother and not his or her father. In fact, however, abusua membership is often assimilative, with people being brought in from outside the group as members. In fact, one feature of *slavery* in the region in the eighteenth and early nineteenth centuries was the assimilation of captives into full membership of the asafo.

In addition to the abusua, Akan societies also developed the ***oman*** (plural: *aman*), or states ruled by chiefs and kings chosen from within leading abusua. The chief, or ***ohene*** (plural: *ahenfo*) of an oman could often exercise a great deal of power, but his actions usually were also monitored, and sometimes overturned, by leading men and women of the community who served as advisors, judges, priests, and even legislators.

From at least the seventeenth century, as well, the common people of the community found a way to participate in the politics of the community and the oman through the development of the *asafo*. These brotherhoods (and possibly sisterhoods) organized people into groups for community labor, defense, firefighting, and other tasks, but they also came to play a role in politics by sometimes opposing the power of the chiefs. In short, Akan society was organized into states, families, and brotherhoods. The people did not live in *tribes*, a term commonly misapplied to the region. Nor were the chiefs arbitrary or despotic rulers. Rather, their power was checked by institutions that represented different classes and communities.

SOCIETAL AND POLITICAL CHANGES: ASANTE AND THE EUROPEANS

Two important changes after the sixteenth century complicated Akan society. The first was the rise of the state of Asante (sometimes called Ashanti) around 1700. Centered several hundred miles north of the coastline, Asante began as a confederation of allied *aman* whose leading families organized for self-defense but whose armies soon defeated many surrounding states and slowly grew to control the valuable gold and kola trades in the region. Later, they also became a powerful force in the slave trade. By the late eighteenth century, the Asante Confederation was organized under a single ruling *abusua* and it loosely controlled the zone extending from the coast to deep into the interior—roughly the same area as the state of Ghana today (see Map 3).

The other important political change of this period was the emergence of Europeans as political players on the coast. Portuguese merchants had arrived in the region as early as 1471 with charters from their king to pursue the trade in gold. They quickly made an alliance with the rulers of the town of Elmina, close to Cape Coast. They were followed by the Dutch in

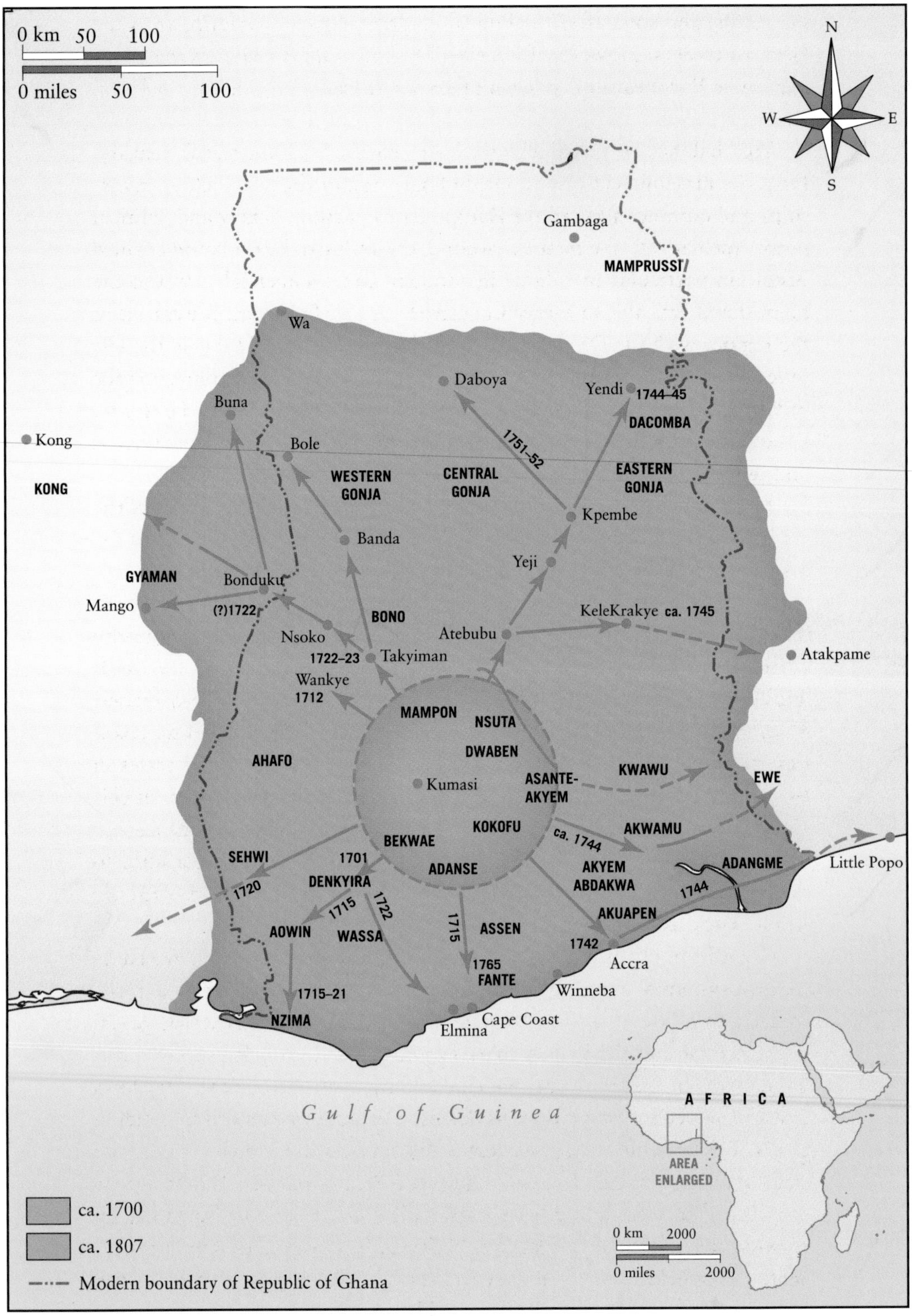
0 km 50 100
0 miles 50 100
N
W
E
S
Gambaga
MAMPRUSSI
Wa
Daboya
Yendi 1744–45
DACOMBA
Buna
Kong
KONG
Bole
WESTERN GONJA
CENTRAL GONJA
1751–52
EASTERN GONJA
Kpembe
Banda
Yeji
GYAMAN
Bonduku
Mango
(?)1722
BONO
KeleKrakye ca. 1745
Nsoko
Atebubu
1722–23
Takyiman
Atakpame
Wankye 1712
MAMPON
NSUTA
DWABEN
AHAFO
Kumasi
ASANTE-AKYEM
KWAWU
EWE
KOKOFU
BEKWAE
ca. 1744
AKWAMU
SEHWI
1701
ADANSE
AKYEM ABDAKWA
ADANGME
Little Popo
1720
DENKYIRA
1715
1722
1715
ASSEN
1744
AKUAPEN
AOWIN
WASSA
1742
1765 FANTE
Accra
Winneba
1715–21
NZIMA
Cape Coast
Elmina
Gulf of Guinea
AFRICA
AREA ENLARGED
0 km 2000
0 miles 2000
ca. 1700
ca. 1807
Modern boundary of Republic of Ghana

MAP 3 The Expansion of the Asante Kingdom, ca. 1700–1807 the 1590s, and soon after the English, French, Danish, Swedish, and even German traders. However, for several centuries local rulers were able to play these Europeans off of each other and effectively limit their political reach.

This balance of power changed around the mid-nineteenth century. First, the development of new technologies and medicines, such as steamships and quinine, allowed the Europeans to pursue military and political power further into the interior. Second, the Industrial Revolution enabled Britain in particular to enlarge its military and commercial power to the point that it was able to eventually drive the other European powers out of the region, with the Danish (1850) and Dutch (1871–1872) being the last to leave. Finally, the emergence of palm oil as a strategic resource for the British led them to invest more energy and effort in controlling the region. Palm oil was useful for two major industrial needs—as machine lubricant and in the production of soap.

The main challenge the British faced was the regional supremacy of the Asante state. Ruling over the principal palm oil–producing regions and the major ports of the area, the Asante kings seemed unchallengeable. Fortunately for the British, however, the rulers (*ahenfo*) of some states (*aman*), including the kings of the coastal town of Cape Coast and their nearby allies, resented Asante power and were willing to assist them. In the 1850s and 1860s, a series of conflicts broke out between the Asante and their allies on the one hand and a British-led coalition on the other. This coalition included the Fante Confederation, a traditional alliance of states in the area around Cape Coast. In the 1860s and 1870s, the leaders of this Confederation largely sought independence from Asante as an independent state allied with Britain. In 1873, the British crown sent a major force to the region and, along with Fante forces and other local allies, pushed the Asante back from the coast.

Out of the chaos left by the Asante retreat, the British managed to create a system of agreements with local rulers that was formalized in the creation of a *Colony* and a *Protectorate*. The **Colony**, where it was generally accepted that the British ruled formally, was legally limited to a few large towns like Cape Coast, which could by controlled by the large forts that had served for generations as defensive establishments and for holding slaves. The bulk of the region became the **Protectorate**, which included the small and large states that had supported Britain in the 1873–1874 war as well as others who had been Asante allies but were now controlled by *ahenfo* sympathetic to British rule. Technically, these states were independent. Nevertheless, they had to accept certain rules imposed by the British including, technically, the abolition of all slavery.

THE BRITISH CIVILIZING MISSION

That the British were, by the late eighteenth century, the biggest proponents of the abolition of slavery worldwide was something of an irony,
since they had in previous centuries been the world's largest slave dealers.
This switch from slave trading to abolitionism in Britain in the nineteenth
century reflected wider changes in British society. The Industrial Revolution that had begun in the eighteenth century had created a new middle-
class society of industrialists, financiers, and even shop owners in Britain
who were wealthy but largely lacked the political clout of the old aristocra-
cy. This class helped to fund a community of enlightenment thinkers who
developed a concept of liberalism. These new ideas celebrated the hard
work and free market economy of the middle class, and allowed them to
represent these values as more virtuous than those of the aristocrats, many
of whom were slave owners. It was a religious as well as secular ideology,
including the notion of *evangelizing*, or convincing others to live according
to their values. It was also a useful political ideology, allowing the middle
class to see themselves as more deserving of governing the country than
the upper classes whom they were seeking to replace. In the late eighteenth
century, the British middle class turned this ideology upon their own working classes as a sort of propaganda campaign, trying to convince them to
support the middle classes and to aspire to live like them.

This internal campaign became international in the early nineteenth
century as members of the British middle class arrived at the notion that
not only were they the superior class in society, but also as a nation the
most "civilized" people of the world. Thus the duty to convince the lower
classes to envy and support the middle classes in Britain morphed into the
concept that the British had a duty to bring their values and "civilization"
to everyone else. This "civilization" included Christian evangelism, a belief
in free trade and free labor rather than slavery, and support for democratic
ideals. It was a powerful set of ideals that found expression in the famous
words of one of the great architects of the empire, Joseph Chamberlain:

> We feel now that our rule over these territories can only be justified
> if we can show that it adds to the happiness and prosperity of the
> people, and I maintain that our rule does, and has, brought security
> and peace and comparative prosperity to countries that never knew
> these blessings before. In carrying out this work of civilization we are
> fulfilling what I believe to be our national mission, and we are finding
> scope for the exercise of these faculties and qualities which have made
> of us a great governing race . . . in almost every instance in which
> the rule of the Queen has been established . . . there has come with it

greater security to life and property, and a material improvement in the condition of the bulk of the population.—Joseph Chamberlain, Speech to the Royal Colonial Institute, London, 31 March, 1897.

Were the British justified in believing that they were more civilized than others, and that they therefore had a right to force or cajole other people to live in ways acceptable to the British middle class? Ironically, while the civilizing mission included a message of "democracy" and freedom, it also found ways to depict Africans and others as being unworthy of self-rule and self-determination. In Britain, the new enlightenment ideology had excluded certain groups—children, those deemed insane or criminal, and women, for example—from enjoying equality. Instead, these groups were to be "protected" and watched over by the male head of household or the British state, which was seen as sort of a national father figure. By the mid-nineteenth century, similar language was being applied in the colonies, where Africans, South Asians, and others were spoken of as being "child-like," "savages," or "feminine" and thus unworthy of full participation or rights. By the 1870s, when Abina lived, these ideas were supported by a pseudoscientific language of racism that sought to scientifically justify their permanent exclusion from rights and thus Britain's rule of the colonies. At the same time, however, it must be recognized that many British administrators, missionaries, and others still truly *believed* that they were acting in the best interests of their African "wards."

THE CIVILIZING MISSION IN THE GOLD COAST

Within the Gold Coast, this sense was reflected partly in the drive by British administrators to try to reorganize local communities along the lines of British, middle-class society. This was especially pronounced in the Colony and specifically the town of Cape Coast. Once ruled by the larger *oman* of Fetu, Cape Coast had achieved its independence in the eighteenth century by exploiting the wealth of its merchants earned through trade with Europeans. But this self-rule was short-lived, as first Asante and later Britain came to claim the town. The British sought to impose new rules on the city, including British-style housing, straight roads, new decision-making bodies, and rules about what behavior was acceptable in the city. In order to pay for these projects, they tried to raise revenues through taxation. The rulers of Cape Coast did not always accept these measures without protest. In 1844, the leading *asafo* signed a protest against a British tax. Then in 1865 John Aggrey, the king of Oguaa (the Fante state in which Cape Coast was located) got into a conflict with the British administrator over who had the right to imprison criminals. He was replaced by the British, who ignored widespread protests.

Despite these conflicts, Europeans and Africans interacted relatively freely in the town on a day-to-day basis. By the 1870s Cape Coast contained a large population of English-speaking Africans and Euro-Africans of mixed heritage. Many of these individuals formed a class of professionals and merchants who were generally supportive of British attitudes, traded and worked with the British administrators and commercial companies, and saw themselves as at least partly British in identity. It was these men who tried to create European-style but independent states such as the Accra Confederation and who wrote a constitution for the Fante Confederation of 1873. Many of their attitudes were reflected in newspapers meant to serve these English-speaking West Africans, like the *African Times*, whose Sierra Leonean editor in 1872 described himself as follows:

> A strenuous upholder of British influence and rule on the West coast of Africa as being the only one possible under which the spread of civilization and Christianity, and a large development of material resources, could ever be effected—*African Times*, Feb 28, 1872, p. 94.

However, such attitudes did not necessarily extend to the lower classes of Cape Coast, and even less so to the population of the Protectorate territories beyond its walls. Even the greatest supporters of British "civilization" often resented the realities of British rule, and administrators faced opposition to many of their actions throughout this era.

SLAVERY IN THE GOLD COAST

In the mid-1870s, an appreciable proportion of that Protectorate population was made up of people whom we can label *slaves*, although that label is somewhat imprecise. A more accurate picture of enslavement in the region must include an historical account that ties it to the history and societies of the region.

Through written, oral, and archaeological sources we know that the Akan and their neighbors had developed a variety of social statuses in the period leading up to the sixteenth century. These can be understood partly by looking again at the various institutions of their societies. For example, individual's identities and access to resources were tied to their membership in an extended family (abusua). What happened to people who were kicked out of their abusua for crimes or transgressions, or whose abusua broke apart due to famine or warfare? Such individuals often came to be attached to new abusua, but often without the rights and privileges of regular members. Although they might carry out the same types of labor as full members of the family, they did not enjoy the same social status or protections, and certainly not the same ability to move around. These individuals might therefore be called *slaves* with some accuracy.

Similarly, the fact that *ahenfo*—chiefs—and other leading men were limited in their power by a web of elders and family obligations meant that if they wished to exert their own personal power, they had to find helpers and dependents who were not loyal to any single abusua but rather to them personally. One way to accomplish this was to create a class of "royal slaves." These individuals had become slaves through the breakup of their families or through warfare and kidnapping, and thus were at the bottom of the social ladder. Yet once they came to serve a chief they often could become quite powerful as warriors, bureaucrats, and advisors. Nevertheless, they too were dependent upon the chiefs and had restricted rights.

Several observations can be made about these Akan institutions that are often grouped under the term *slavery*. First, in contrast to plantation slavery in the Americas, Akan "slavery" was not necessarily or primarily economic, but rather political and social. Slaves may have worked as agricultural laborers and gold miners, but they usually did so alongside the families and individuals to whom they belonged. Second, slavery of this sort remained very limited until the late seventeenth century. Finally, slavery in the Gold Coast was generally assimilative, in that the enslaved could become full members of the society—and even family—in which they lived over the course of their lives or perhaps a few generations.

THE ATLANTIC SLAVE TRADE AND ABOLITION

The Atlantic slave trade changed this gradually but dramatically. We can begin to trace these changes to the seventeenth century, for although some inhabitants of the region were enslaved and carried to the Americas as early as the 1500s, it was not until the 1670s that Europeans really saw the Gold Coast as a place to obtain slaves. Around that date—the height of sugar demand in Europe—Europeans became willing to pay very high prices for African laborers to work in the sugar plantations of Brazil, Louisiana, and the Caribbean. As a result, individuals in the Gold Coast willing to provide European slavers with captives could reap enormous profits. By the 1790s, European and American slave traders were embarking about 74,000 enslaved Africans per year from the region. Some large states, like Asante, became key providers of captives. Many of these were obtained from deep in the interior, where Asante armies captured entire communities and forced weaker states to provide enslaved youths as tribute to the Asante crown. In their greed, some chiefs and other Africans also changed the laws and norms of their societies to find ways to sell their own people as slaves. Such "crimes" as defaulting on a debt or committing adultery became punishable by enslavement and sale in some cases. At the same time, European and American ideas of slavery as a permanent institution became prevalent in the Gold Coast, especially as some coastal Africans began to use slaves to produce grain, palm oil, and other products on large farms for sale to Europeans.

Most of the Africans sold into the Atlantic slave trade from this region were men. Not only did American buyers prefer males, but also powerful Africans preferred to retain women (whom they perceived as harder workers and potential wives) within their societies. Thus slavery came more and more to be a "female" condition in the region. When the British banned the slave trade in 1807, and later criminalized slavery in the newly created Colony and Protectorate in 1874, this trend increased. There were several reasons for this, but the main one was that women were seen as being less able to run away or to report their masters and mistresses to the British.

In fact, most British administrators were uninterested in truly eliminating slavery in the region. Although many of them can be loosely called abolitionists, they were in reality opposed to actively rooting out slavery for several reasons. First, they recognized that the wealth of the colony and its political stability relied on their alliance with local men who were slave owners, and did not wish to alienate this class. Second, they feared that actively liberating enslaved people would cause chaos, which they wished to avoid. Finally, they convinced themselves that slavery in the region was "not that bad" and more like a parent-child relationship than plantation slavery in the Americas.

As a result, the laws banning slavery that came into effect in 1875 made it possible for any slave to liberate himself or herself, but did not call for British administrators to actively pursue slave owners or free slaves. This placed the burden on the enslaved to go through a number of difficult steps to liberate himself or herself, slowing down the process of emancipation immensely. It also led to the perception among slave owners that adults, especially men, would make bad slaves since they were most likely to be able to run away, go to court, or otherwise escape. Thus, after 1875, more and more children, especially girls, were enslaved outside the Colony and Protectorate and brought in to serve as slaves.

For these young Africans, achieving liberation was a difficult process. It entailed running away to a society about which they knew very little and where they knew few people, searching out a British magistrate or some other protector who probably cared little about them and whose life and viewpoints were unintelligible, and somehow obtaining their aid. That some of them still managed to do so is an incredible story.

ABINA MANSAH AND THE IMPORTANT MEN

Abina Mansah was one of these young girls. From her testimony, we know quite a bit about her life before she became the "property" of Quamina Eddoo. We know that she had been captured or kidnapped in Asante territory, and enslaved at two residences in Asante, first in the capital city of Coomassie [Kumasi] at the home of Eddoo Buffoe and then again in the Asante province of Adansi [Adanse] (see Map 4). At some point, she was then purchased by a trader named Yowawhah [Yaw Awoah] and traveled with him to the town of Salt Pond, not far from Cape Coast and legally within the borders of the Colony. In Salt Pond, Yowawhah then appears to have secretly sold her to Quamina Eddoo, who turned her over to his sister Eccoah. After several weeks, she was told that she was to marry Tandoe, at which point she ran away to her "countrypeople" in Cape Coast—probably others from the region of Asante in which she had been born. They in turn led her to Davis, who helped her to appear before the court.

Most of this story revolves around Abina's relationship to four important men—Quamina Eddoo, William Melton, James Davis, and James Hutton Brew. Davis played a pivotal role in helping Abina, not only because he seems to have taken her into his care (under conditions about which we know no details), but also because he became her attorney in the courtroom. Much of what is written about Davis in this story is a composite of evidence about other young men like him. As a court interpreter, Davis was likely educated at a mission school whose curriculum would have included English. He also spoke several other languages. He could write, and was likely a Christian. He probably was of mixed heritage, with at least one European ancestor. Although at the bottom of the middle classes of Cape Coast, Davis was employed, seems to have been related to an important local merchant family, and understood how to speak the language of the court and appeal to the morality of the judge.

That judge was William Melton, a minor career official of the British Colonial Office. In fact, we don't know that much about Melton, although it's likely that his papers exist somewhere in Britain and that further research in the British archives could tell us more about him. Melton was not trained as a judge, but in his capacity as judge he was reasonably fair, at least as far as cases involving enslavement were concerned. He ruled in favor of plaintiffs who claimed to have been enslaved almost as often as in favor of their alleged masters, and frequently turned to local advisors to help him in his decisions. Unfortunately, those advisors and jurors tended to be powerful men who were sympathetic to slave ownership and not to young, female slaves.

We have imagined Melton's positions in this **graphic history** based partly on the record of his decisions and partly on a profile of other minor

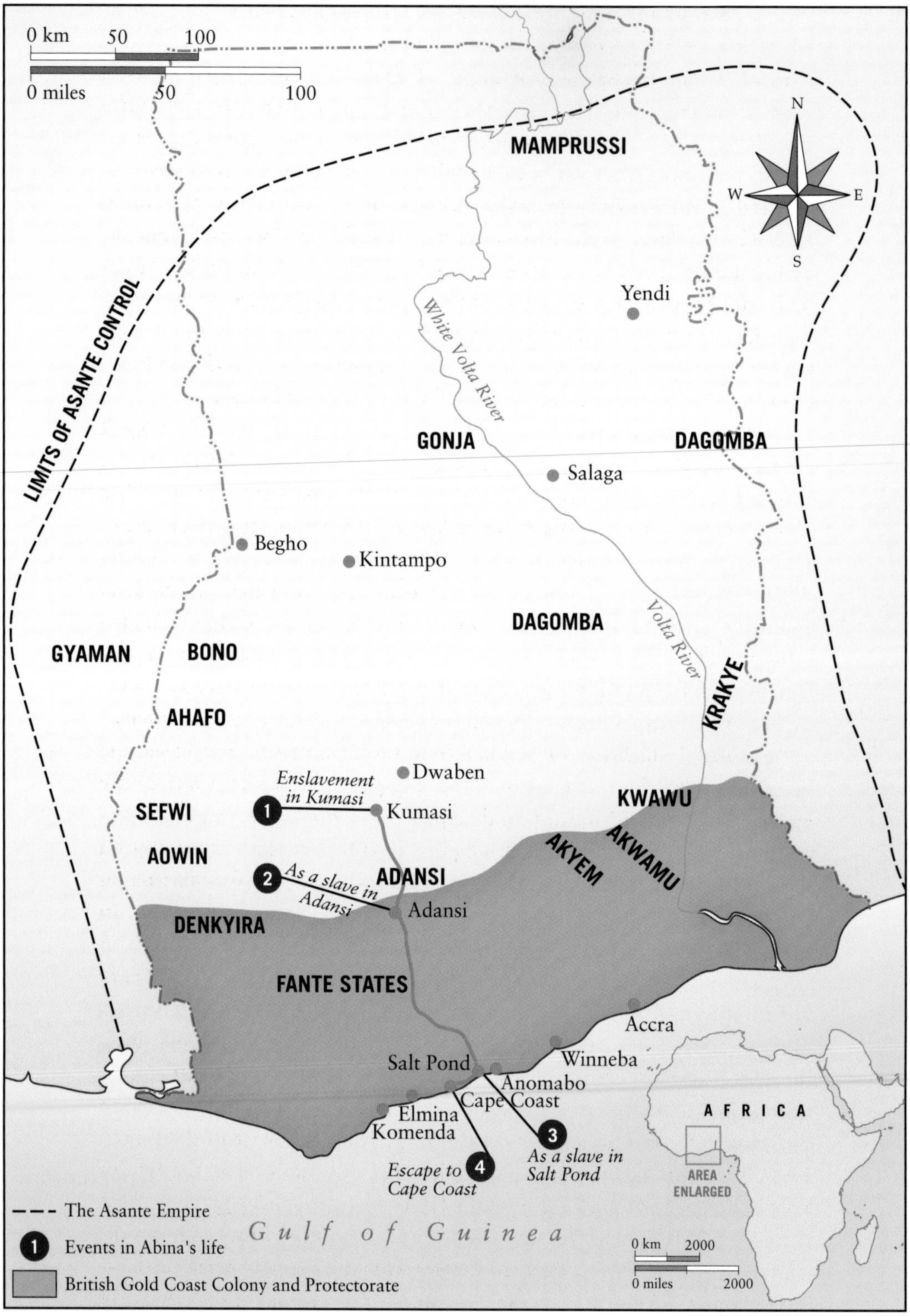
0 km 50 100
0 miles 50 100
N
W
E
S
LIMITS OF ASANTE CONTROL
MAMPRUSSI
Yendi
White Volta River
GONJA
DAGOMBA
Salaga
Begho
Kintampo
DAGOMBA
Volta River
GYAMAN
BONO
AHAFO
KRAKYE
Dwaben
Enslavement in Kumasi
1
Kumasi
KWAWU
SEFWI
AOWIN
AKYEM
AKWAMU
2
As a slave in Adansi
ADANSI
Adansi
DENKYIRA
FANTE STATES
Accra
Winneba
Salt Pond
Anomabo
Cape Coast
Elmina
Komenda
3
As a slave in Salt Pond
4
Escape to Cape Coast
AFRICA
AREA ENLARGED
The Asante Empire
Events in Abina's life
British Gold Coast Colony and Protectorate
Gulf of Guinea
0 km 2000
0 miles 2000

MAP 4 Asante and the Gold Coast, ca. 1876

officials serving on the Gold Coast during this period. Most were evangelical Christians from the British middle classes who spent only a short time in each of several overseas colonies and who believed in a **paternalistic** sense of fathers both as wielding great power and sacred responsibility within the family. They applied this belief both to African men, whom they trusted more than women and children, and to the British Empire as the "father" of Africans generally. Because of this worldview, they often believed that slaves could be legitimately described as "wards," "apprentices," "foster" children, or even "wives," and frequently declined to liberate them or to punish the owners unless physical abuse could be proved or the evidence was beyond dispute. Even so, it must be noted that in Britain some physical punishment of children and forcing them to work was legal, and many British magistrates condoned this in the Gold Coast as well.

Melton seems to have been ambivalent about cases involving alleged slavery, and this was especially pronounced in this case because of the presence of James Hutton Brew. We know more about Brew than any other person in this story. The only trained lawyer among the "important men" with whom Abina interacted, Brew was the descendant of a Scottish merchant who had married into a powerful local family of chiefs and traders. James Hutton Brew was related to many important local leaders, and also had strong ties to the British authorities. Yet he was also seen by some (although not Melton) as being somewhat suspect. Not only did many British of the time distrust people of mixed heritage, whom they saw as "uppity" or "polluted," but Brew himself had been involved in a scheme called the Fante Confederation in the early 1870s. The goal of this plan was to create an independent local state around Cape Coast. While Brew and his compatriots had hoped to get British support for this state, the administration had in fact seen it as a threat and shut it down quickly, briefly imprisoning Brew and others. Yet this did not mean that Brew was anti-European. In fact, he and the other conspirators had modeled their proposed state on Britain and Germany, and his writings suggest that he truly believed that British "civilization" had much to offer Africans.

Brew was clearly an effective representative for Quamina Eddoo, about whom we know much less. Clearly, Eddoo was a wealthy country "gentleman" who owned many slaves and other dependents, interacted with merchants and traders, and could afford the leading lawyer in the region. Yet he was probably illiterate, and today, nobody who lives in the area of Saltpond, where he lived more than a hundred years ago, appears to know of him. Like Abina, he has virtually disappeared from history as it is written today, and thus he cannot be numbered among the "important men"—Davis, Brew, and Hutton—who dominate the proceedings of the court case that was supposedly between Eddoo and Abina.

PART IV

READING GUIDE

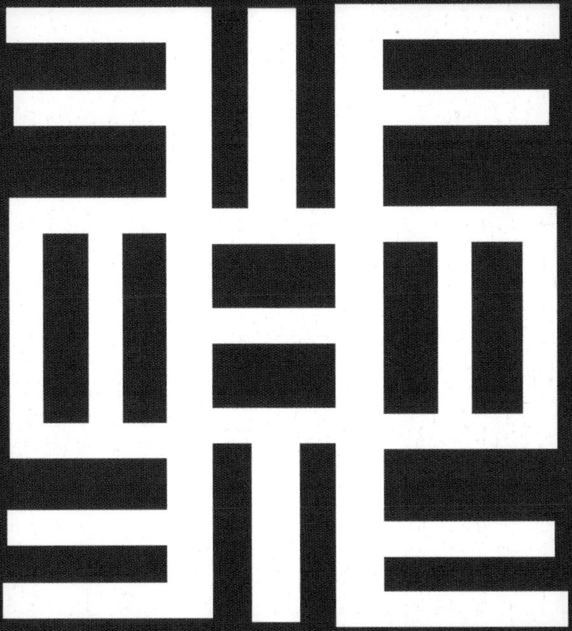

NEA ONNIM NO SUA A, OHU

"HE WHO DOES NOT KNOW CAN KNOW FROM LEARNING"

In Part III of this book, we gave you a sense of the social environment and history surrounding the events portrayed in *Abina and the Important Men*. That background was reconstructed by the author, who put together evidence from primary sources (documents and oral histories collected in the archives and communities of Ghana) and secondary sources (scholarly works by experts on the region's history).

However, historians do more than just reconstruct what they think happened in the past. They also interpret past events. No two authors or two artists would interpret a document like Abina Mansah's testimony in entirely the same ways. Nor should they. Interpreters of the past, like the author and illustrator of this volume, have a public role to play in helping us to make sense of the past in light of our own lives and present experiences. So, instead of just reconstructing the past, we help our readers to construct meaning from those pasts that are relevant today.

Yet historians do not have total freedom in their interpretations of past events. We also have responsibilities. We have a duty to the people who lived through those events to talk about their experiences accurately and perhaps empathetically. We also have a duty to our readers to help them to construct their own understandings of the past rather than simply imposing ours upon them. For that reason, Part IV of this book is a guide to the issues of philosophy, ethics, and methods that we faced in turning a document from 1876 into a graphic history in 2011. In the following pages, we grapple with three questions: Whose story is this? Is it a true story? Is it an authentic story? In response to each question, we present a series of related thoughts and issues in increasingly complex levels. The first level of each explanation is meant to be open to all readers. In the second level, we weave in more complex themes and ideas for more advanced readers. Finally, in the third level of each response, we dig deep into the issues, methods, and morals surrounding the interpretation of Abina Mansah's testimony. While some readers may find the more advanced sections difficult, it is our hope that they will revisit this book many times and explore those topics over time.

WHOSE STORY IS THIS?

LEVEL 1: A STAIRCASE OF VOICES

The first question we must ask is, "Whose story is *Abina and the Important Men*"? Like most histories, the story in this volume has multiple characters, all of whom were real people and who have a right to claim some ownership of any account of their lives. There are at least two accounts of the story in question. The first is the transcript on which this book is based. The second is the graphic history itself. Neither the anonymous clerk (possibly Melton himself) who wrote the transcript in 1876, nor the historian who wrote the text of this book, nor the artist who illustrated it were purely objective observers. Rather, each interpreted the events of the story in their own way.

Thus the first answer to the question must be that many people can claim to have participated in the production of this story—Abina and the other actors in the story, the clerk, the historian, and the artist. These individuals can be seen to be stairs in a staircase of voices leading from Abina, who brought the case to court and initiated the story, to the reader. Yet from the top stair, it is difficult to see what the stairs beneath look like. In order to get back to the first stair—to Abina—the reader has to be able to move down through the stairs like an archaeologist excavating the distant past by carefully removing and analyzing each layer of soil.

The first layer that must be removed is the one created by the collaborators on this book—the author and the illustrator. As we will discuss in a following section, we have tried to present a reasonably accurate picture of the events described in the transcript. Nevertheless, we know that we have put our own stamp upon the story. The author, especially, approached this story with a particular empathy for Abina. He saw this story as inspirational, for it revealed how a young woman in the lowest rungs of society could still fight for her freedom. He also saw it as a vehicle for explaining the human costs, as well as the historical complexities, of the slave trade, colonialism, and the free-market demand for goods like palm oil. The reader may agree that these are admirable goals, but the author still must acknowledge that they reflect today's moral standards in the United States, and may not have been the perspectives of any of the actors in the past. In presenting these themes, the author chose to organize Abina's testimony along the lines of a plot that speaks to him, and to emphasize certain points by putting words in the mouths of Abina, Davis, Melton, and others that they may not have said. The author then produced a script that was interpreted in images by the artist, who depicted some people more sympathetically than others and generally helped to imagine the story along the plotlines proposed by the author.

If we wish to remove the author's and artist's interpretation of events, we can look back to the transcript itself, which is the only direct evidence of events in Abina's life (see Figure 1). However, the transcript is not an exact record of Abina's testimony either. Like most people of her time—and in contrast to Davis, Melton, and Brew—Abina probably could not write. However, in British courts of law on the Gold Coast, records were usually not kept by the lawyers or the judge, but rather by an official clerk. Yet in *Regina v. Quamina Eddoo* (Abina's case—*Regina* is Latin for "Queen" and refers to Queen Victoria, who was the ruling monarch of Great Britain at that time), the usual clerk of the court seems to have been missing. It's possible that Davis, who was a court interpreter, was also the clerk but he could not keep records because he was also serving as legal counsel to Abina.

This mystery may be a good thing, for whoever kept the records that day took extensive notes. The testimony in Abina's case that is much longer and much more detailed than in comparable cases, forming a large enough story for us to work with. It seems likely that Melton himself took the notes, as the handwriting in this case seems to match handwriting in notes Melton wrote elsewhere. But Melton, of course, was not a disinterested observer. He had much at stake in this case—including, perhaps, the political stability of the region and his own career. He probably did not write down the words of Abina or other participants verbatim, as these might not have suited his purpose. And is it likely he could not have even if he wanted to. Most court clerks of the time, whether trained or not, had difficulty following rapid conversation and frequently made errors or omissions. An error can be found, for example, on page 107 of the transcript, where Abina is reported to have said that the other girls were "fed, but not fed." The second "fed" should probably be "paid." Thus in turning the testimony of Abina and others into a court transcript, Melton by mistake or on purpose probably shaped the document and the story it told.

Melton was also a key voice within the transcript in his role as judge, or magistrate. As the final decision maker, he was the one who had to be won over by the participants, and as a result he defined the rules of engagement. Based on the record of his judgments in other cases, we know that Melton seems to have held a somewhat typical British understanding of "slavery." In the first place, he defined enslavement in economic terms and thus looked for proof that the person in question was bought and worked unpaid. Yet he also saw slavery as a breaking of the rules of fatherhood. Adult males, he seems to have believed, had the right to compel children (their own offspring, apprentices, or wards) to work, as well as to punish them physically. Slavery, in his view, was evident when this relationship crossed some sort of limits—when the work was inappropriate for the child or when the physical punishment was abusive. This view of adult males as

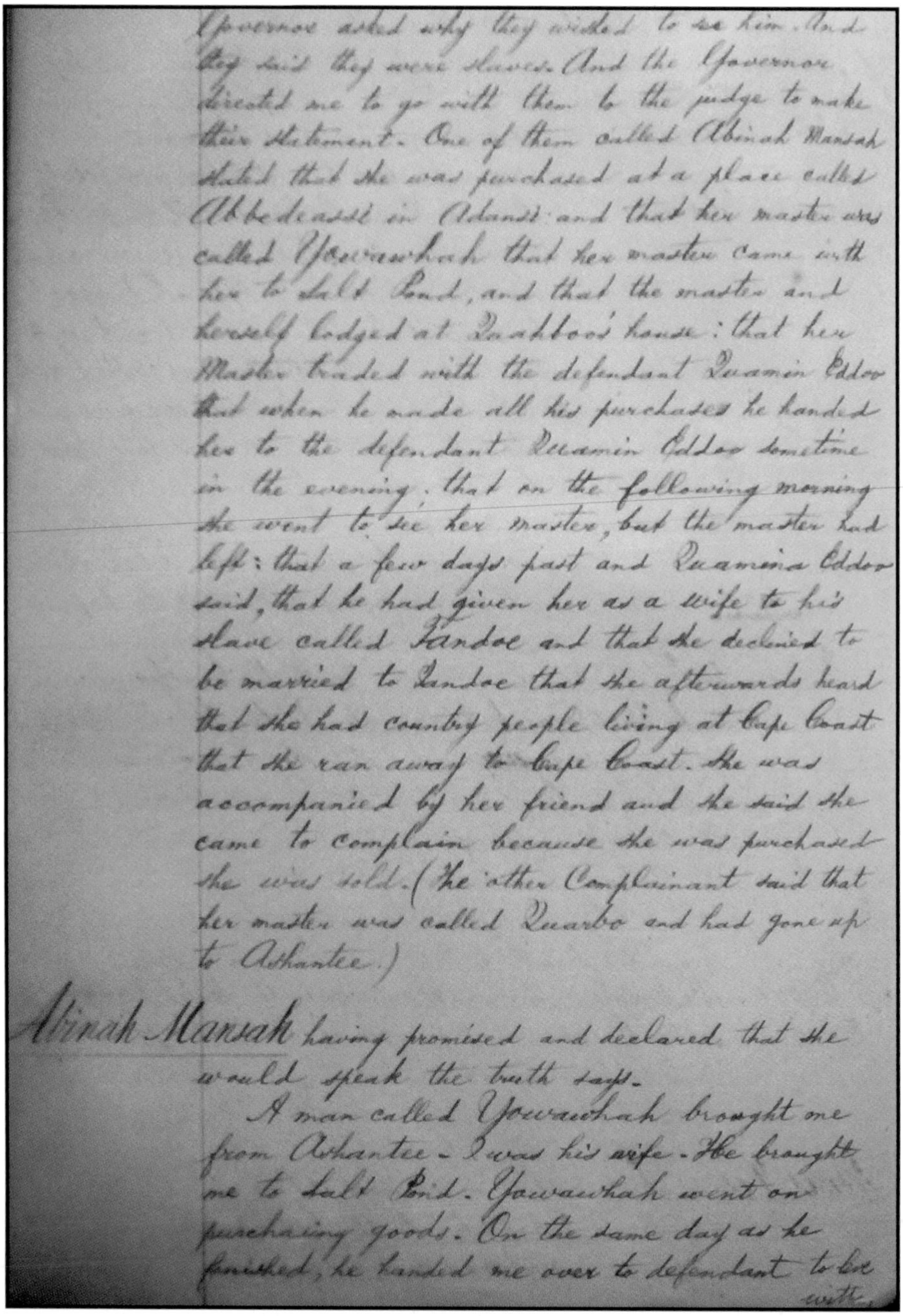

Governor asked why they wished to see him. And
they said they were slaves. And the Governor
directed me to go with them to the judge to make
their statement. One of them called Abinah Mansah
stated that she was purchased at a place called
Abbedeassie in Adansi: and that her master was
called Yowawhah that her master came with
her to Salt Pond, and that the master and
herself lodged at Quabboo's house: that her
Master traded with the defendant Quamin Eddoo
that when he made all his purchases he handed
her to the defendant Quamin Eddoo sometime
in the evening. that on the following morning
she went to see her master, but the master had
left: that a few days past and Quamina Eddoo
said, that he had given her as a wife to his
slave called Tandoe and that she declined to
be married to Tandoe that she afterwards heard
that she had country people living at Cape Coast
that she ran away to Cape Coast. She was
accompanied by her friend and she said she
came to complain because she was purchased
she was sold. (The other Complainant said that
her master was called Quarbo and had gone up
to Ashantee.)

Abinah Mansah having promised and declared that she
would speak the truth says.
A man called Yowawhah brought me
from Ashantee - I was his wife. He brought
me to Salt Pond. Yowawhah went on
purchasing goods. On the same day as he
finished, he handed me over to defendant to live
with,

FIGURE 1 SCT 5-4-19 *Regina v. Quamina Eddoo*, 10 Nov 1876. This is the file in which Abina's testimony appears. By 1876, British handwriting and notational style had largely been standardized through formal education—men of Melton's class would have been educated in private schools, but Britain also introduced mandatory schooling in 1870. Education largely took the form of rote learning, and penmanship was taught through endless repetition. Readers may note that the scribe (or Melton) spells Abina's name here as "Abinah." British spelling of African names was largely phonetic. For example, Kwame and Kweku were often rendered "Qwame" or Quecue." Many colonial spellings have been abandoned by Ghanaians, like the "h" at the end of Abina.

"fathers," with duties to protect and to rule, was common to Britons both at home and abroad in this period. Melton also shared with many other British officials in Africa a need to describe and interpret African rituals and customs, which often influenced his legal judgments. For example, Melton witnessed young Akan husbands-to-be giving ritualistic gifts to their future in-laws and decided that Africans "bought" their wives. And he was clearly very interested in the rituals of "cutting beads" and "giving cloth" mentioned in the trial. Yet he also filtered local customs through his own lens of nineteenth-century European values, mentioning concepts like "free will," which was then in vogue in British philosophical circles.

James Davis and James Hutton Brew both had some understanding of Melton's legal and philosophical views, and they catered to them during the trial, creating a powerful shared language of "law" and "civilization" that everyone could understand, with the obvious exception of Abina. Oddly, however, Abina's inability to understand may provide an opportunity to excavate her voice from beneath those of the important men. For example, Abina rejects Melton's formulaic interpretation of slavery, and instead tries to speak from the heart about her own experiences. She deflects a complex question by saying simply that "when a free person is sitting down at ease the slave is working," and explains what slavery meant to her: "I had been sold and I had no will of my own and I could not look after my body and health." When asked to comment on whether the other girls in the house might have been slaves—in order to paint her as merely a complainer—she said she could not tell how Eddoo had treated them, "but as for me he did nothing good for me." Some of these quotes may actually be proverbs that were widespread in local society, and may represent a wider "voice" or "truth" than Abina's alone. Nevertheless, it is these moments that help make Abina's story enduring despite the many layers that cover up her voice.

LEVEL 2: SILENCES

While it's possible to look at this story as a staircase of voices *added* on top of one another, it's also important to realize that something was also *lost* at each step of the process. In order to explain this seeming incongruity, we can usefully turn to historian Michel-Rolph Trouillot's argument that history involves the creation of silences as well as voices. In his influential book *Silencing the Past*, Trouillot (currently a professor of anthropology and social sciences at the University of Chicago) engages the issue of the ways in which "history" is produced by professional historians.[1] Like many other philosophers of the past few decades, Trouillot argues

---

1   Michel-Rolph Trouillot, *Silencing the Past: Power and the Production of History* (Boston: Beacon Press, 1995).

that historians don't just *reconstruct* the past like detectives searching for clues as to what happened, but they also *construct* the past by putting their own interpretations and spin on their accounts of the past. Moreover, Trouillot argues that because historians' interpretations tend to be accepted, they are particularly powerful in shaping understandings of the past, and also in legitimizing or discounting certain versions of that past. Thus, he points out, historians are part of the process by which some voices come to be featured in authoritative accounts of the past and others get left out.

Trouillot specifically suggests that this process of "silencing" some voices has four stages. First, some people's perspectives never get recorded. This is especially true of the illiterate, the poor, women, and in some cases people of color—in short, Abina. Second, not all records that are put into archives are saved: Some documents get thrown away; others deteriorate, often because they are considered to have little value. Third, historians choose to feature some sources and voices and to ignore others when they write about the past. Finally, some accounts of the past come to be seen as "classics" or "important," while others are discounted.

Arguably, Abina's voice was silenced in the first stage of the process in that she did not write her own account of what happened. Yet, as we have argued above, by going to court and having her story heard and recorded, Abina made sure that she would not be silenced forever. Without that effort, she—like so many other young, enslaved females—might have disappeared from history forever. As a direct result of her insistence on going to court, and with a little luck, we *can* now hear her. Of course, it is too simple to suggest that the mere finding or even printing of Abina's testimony reverses the silencing. Instead, excavating her voice from within the document requires that we also confront the limitations and processes of representation and translation by which her testimony was turned into a transcript and then a graphic history.

LEVEL 3: REPRESENTATION AND TRANSLATION

This exploration of the issues of representation and translation continue our theme of discussing the relationship between power and knowledge in the writing of history generally and the story of *Abina and the Important Men* specifically. This topic is vital to addressing the questions of accuracy and authenticity in the next sections of this volume. Let's take a moment to examine the graphic history in two ways.

On the one hand, *Abina and the Important Men* is a representation of Abina's story, and not the story itself. The word *representation* here can be taken to mean two things. First, Abina did not present her story first hand. Instead, while she verbally presented her story in court, it was the clerk, whether Melton or someone else, who *re-presented* it to us in the transcript, in written form. Then the author and artist of this volume re-presented it once again to the reader. It is vital to understand that no matter how much we (the author and illustrator) or the clerk valued accuracy we have interfered with the story as Abina first told it.[2] But there is also a second understanding of *representation*, similar to the way in which a politician represents his or her district, for example. By this definition, the author and illustrator serve as Abina's representatives, since she cannot speak for herself. Are we presenting her accurately, in a manner that accords with her wishes? We will never be able to fully know. In addition, we must acknowledge that we have more power than Abina in this representation because we have the ability to write, illustrate, and publish her story, something she could never do.[3] Thus we have a particular responsibility to try not to overwrite Abina's story with our own.

On the other hand, what we are doing is as a translation from Abina's world to our own. One of the issues we confronted in writing and illustrating this story accurately was how to interpret Abina's words in the transcript because they sounded strange to our ears. In part, this is because Abina's words were translated from her language (probably Asante Twi, although she seems to have used some words that come from the Ewe language) to English. In part, it has to do with the fact that the English vernacular at the time was different from what it is today. It also probably owes something to Melton's (or the clerk of the day's) rapid and inaccurate transcription. Finally, it is a consequence of the differences between oral and written storytelling, as we are turning spoken word into written text and image, and these two communication methods have different rhythms and styles.

Thus, we continually had to grapple with the issue of how to translate Abina's story from the language and context of the past to our own world. We felt that we had a responsibility to keep the story Abina's, but at the same time we also had a responsibility to our audience to make a volume that was readable and understandable to those who might not want to immerse themselves in years of study of the nineteenth-century Gold Coast. Thus we had to balance the desire to "translate" the story into a modern idiom without sacrificing those qualities that made it Abina's story and not our own. This tension also connects to the issue of "accuracy," which we discuss next.

---

2 Edward Said, *Orientalism* (New York: Vintage, 1979), 21.

3 Gayatri Chakravorty Spivak, "Can the Subaltern Speak?," in *Marxism and the Interpretation of Culture*, ed. Cary Nelson and Lawrence Grossberg (Urbana: University of Illinois Press, 1988), 271–313.

IS THIS A "TRUE" STORY?

LEVEL 1: RECONSTRUCTING ABINA'S STORY

One of the principal tasks of the historian is to strive to **reconstruct** the past. In other words, historians recognize that events occurred in the past, and part of our job is to try to determine what happened and why. We generally begin this task by conducting *research*. This usually means going to the *archive* or into *the field*. Archives are sites where documents, photographs, and other records from and of the past are stored, organized, and made available for scholarly use. Many of these archives are official: The Library of Congress in Washington D.C. is the most famous archive in the United States, and Abina's case was located in the National Archives of Ghana. However, many archives are unofficial collections of family or organizational papers. Increasingly, archives are digitized and can be found online. *The field* is the term that researchers use when they are collecting nonarchived material, especially oral testimony and archaeological remains.

Of course, the field and the archive are not neutral places. Both are more likely to retain some documents or stories than others. Most archives are full of the writings of "important men," for example, and contain few records of the unimportant. Similarly, oral traditions and archaeological remains are not all preserved at the same rate, and many of the stories and perspectives of everyday people get lost over time. In fact, the archive and the field are both places where views of the past are contested every day. Both professional archivists and people on the street rearrange memories and documents, store some with care, and lose others. Sometimes this is purposeful, and other times merely the result of coincidence or circumstance.

For example, the archives in Ghana once contained many records that over the years have been lost for various reasons. Several of the court documents from the period after Abina's life were stored beneath a leaky pipe and have decayed completely. Other documents were written on highly acidic paper, which, combined with the ink that was used, has caused them to slowly deteriorate to the point where they are no longer readable. Still other documents were allegedly sold to private individuals, including tourists, during the 1980s, when archival staff could barely afford to keep up the building in which they were housed.

Because of all these issues, it is impossible for any historian to state truthfully that he or she can tell you "the past as it happened." This is true even when there are many records available, for it would be impossible to record the perspectives of every single person who witnessed an event. Nevertheless, historians generally believe that it is possible to understand certain things about the past, and that there are rules and practices we can follow that increase the likelihood that our reconstructions of the past are accurate interpretations.

These practices begin with the historian and his or her attitude toward the evidence. No historian approaches a study of the past completely objectively and dispassionately. For example, the interpretation of *Regina v. Quamina Eddoo*, on which this book is based, is certainly colored by the author's knowledge of the horrors of colonialism and slavery. Nevertheless, it is usually possible to limit the significance of any bias and reach a reasonable conclusion through meticulous research, careful recording, and the placing of all evidence in the correct context.

These practices require the historian to deal with his or her sources extremely carefully. Once, history was largely defined as a craft by the reading of written documents from the past. More recently, historians have learned to work with a variety of sources, including archaeological remains, language, oral traditions, and memories, to name a few. In general, the best practice for investigating the events of the past and determining their causes is to bring together as many of these sources as possible. By doing so, it is possible to create a broad picture of a place and time in the past. These sources can then be read as evidence of what happened to cause a given event, what people were thinking or feeling about the event, and how they experienced it. Each type of source requires a specific set of practices to limit errors in interpretation, and historians are learning more about how to handle these sources all the time.

Of course, the best source in the world is useless if it is poorly misunderstood or if the historian misrecords the evidence. There have been occasions in the past in which historical analyses were incorrect simply because the historian miscopied a statement from a document. In order to avoid those mistakes in this volume, the author had the main original document—the court transcript—carefully photographed. He then copied it onto paper, asking a graduate student to check the copy for errors.

Of course, the court transcript by itself is difficult to interpret without a wealth of data that helps us to understand what it means. For example, what is the meaning of the removal of Abina's beads or the giving of cloth? In order to answer these questions, the author discussed these topics with Ghanaians, both professional historians and other inhabitants of the region, and sought out additional documents that might provide answers to these questions. Even so, the interpretation presented in the graphic novel is not definitive, since it is based on only a few sources. Nevertheless, it does demonstrate the importance of relating a single document to a whole range of sources wherever possible.

The issue of accurately representing the past in this volume was complicated by the illustrator's need to represent Abina's world graphically.

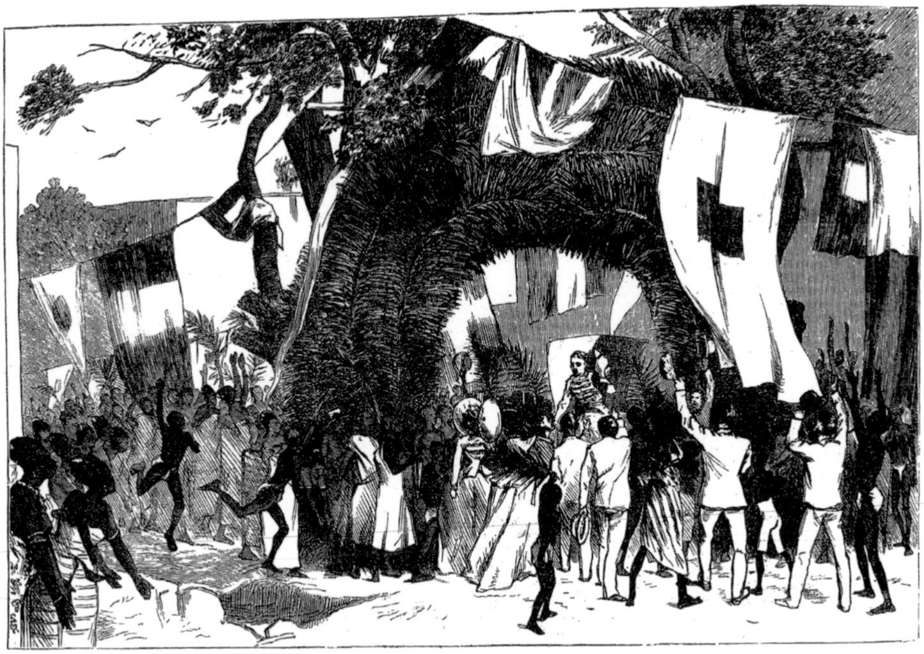

HAULING SIR GARNET WOLSELEY UP TO GOVERNMENT HOUSE

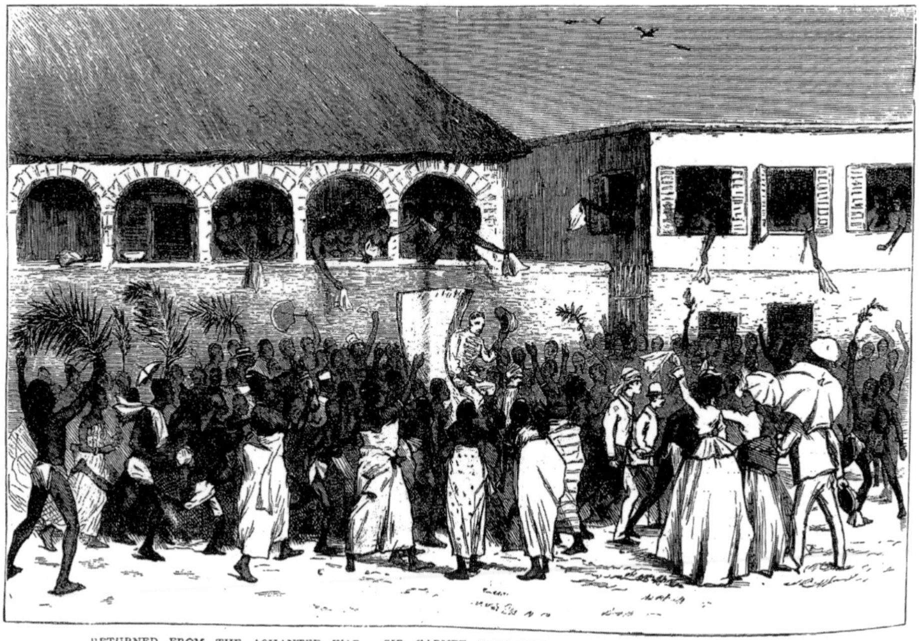

RETURNED FROM THE ASHANTEE WAR SIR GARNET WOLSELEY'S RECEPTION BY THE NATIVE LADIES

FIGURE 2 "The Ashantee War—Return of Sir Garnet Wolseley to Cape Coast Town," Graphic (London), April 11, 1874, p. 330. Images such as this were invaluable in providing information about the time and place and the people who inhabited it. Illustrator Liz Clarke looked at many pictures of both historical and contemporary Ghana to better understand its visual identity. This image specifically offered details about the style of clothing and architecture of the time. The exterior of Davis's house is modeled on the one at bottom right. © The British Library Board. (HS.74/1099)

A written history of Abina might reasonably omit the question of what Quamina Eddoo's house looked like, or what kind of furniture might have been in Cape Coast Castle, or what clothing Abina likely wore. A graphic history cannot do so, however. The illustrator and author had to find and consult paintings, illustrations, and even photographs from that period to provide the necessary visual information for the reader (see Figure 2).

It is worthwhile to spend a moment considering two specific places in the text where we faced particular issues of accuracy and only partially resolved them. The first has to do with the deposition featured on page 13 of the graphic novel, in which Abina attests to the fact that she was sold by Yaw Awoah, enslaved by Quamina Eddoo, and told to marry Tando or else suffer a flogging. In fact, the deposition has been lost. We infer its presence by a question, early in the trial, that Davis posed to Abina: "What is read to you now did you not make that statement?" The contents of the statement are unclear, although from the topics leading up to Davis's question and based on his knowledge of the law at the time, it probably included the fact that Abina Mansah had been brought into the Protectorate illegally, had been sold, and had been threatened with physical punishment. However, we cannot be sure.

The second episode that needs some elaboration has to do with the jury discussion. We in fact know nothing about this jury specifically or what they deliberated. We know who was likely to have been asked to sit on a jury during this period, based on other cases in which the names of the jurors are actually listed. Those jurors we can identify were all men, and usually either chiefly officeholders or leading "educated men"—English-speaking professionals like Brew. We have some idea as to the arguments such men had presented in 1874 to try to stop emancipation (see Part III), and we demonstrate those on pages 68–69. In general, these arguments were either that slavery in the Gold Coast was customary and rather benign, with the master as a father figure protecting young people rather than exploiting them, or that disrupting the slave-labor economy would slow down the region's economic development. Slave owners had learned that these were the arguments most accepted by British magistrates and officials. We do not know that any of the jurors said these things during the deliberations in Abina's case, but it seems likely.

As these examples illustrate, it is impossible to know the "whole truth" about any event, especially one with as few direct sources as this court case. In order to tell the story, therefore, we have had to employ techniques such as referring to similar sources and deducing the contents of documents from references in other sources. These are not exact practices, but without them it would be impossible to construct even an approximate interpretation of Abina's experiences.

LEVEL 2: DECONSTRUCTING THE COURTROOM TRANSCRIPT

Of course, historians don't just reconstruct the past from documents. They also **deconstruct** narratives of the past. Deconstruction is a term that often sounds like some sort of trendy, high-theory concept of little practical use. In fact, however, deconstruction is a way of getting at *truths* beyond the obvious, and is therefore highly useful in expanding the range of information we can extract out of documents, images, and other sources from the past.

Most sources contain intentional messages. That is to say, they were produced by some person or persons for the purpose of conveying information to an audience. Oral, written, and visual sources can all contain intentional messages. Whether a document like the U.S. Constitution, a folk story like "Little Red Riding Hood," or a painting like the ceiling of the Sistine Chapel, all were meant to communicate to an audience. Often, the meaning is open to debate, as is evidenced by the ongoing dispute of the intentions of the framers of the U.S. Constitution that still shapes politics in the United States today. Nevertheless, it is clear that there *are* intentional messages in this document. We call the practice of seeking to understand the information or messages that the authors of the text wanted to convey to their audience **reading with the grain**. Reading with the grain is an important skill to develop, as it requires the researcher to try to understand the writers' ideas and purpose and to see the world from his or her perspective.

However, texts also contain messages that their authors did not intend to convey to their audience. Often these messages are sets of assumptions. For example, when Abina testified to the giving of cloth or the breaking of her beads, she assumed her audience would know what that meant—that it signified a transfer in her "belonging," either within a family group or to a master. She did not feel the need to explain the meaning of these messages. Of course, Melton had no idea that these acts were metaphors for belonging, because he did not speak the same language and operate with the same set of assumptions as Abina. So, too, the historian today might easily gloss over these events described by Abina, seeing them as acts of violence but nothing more, if he or she merely read the court transcript with the grain. By definition, these assumptions are *not* explicitly stated in the text because they are assumed by the author to be universal truths that anyone (or at least the audience) would immediately recognize.

It is necessary, therefore, to **read against the grain**—or to deconstruct our sources—in order to gain access to the assumptions. The practice of deconstruction generally involves a series of steps. The first of these is to establish the origins, author, and other evidentiary issues about the text and to read it with the grain. It is especially important to know as much as possible about the author—his or her status in society, life experiences, political and cultural outlook, and so forth. This is because the assumptions we are looking for are usually generated communally and shared among a group. In the case of the "important men" in this story, for example, a British version of paternalism (the legitimate role of the father or other adult male figure as protector and punisher) seems to have been shared because of the shared life experiences of Davis, Melton, and Brew. Abina, however, did not have the same set of assumptions.

The next step in deconstruction requires the researcher to search for assumptions and figurative language—metaphors, similes, stereotypes, and the like. Often, it is useful to look at a range of documents as a way of identifying language that is commonly used by many people in the same society or social group. At the same time, it is important to read the document closely to see where explanations end and assumptions begin—in other words, to search out the points that the author assumes need no explanation. The famous anthropologist Clifford Geertz (1926–2006) explains this problem by using the example of winks, and points out the difficulty of an outsider understanding the meaning of a wink as a gesture. Only by investigating the many roles of the wink in a society—lascivious, indicating agreement, mocking—and by understanding the exact situation in which a particular wink takes place can the outsider hope to understand what the wink actually means.[4]

The transcript of Abina's testimony occupies a middle ground between intentional and inadvertent sources, since it was recorded purposefully but not necessarily with the intent that it be read in the future, let alone turned into a graphic history. Nevertheless, through deconstruction, it is possible to identify two very different sets of assumptions that were operating in the courtroom, and thus two very different versions of "truth."

The first—and dominant—set of assumptions evident in the transcript is a construction of the world that defined Melton, shared to a certain extent by Brew, and aspired to by Davis. This view might be called "Whiggish," after the slang term "**Whig**," for the liberal, middle-class political alignment of the time. In this view, progress is possible along rational terms. Good order is represented by rational people—especially adult men—acting on behalf of those assumed to be less rational than they, especially children, the disabled, and women. By 1876, many middle-class Britons adopted a view in which Africans and other non-Europeans (and the Irish and Eastern and Southern Europeans as well) were seen as being less rational than the Britons and other northern Europeans. This racialized view of peoples from different social and cultural backgrounds still

---

4   Clifford Geertz, *The Interpretation of Cultures* (New York: Basic Books, 1977), 6–7. Geertz is himself building on the work of philosopher Gilbert Ryle.

persists in Europe and America today. However, *race* was largely defined at this time through the idea of *rationality*, and men such as Brew and Davis seem to have interpreted being *civilized* in an English sense, in which civilized individuals can make rational decisions.

For Britons and others in the late nineteenth century who espoused this view, slavery was generally seen as a negative institution—something of a reversal from earlier decades—in that it held back progress and conflicted with "free labor," "the free market," and other desirable economic institutions. Moreover, slavery represented the opposite of rationality since it was irrational and restricted the liberal, capitalist system of labor and society. Indeed, the word *free* is perhaps the hallmark of the Whiggish perspective. This is expressed in the transcript not only by Melton's understanding of slavery as the opposite of freedom, but by his interesting question, early in Abina's testimony, of whether she had "free will." *Free will* was a term that had been in vogue in Britain, and was discussed by many of the leading bourgeois British intellectuals, including John Locke (1632–1704), David Hume (1711–1776), and John Stuart Mill (1806–1873). Indeed, Mill at least had queried whether non-Europeans could be said to have free will at all. By asking about this concept, Melton appears to have been getting at the heart of the "truth" of the matter, as far as the Whiggish view of slavery was concerned—was Abina free, or was she constrained, restrained, and captive? By reading the document against the grain, we can see Melton's assumptions, and those he shared with Davis and Brew, about how the world worked.

The specific philosophical concept of free will, however, had little meaning to Abina because Abina operated outside of the Whiggish assumptions of the way the world did and should work. In fact, she did not come to court to achieve her freedom. She had already done so by successfully fleeing to Cape Coast. Nor does she seem to have been in much danger of being recaptured. There are few records of slave owners from the countryside successfully reclaiming their former captives in Cape Coast, and it's not likely that this was a great risk. We can instead believe that Abina had come to court to tell a different "truth."

Abina's truth emerges from closely reading some of her statements, several of which are featured as full pages in the graphic history. First, reading with the grain, we can see that Abina tries to convey her enslavement to Melton and the men of the courtroom, not in some abstract sense of not being *free* but as something experienced bodily and psychologically. Thus she complains that she "could not look after [her] body and health." She rejects Brew's questions about the status of the other girls in the house by saying she knew little of their long-term experiences: "But *as for me* he did nothing good for me . . . and I ran away." The episodes on which she chooses to focus are also both physically and psychologically affecting—the violent cutting of the beads, the threat of flogging, the forced engagement to Tandoe. These episodes, and their lingering effects, are part of Abina's "truth."

This brings us to the question of why Abina chose to litigate against her former owner in the first place. Assuming she was facing little threat of reenslavement (a possibility she does not even mention), she must have had a deeper purpose for bringing him to court. It is our interpretation that Abina's testimony is a plea to be heard, a willingness to bear witness against injustice, and an attempt to deal with the pain of surviving such a violent system. As such, it reflects both the strength of a remarkable individual and the suffering of a whole class of people over time.

LEVEL 3: RECONSTRUCTING ABINA'S "TRUTHS" OR CONSTRUCTING OUR OWN?

Yet does the above conclusion really reflect Abina's message, or have we imposed on this story a message based on our values, stories, and moral codes? Is this truly what Abina was thinking, or have we created a heroine who suits our own needs? In other words, have we really reconstructed Abina's "truth" by deconstructing her message, or have we constructed a story that reflects our truths today?

Some scholars argue that reconstructing the past is impossible, and that both the tasks of reconstruction and deconstruction lead us only to create versions of the past that are meaningful to us but would be unrecognizable to people living in the past. They argue, in fact, that historians really only **construct** pasts. In the extreme, proponents of this argument suggest that there is no such thing as *truth*, only interpretations, or as the French theorist Jacques Derrida (1930–2004) wrote, perhaps "there is nothing outside of the text."[5] In this theory, all language and writing, including history, is merely a representation of the world that is meaningful to the writer.

Such a view is of limited use to the historian. To be sure, it is important that historians recognize the difference between *events* that happened in the past and *interpretations* of those events. There is general agreement among the current generation of historians, for example, that history can be neither truly objective nor entirely authoritative. Nevertheless, most historians (if not scholars in all other fields) agree that it is possible to strive to capture some message, metaphor, or "truth" about the past.

Of more immediate importance to us here is the work of historian and literary critic Hayden White (currently a professor emeritus at the University of California, Santa Cruz). Building on the idea that historians,

---

5   Jacques Derrida, *Of Grammatology* (Baltimore: Johns Hopkins University Press, 1998). Originally printed 1976.

like other humans, are caught in webs of meaning and not entirely free to interpret the past outside of their own social situation, White suggests that we interpret history through a limited set of ideologies available to us, and thus have only a few plots into which we try to fit past narratives and events. He focuses especially on historians trained in the period since the emergence of professional history in the late nineteenth century, and argues that all histories in the Western tradition since then are written from anarchist, conservative, radical, or liberal ideologies. He then connects these ideologies to just four plots. One of these is what White calls the "romantic" plot, which embodies certain values in an individual and then celebrates their victory over a series of challenges and obstacles. In particular, these values are the values of the author and some segment of his or her society.[6] So, for example, it's possible to argue that the interpretation of Abina's story in this book tells us more about the author's and illustrator's values of *freedom*, multicultural diversity, and gender equity than anything about nineteenth-century West Africa.

This is perhaps accurate. However, anthropologist Jan Vansina (currently a professor of anthropology and history at the University of Wisconsin, Madison) and historian Carolyn Hamilton (professor of social anthropology at the University of Cape Town, South Africa) have both pointed to the fact that stories aren't just made up out of nowhere. There are continuities to interpretations over time and across multiple narrators and authors. In fact, some voices in the historical record seem to yell out and to say exactly what they mean, with relatively little room for free interpretation. Abina's voice is one of these. In the courtroom, she is forceful enough to receive unquestionably the most extensive treatment given by any testifying female former slave in a Gold Coast colonial court. Her words are powerful enough to form a consistent message that is a desire to be heard as well as to be free. It is for this reason, and through our attempts to provide broad contextualization and careful qualification of our work, that we are confident enough to say that her message is present in our interpretation.

IS THIS "AUTHENTIC" HISTORY?

LEVEL 1: LOCAL FORMS OF HISTORY-TELLING

There is something special about a story of a family's past told by a grandmother or grandfather in the kitchen on a special family day. When these

---

6   Hayden White, *Metahistory: The Historical Imagination in Nineteenth-Century Europe* (Baltimore: Johns Hopkins University Press, 1973).

histories are told to us, we rarely question whether they are exactly *ac-curate* or what *message* they convey. Their value lies somewhere else, in the sense of community they create and the continuity of existence they reinforce. This value can be expressed by their *authenticity*. The concept of authenticity suggests that the rituals and ways we pass on information about the past are part of a wider sense of who we are as families, communities, and nations.

There is a catch, however. Neither a scholarly article nor a textbook nor even a graphic history fits within the way that most people in Cape Coast and its surrounding regions talk about who they are. Perhaps it is appropriate to illustrate this point with an argument. Several years ago, I (Trevor) was conducting interviews around Cape Coast to find out what people knew about an event that had happened during roughly 1867 to 1873, ending barely three years before Abina's court case. Called the **Fante Confederation**, it was quite a famous event, often cited in African history textbooks and Ghanaian official histories. Moreover, the Akan speakers of the Cape Coast region tend to very effectively pass on oral histories of important events. Therefore, I had reasonable expectations of learning something. Yet time and again, the everyday people of the region reported that they knew nothing of it. I finally found some individuals who *were* able to tell me what they knew about the events. Yet their stories were all oddly familiar, and it turned out that they were merely repeating the lessons they learned from their high school textbooks. So here we had a story that scholars and the government claimed had "historical importance" to the region, and yet it was not reproduced in the popular ways of talking about the past.

Indeed, there are several pathways in the Gold Coast by which the past is discussed. These range from rumors and family stories passed along informally from generation to generation, to proverbs, to epic foundation myths and historical narratives of central social importance ritually related to the public, or in secret ceremonies by members of *asafo* companies. Perhaps the highest status of these processes of transmission, however, is through the state linguist of each of the small *aman* (plural of oman), or "traditional areas" of the country. These state linguists have the Akan name **okyeame**, and they are individuals whose job it is to recall past events and parables for the use of the community and its rulers.

Most *aman* have several linguists, each representing an *abusua* (matrilineal group) within the community. One is usually considered the *chief linguist* and represents the entire state. Part of the linguists' job is to commune with the ancestors, a role that carries a great deal of responsibility for relating stories about the past as advice for contemporary rulers and members of society. In some situations, linguists act as private advisors; in others, their role is very public—for example, in the rituals that define the calendar, the stages of life, and the public identity of the community. Often, they are called upon to speak at these events, both in prayer and in story.

The historical narratives related by the okyeame bear only a limited relationship to those of the history textbooks of Western societies. For one thing, they are only rarely chronological, instead jumping backward and forward in time to make important points. They are rarely written, but rather spoken and sung, sometimes both together. Often, they take the shape of performances, and even include props. Both the singing and the props are meant to help aid the memory of the linguist in order to maintain accuracy, but the spoken sections are there to purposefully allow the linguist to adapt the story to the situation in which it is being told. Thus a certain amount of improvisation is prized, unlike in our formal histories. On the other hand, like many of our own histories, their stories contain lessons or morals, are represented as having some sort of "truths," and are believed to be of educational value, especially for training the young and new members of society.

In *Abina and the Important Men*, we are moving away from the formal history textbook model, but we are certainly not claiming to have effectively reproduced the narrative styles or skills of the *okyeame*. A graphic history is a type of history all its own and different from both. However, in our use of flashbacks and our attempt to combine writing and graphics, we have tried to gain access to a cadence and techniques that would be familiar to many southern Ghanaians today. We have done this partly in recognition of a duty to write a history of Ghanaians that would be recognizable and useful *by* Ghanaians today. Indeed, it is our plan that this book will be made available in Ghana to a Ghanaian audience.

LEVEL 2: THE PERSONAL AND THE COLLECTIVE AUTHENTIC

Another level of authenticity has us asking whether Abina or her contemporaries would recognize her in this story. Of course, this question links up with many of the methodological and philosophical issues raised in earlier sections. It also connects to two of the main approaches to the study of the past in the discipline today—**social history** and **cultural history**.

Social history, which emerged out of the political and social developments of the 1960s, developed as a method to understand the experience of large groups of people, largely through the categories of race, class, and gender. It successfully shifted the focus away from the histories of a few elite men (and women), and by looking at everyday behaviors—consumption, entertainment, work, child rearing, sexuality—it came much closer than earlier elite, political models of history to describing an experience that would have been recognizable to most members of a society.

By the 1970s and 1980s, however, some historians identified certain limitations to social history. Specifically, while describing the experiences and behaviors of large groups of people, social historians were less successful in looking at individual variations in both experience and perspective. Influenced by innovations in the field of anthropology, these historians began to focus on "culture" as a central theme. These scholars, like Peter Burke (emeritus professor of cultural history at the University of Cambridge) and Lynne Hunt (currently a professor of history at the University of California, Los Angeles) focused less on the shared experiences categories or groups of people and more on the ways in which individuals related to these collective institutions and behaviors. In doing so, they brought to the fore the idea of *culture*. Cultural historians largely see culture as a package or web of ideas, meaning, and expressions. Individuals, they argue, get caught up in these webs and are not entirely free to act exactly as they want. However, they also relate to them in particular ways and from unique perspectives, and thus make very personal choices. For cultural historians, it is not possible to reduce the individual to a face in the crowd. Just as social historians had sought to write new histories in which groups other than elites could recognize themselves, cultural historians constructed pasts in which individuals might recognize themselves. Yet cultural history also has limitations. One of these is that by seeking individual experiences, cultural historians often end up focusing on the fringes, and not adequately describing the experiences of most people.[7]

Of course, it is possible to make the argument that both of these approaches aim at greater accuracy, rather than some distinct type of authenticity. But this would ignore the motivations that drove both social and later cultural historians. Social historians have frequently focused on class, race, and gender from Marxian, feminist, antiracialist, and other such political positions. They seek to understand the operations of power by elites upon less powerful groups of people and to chronicle and/or commemorate the everyday experiences or grassroots rebellions of these groups. Similarly, cultural historians' decisions to focus on the fringes are often exacerbated by their desire to highlight the oppression suffered by individuals who are seen as being outside of the norm. It is often this aim that drives their emphasis on human variation.

---

7   Paula Fass, "Cultural History/Social History: Some Reflections on a Continuing Dialogue," *Journal of Social History*, 37 (2003), 39–46.

In writing *Abina*, we are seeking a certain authenticity in the model of both a social and a cultural history. On the one hand, we are using Abina as a vehicle for describing the behaviors and experiences of a large group of people—enslaved girls in late nineteenth-century Gold Coast. There are statistical data to show that this group existed in substantial numbers, and court records are the main sources for us to understand their lives. The data from these court records, developed through social history methodologies, illustrate many of the things experienced by Abina—for example, violence, employment, living conditions, and sexual exploitation. Moreover, we sympathize with members of this exploited class and argue that it is of value to know about their experiences.

At the same time, *Abina and the Important Men* is very much a cultural history. First, Abina cannot be assumed to be just like every other enslaved, young female African living in the Gold Coast in 1876. Indeed, she was probably quite exceptional. Thus, we are using her words to try to understand her individual experiences and personal purposes that drive her actions. In doing so, we are also sympathizing with Abina specifically, and committing ourselves to try to understand the case through *her* eyes.

LEVEL 3: HISTORY AS A FORUM OR A TEMPLE

The search for authenticity has certain limitations, and indeed potential dangers. Most important, it can turn history into **heritage**. There is a difference between the two. For all of its problems, *history* at least aspires to critically question the narratives of the past and provide evidence about them. By contrast, *heritage* is an uncritical celebration of history, an attempt to build up in-group identification. This often takes the guise of attacks on other groups. *Authenticity* in the guise of heritage can often be highly orthodox, leading to attacks on those deemed *unauthentic* or different. Moreover, because the search for authenticity doesn't always prize accuracy, it can frequently lead us away from learning as much as we possibly can.

The important point here is that history is constantly contested among various groups, each with a stake in portraying its events and experiences in particular ways. But it isn't actually really a problem that history is contested; this is the way that human societies work, after all. However, the question remains as to how historians should react to these contests. Should we pick a side and jump in? Or should we rather strive to be objective and sit above the debate? This is a problem that is at the heart of the public role of the historian.

One useful way into this question comes from the part of our profession that deals with museums. Museums that deal with history, of course, also deal with heritage. Once, museums would have claimed to represent neutral exhibits, in which the facts spoke for themselves. In reality, however, there is no such thing as a truly neutral museum or exhibit. Just as with scholarly books, "facts" and objects in a museum are always presented in such a way and accompanied by such devices as written or audio captions and catalogs as to tell a story that has a plot or point of view. Most such exhibits are meant to somehow reinforce the "authentic" heritage story of a group—the "nation of immigrants" story at Ellis Island, for example, or the "brave Texans" story at the Alamo. By contrast, evidence that contradicts this narrative is ignored or hidden.[8] In such cases, the museum becomes a "temple" where people of a particular group can celebrate or commemorate their "authentic" story of their past.

The problems with this type of presentation came to the fore in the United States in a debate in the early 1990s over the presentation of an exhibit dealing with the dropping of two nuclear bombs on Japan. The exhibit was being planned for the Smithsonian Air and Space Museum in Washington DC, and the museum's director wanted to avoid making the exhibit into a heritage temple. Instead, he wanted it to become a forum in which opposing views on the dropping of the two bombs could be presented and visitors to the museum could be asked to reflect critically on the events. This proposal drew the ire of several groups of "patriots," and especially groups representing military veterans, who felt that such an approach sullied the contributions of those in the military to the winning of the war. They pushed for an approach that would celebrate military service.[9] By contrast, a large group of professional historians campaigned to keep the exhibit as a forum by including multiple viewpoints.

A somewhat similar debate has taken place over the years at Cape Coast Castle, the site where Abina's case against Quamina Eddoo was heard. The museum is now a United Nations (UNESCO) World Heritage site and houses a museum. There has been a great deal of debate as to the form and content of that museum. As a major site at which Africans were sold to European and American slave ship captains, the castle is a site of pilgrimage and heritage for many African-Americans and Africans of the diaspora. The main story they want to see represented at the museum, of

---

8   Richard R. Flores, "The Alamo: Myth, Public History, and the Politics of Inclusion," in *Contested Histories in Public Space: Memory, Race, and Nation*, ed. Daniel J. Walkowitz and Lisa Maya Knauer (Durham, NC: Duke University Press, 2009), 123–135.

9   Edward T. Linenthal, "Anatomy of a Controversy," in *History Wars: The Enola Gay and Other Battles for America's Past*, ed. Edward Linenthal and Tom Englehardt (New York: Metropolitan, 1996), 9–62.

course, has to do with Cape Coast Castle's role as a slave-trading station. Many of these heritage visitors also want to make sure the castle remains unrestored and in dilapidated condition appropriate to a story of suffering and persecution. This means that the room where Abina's case was probably held, for example, remains unfurnished and unrestored. By contrast, many Ghanaians today see Cape Coast Castle as a symbol of colonial persecution rather than of the slave trade. Some Ghanaians believe the museum should be restored to the furniture and condition of the colonial period, to better illustrate how the colonizers lived and governed the region. Finally, the staff members of the museum wish to present a national story in the museum covering the long history of the castle and local community, rather than focusing solely on the slave trade era.[10] Central to this debate is the question of the role of Africans in the Atlantic slave trade at this museum. Some tour guide operators in the area, for example, would prefer not to acknowledge that Africans were active participants in selling other Africans because this conflicts with a story of African/African-American unity that is at the core of the way that they present a heritage story of the region to visitors. Most of the museum staff, however, is trained to present the *empirical truth*—that is, that there *is* evidence of Africans participating in the slave trade, if not in the same ways as Europeans. To their credit, some official museum guides have even learned how to make a *forum* of the issue, presenting multiple sides of the scholarly and popular debate over the topic.

Abina and the Important Men is intended to be a similar forum to the past, if in a printed, graphic form. To be sure, the author and illustrator speak with the authority of the historian and get to tell the main narrative of the story in a way that we like. However, we acknowledge that there are many issues within that need a more complex resolution than a single story can provide. How should we view Melton and British claims to "civilization," for example? Should we give Britain credit for legally abolishing slavery in its holding on the Gold Coast, or point out the limitations and hypocrisies of their policies? How should we view Quamina Eddoo and other Africans who, by the nineteenth century, profited from the labor of young Africans themselves? What about Brew, a onetime leader of a local nationalist movement, at once believing in self-rule and self-worth of Africans and yet aspiring to European values and styles of living, and speaking of moral values while defending a slave owner?

It would be all too easy to make a story of Abina and her encounter with a group of powerful men into a temple to her and to the practices and

---

10   Edward M. Bruner, "Tourism in Ghana: The Representation of Slavery and the Return of the Black Diaspora," *American Anthropologist*, 98 (1996), 290–304.

authority of professional historians. We have chosen to avoid that route, and to reveal to you the limitations of our work and the complexities of the story instead. Thus we offer *Abina and the Important Men* to you as a forum, for better or for worse. If we are authentic to no particular view of the past, we hope that we have given the reader something to think about.

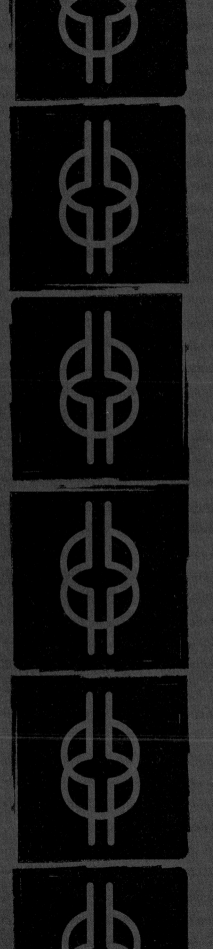

PART V
ABINA IN THE CLASSROOM

NYANSAPO
"WISDOM KNOT"

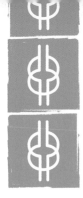

ABINA FOR THE WORLD HISTORY CLASSROOM

One of the major trends in the teaching of history in the United States in the last few decades has been the rise of **world history**. There are real-world reasons for this shift. Just as World War I helped to strengthen interest in Europe and solidify the creation of Western Civilization courses—still offered at many colleges and universities in the United States—so too the Cold War and the increasing scope of American involvement in the world spurred the growth of global history courses, while internal politics and issues such as the role of multiculturalism helped specifically to foster a "new world history" in the 1990s.[1] This version of world history focuses specifically on the connections among and between various groups and societies on a global scale. In the view of these practitioners, "world history is the story of connections within the global human community. The world historian's work is to portray the crossing of boundaries and the linking of systems in the human past." [2] It is this sort of global history that is largely enshrined in curricula, textbooks, and course syllabi for most world history courses at the high school (AP) and university survey levels.

In an influential 1999 article, A. G. Hopkins, a British historian of globalization and empire, argued that one of the key ways to understanding a global history is through an exploration of empire.[3] He is just one of many scholars who have argued that just as it's impossible to understand the

---

1   Gilbert Allardyce, "The Rise and Fall of the Western Civilization Course," *American Historical Review*, 87 (1982), 695–725. Gilbert Allardyce, "Toward World History: American Historians and the Coming of the World History Course," *Journal of World History*, 1 (1990), 23–76. Trevor Getz, "World History and the Rainbow Nation: Educating Values in the United States and South Africa," in *Memory, Public History & Representations of the Past: Africa & Its Diasporas*, ed. Audra Diptee and David Trotman (New York and London: Continuum Books, 2011).

2   Patrick Manning *Navigating World History: Historians Create a Global Past* (New York: Palgrave Macmillan, 2003), 3. Manning is president and chairman of the Board of the World History Network, former editor of H-World, and has consulted for more than a dozen universities on their world history programs.

3   A. G. Hopkins, "Back to the Future: From National History to Imperial History," *Past and Present*, 164 (Aug. 1999), 198–243.

histories of colonies—like the Gold Coast, or modern-day Ghana—without reference to colonialism, so too we cannot understand the histories of imperial capitals like Britain without looking at their empires. Exhorting us to see empire as a "single frame of reference," these scholars point out that the flow of ideas, people, concepts, goods, diseases, and species in the last five hundred years has often happened along the lines of communication, control, and trade that make up empires.[4]

In *Abina and the Important Men*, for example, we see the flow of many different ideas and things between Britain and the Gold Coast. Men and sometimes women like Melton—who came from Britain, held positions of influence in the Gold Coast Colony and Protectorate, and later moved on to other colonies, bringing ideas and ways of living with them. Brew is an even better example of a truly imperial history. Born in the Gold Coast to the daughter of an *ohene* (chief) and the son of a leading Euro-African slave trader, Brew studied law in Britain before returning to the Gold Coast. He had a great impact in the region, where he tried in the early 1870s to create a state modeled on British and German political institutions, known as the Fante Confederation. He also wrote for several newspapers, and some of his work was published in Britain.

Learning about these sorts of cosmopolitan, transnational histories helps us to view the world more accurately. The global past is not just about a bunch of competing nation-state blocks, but about human stories that cross boundaries as often as they put them up. It is for this reason that leading world historians have proposed that world history is "good for us." Here, for example, are the words of two leading modern world historians. First, William H. McNeill, one of the founding fathers of the field:

> Instead of enhancing conflicts, as parochial historiography inevitably does, world history might be expected to diminish the lethality of group encounters by cultivating a sense of individual identification with the triumphs and tribulations of humanity as a whole. This, indeed, strikes me as the moral duty of the historical profession in our time. We need to develop an ecumenical history, with plenty of room for human diversity in all its complexity.[5]

---

4   For a survey of this type of approach, see Trevor Getz and Heather Streets-Salter, *Modern Imperialism and Colonialism: A Global History* (Upper Saddle River, NJ: Prentice Hall, 2010).

5   William H. McNeill, "Mythistory, or Truth, Myth, History, and Historians," *American Historical Review*, 91 (1986), 1–10.

Next, the current editor of the *Journal of World History*, Jerry H. Bentley:

> Another argument for studying world history is that it is moral, in
> that it has to do with the kinds of personal conduct and public policy
> that are appropriate for the contemporary world. . . . [W]orld his-
> tory has unusual practical value because of its potential to acquaint
> students, citizens, and policy makers with cultural and social differ-
> ences, and furthermore to facilitate constructive engagement with dif-
> ferent peoples and societies.[6]

Yet in order to do this, world history has to appreciate not only the connections among societies and individuals but also the variety of life experiences in the world. In other words, we must appreciate the different ways
that people have in the past lived their lives and not try to make a single,
universal story of them. As African historian Joe Miller has argued, "Until
'world' historians incorporate Africa on its own terms, and focus also on
the unique aspects of other world regions . . . the logic of progressive world
history is condemned to obscure the dynamism of a truly global past."[7]
Therefore, it is our argument that Abina's story is of value not only because
of the ideas of Melton and Brew, which were forged connections across the
Atlantic and between Britain and West Africa, but also for Abina's very
different life experiences and perspectives. As we can see in the transcript,
Abina's life was not easily summed up by British notions of *free will* or
definitions of *slavery*. She sought, instead, to make her own wishes and
needs understood in the courtroom. In doing so, she reminded us, as well
as the men in the courtroom, that we live in a world of great diversity and
in order to function and flourish within it we must listen and learn from
others, no matter how powerful or powerless. Hopefully, this is will become a new type of world history, not a single global narrative but rather
an exploration of the many stories and perspectives that make up the human past. Thus while we urge the instructor to use this book to highlight
the connections across oceans and societies forged by the British Empire,
we also hope that teachers will help their students to understand the value
of listening for voices like Abina's and the value they bring in teaching us
to look at contemporary and historical situations from the viewpoints of
all of the actors.

---

6   Jerry Bentley, "Why Study World History?," *World History Connected*, 5 (2007), 4.

7   Miller, Joseph C., "Beyond Blacks, Bondage, and Blame: Why a Multi-centric World
History Needs Africa," draft originally prepared for a talk at Carleton College, March 9,
2005.

ABINA FOR THE AFRICAN HISTORY/AFRICAN STUDIES CLASSROOM

African history and African studies courses play a variety of roles in higher education. Knowledge about African pasts and present are important aspects of a liberal education program, and survey courses especially are gateways for students to the deeper pursuit of African area studies. However, *Abina and the Important Men* is designed not solely to supplement the content of African history and African studies courses, but also to help students to gain access to a package of skills, theoretical frameworks, and philosophical and ethical issues that help them develop as global citizens and critical consumers of narratives about the past and the present.

In helping students to develop critical methodologies, the interdisciplinary study of African pasts has a number of advantages over "mainstream" U.S. and European history courses. First, studying Africa is particularly useful for learning to question widely made assumptions about people and places. The western "gaze" on Africa is replete with signs and codes—the **noble savage** and the **people without history**, of course, but also the "unthinking environmentalists" and the "traditional societies."[8] Both teaching students to understand where these narratives come from in particular historical and contemporary settings and challenging them to compare the sign or code to the evidence can impart to students skills that will help them become more aware of the ways they are "consuming messages" that fill the world around them—from the media, from governments, or from other sources. Seeing the images in *Abina* and reading her words can help students to question their ideas of Africans as people who are live "tribes," and in "villages." They can instead see the more cosmopolitan and diverse life experiences of ordinary Africans. This effort is not motivated by political correctness, but rather an effort to promote a more accurate and complex envisioning of African pasts.

Of course, we can do this only because African history has developed a wide range of methods for reconstructing the past—through linguistic, ethnographic, archaeological, and archaeobotanical sources, for example.[9] The techniques developed by Africanists to read these varied sources have

---

8   See Curt Keim, *Mistaking Africa: Curiosities and Inventions of the American Mind* (Boulder, CO: Westview Press, 1999). For an online article, see Jonathan Reynolds, "So Many Africa, So Little Time: Doing Justice to Africa in the World History Survey," *World History Connected*, 2 (2004), http://worldhistoryconnected.press.illinois.edu/2.1/reynolds .html.

9   See John Edward Philips, ed., *Writing African History* (Rochester, NY: University of Rochester Press, 2006).

helped us to reconstruct not only the past of this continent, but the human past elsewhere. Alongside new sources, however, Africanists and allied scholars have developed new techniques for reading older sources in new ways. Through these techniques of "reading against the grain," we can investigate the deeper meaning behind the intentions of powerful men who wrote many of the documents describing Africa in the colonial and other periods, and gain access to the lives of those who were not literate or whose writing was not deemed important enough to preserve. These techniques make documents like court cases important again, and *Abina and the Important Men* is one example for students of a way to read a document to discover the hidden voices within it, and to draw out their meanings.

ABINA AND COLONIALISM

Of course, Abina's story also tells us a lot about topics specific to the time and place in which the book is set. One of these topics is **colonialism**. It is difficult to overestimate the impact of colonialism on the world generally, and on Africa specifically. In essence, colonialism was a reordering of societies. If the change that came with colonial rule was never total, it was nevertheless quite massive, and nowhere more than in Africa from the late nineteenth through the twentieth century.

Colonialism can be understood in many ways. Economically, these include the extraction of raw materials from the colonies in return for finished products. Many of these raw materials were carried by young people like Abina, who was employed by one of her masters to carry palm oil or other industrial raw materials to the coast. Politically, colonialism involved the destruction of local systems of power and authority and the creation of a new system in which a small, external group wielded great power through force and often also alliance with small, local groups. In Abina's world, this relationship was highly gendered—British men made alliances with some African men, who often either embraced British culture or found ways to profit from it.

We also understand colonialism as a cultural process of violence, one in which European people and Western ideals and culture came to be held up as superior and central, while ideas and people from elsewhere were depicted as inferior and peripheral.[10] One result of this process was the creation of hierarchies and segregation of peoples, genders, cultures, and ideas. Another

---

10   Partha Chatterjee, *The Nation and Its Fragments: Colonial and Postcolonial Histories* (Princeton, NJ: Princeton University Press, 1993). Achille Mbembe, *On the Postcolony* (Berkeley: University of California Press, 2001).

was the forcible imposition of Western ideals of gender, race, and culture upon the colonized. By placing themselves on top of this hierarchy, the colonizers claimed the right to "gaze" at colonized people: to describe them, to know them, and to speak for them without allowing them to speak back.[11]

The court case in which Abina participated is a good example of this. Language and power in the courtroom center around Melton, although with the connivance or cooperation of the other important men. Brew collaborates openly with a system that he has, for better or worse, come to embrace as his own pathway forward in society. Davis appears to have truly believed in British notions of justice and "civilization." Quamina Eddoo colludes more opportunistically, for the system favors his authority and power. These men all understand Melton's language and acknowledge his power, and are able to negotiate meaning in his presence. It is Abina who is left out of the negotiations in this colonial space. This becomes a fitting metaphor for the greater oppression of women, the young, the poor, and the powerless that resulted from colonialism.

ABINA AND THE HISTORY OF SLAVERY

Abina's testimony and the events surrounding it also raise several philosophical issues surrounding the study of enslavement. Two of these have to do with the meaning of *slave*. Slavery has been studied in the past as both an identity and a status. At times, the lives of the enslaved have been reduced to the simple category of *slave*, and while this has meant that their victimhood has been acknowledged, the result has often been an avoidance of their agency. Yet, as Abina's story shows, slaves retained their humanity and their actions and understandings were complex and nuanced. Like all other humans, they sought to understand the world around them, and did so emotionally as well as intellectually. Reducing them to simply victims impoverishes their histories and memories.

Abina's story also teaches us to think deeply about the diversity of experiences that we tend to lump together under the title *slavery*. Even during the nineteenth century, some Europeans recognized that slavery as an institution in West Africa seemed often to be rather different than plantation slavery in the Caribbean or the American South. Of course, these were often merchants and colonial officials arguing against emancipation, and their theories that African slavery was "benign" were usually attempts to maintain the status quo for economic or political reasons. Later commentators, and especially

---

11   The classic study is Edward W. Said, *Orientalism* (New York: Vintage Books, 1978).

scholars, were somewhat less obviously motivated by greed or political as-
piration when they noted that West African forms of "slavery" ranged from
purely ritual relationships to much more complex economic ties. One of
the breakthroughs in studying African forms of dependency came from the
French anthropologist Claude Meillassoux (1925–2005), who taught Western readers something most West Africans knew—that enslavement in the
region often had something to do with kinship, and that most of the enslaved
were distinguished within West African societies by not belonging within
any family, but instead belonging *to* individuals and families.[12] Similarly,
the sociologist Orlando Patterson (currently at Harvard University) showed
that slavery was a social as well as an economic institution, and helped to
usher in a new understanding of slavery outside of economic history.[13] Yet
easy definitions of slavery, even in this region, remain elusive. The numerous
experiences and social institutions that we meld into the category *slave* were
historically very diverse and often had little in common with one another.

Having said that, Abina's story is particularly interesting for the way in
which two particular understandings of *slavery* come together in one place
and time. On the one hand, there is the middle-class British understanding,
typified by Melton, that put together liberal notions of labor, knowledge
of Caribbean slavery practiced by Britons for several centuries, and ethnographic observation of Africans in a sort of normative formula of slavery as
economic, paternalistic, physically violent, segregated, and discriminatory
in terms of human rights. On the other hand, Abina's understanding of *her*
enslavement as a denial of identity and status, psychologically violent more
often than physically, and, more than anything else, personal, comes into
play as well.

GENDERING ABINA'S STORY

The courtroom from which Abina's testimony emerged was also a place
in which different understandings of the role of gender collided. Thus it
serves as a useful example of the ways in which our studies of the world
must be "gendered." What we mean by that is that gender is an integral
part of the human experience in any society and time period, and when we
avoid studying it, we often miss part of the story.

---

12   Claude Meillassoux, *The Anthropology of Slavery: The Womb of Iron and Gold* (Chicago: University of Chicago Press, 1992).

13   Orlando Patterson, *Slavery and Social Death: A Comparative Study* (Cambridge, MA:
Harvard University Press, 1992).

Abina's story must be gendered in at least two ways. First, the British society from which Melton was operating was deeply paternalistic. It was seen as being natural for the family, the state, and indeed the empire to be run by "father" figures whose duty it was to both protect their children/wards/women and to also make decisions for them.[14] This conceptualization, which was promoted as both a secular and religious value, operated through the decisions and assumptions that were made. For example, Melton easily accepted the defense that slaves were the wives, adopted children, or other wards of powerful or rich local men. Similarly, many other magistrates in Cape Coast Colony were willing to accept that violence against the enslaved was really just the punishment of unruly children, so long as they deemed it to be within acceptable limits by the standards of British society of this period.

This brings us to the second way in which this story must be gendered. As was discussed earlier, colonialism in nineteenth-century Africa largely took the form of an alliance between European men and a select group of African men. In the process, women gradually lost many of the institutions and beliefs that protected them. Much of this story occurs outside of the particular book.[15] However, one way in which this process occurred was the feminization of enslavement, a process by which women came to be deemed as "preferable" slaves because they were seen as less protected by the new colonial rules than by older social rules. Colonial officials could be convinced that women were wives rather than slaves, and, more significant, they recognized a father's rights to his "children." Thus even if female slaves wished to depart, they often could do so only if they gave up rights to their child, regardless of whether their enslaver was his or her biological father.

By recognizing the ways in which Abina's story is gendered, we can understand the ways in which gender is constructed in particular places and times, is integral to society, and is a useful category for understanding the past.

---

14   Philippa Levina, *Gender and Empire* (Oxford: Oxford University Press, 2004).

15   For this region, see Jean Allman and Victoria Tashjian, *I Will Not Eat Stone: A Women's History of Colonial Asante* (New York: Heinemann, 2000).

READING QUESTIONS

INTRODUCTORY QUESTIONS, FOR STUDENTS AT ALL LEVELS

Answer the following questions by focusing on the original transcript and referring when necessary to the graphic interpretation.

1. What questions does Magistrate Melton ask to try to determine whether Abina Mansah was *really* a slave? Why do you think he asks these questions?

2. Why do you think Abina Mansah did not know that Yowahwah had sold her to Quamina Eddoo at first? Why do you think the transaction was hidden from her?

3. Why do you think it is of value for us to learn about people from the past, like Abina Mansah, who weren't important political leaders or leading social or military figures?

4. Why do you think Abina Mansah decided to take her former master to court? What was her objective? What evidence from the court transcript supports your interpretation?

The following questions are based largely on the reading guide, although you will find it useful to refer to other sections of the book as well.

5. What was the "civilizing mission" as presented in this volume, and where do we find it the transcript and graphic history?

6. Consider the idea that the graphic history of Abina is the product of a "staircase" of voices. Whose voices are present in the graphic history? How did each person help to shape and produce it?

7. The transcript of Abina's testimony was intentionally produced. Why do you think such cases were recorded? Who was the intended audience? What "message" did Melton want them to take away from the transcript?

8. How do the authors try to ensure that the graphic history gives an accurate representation of the place and time in which it is set?

9. Would you consider the Gold Coast okyeame, described in Part IV, a historian? Why, or why not? What is a historian?

QUESTIONS FOR STUDENTS AT THE UNIVERSITY OR COLLEGE LEVEL

Answer the following questions by focusing on the original transcript and referring when necessary to the graphic interpretation.

10. What do the questions Melton asks Abina tell us about his conception of slavery?

11. Read through the trial, and identify points at which Abina Mansah misunderstands, is unable to answer, or contradicts the questions asked by Melton, Davis, and Brew. Why are these moments so important to hearing Abina's perspective? What do they tell us about the different ways in which each participant understood slavery?

12. Consider Abina's statement "If when Yowahwah gave me to defendant to keep the defendant had not given me in marriage to Tandoe I would not have entertained such an idea that I had been sold. *Because defendant gave me in marriage I knew that I had been sold.*" How did Quamina Eddoo's actions in giving Abina to Tandoe in marriage alert her to the fact that she had been sold and had the status of a slave in his household?

13. James Davis, who was probably of mixed European and African heritage, acted both as the court interpreter and the defense attorney. In

the graphic novel, we represent him as having coached, shaped, or edited Abina Mansah's original statement and testimony. Do you agree? Why, or why not?

The following questions are based largely on the reading guide, although you will find it useful to refer to other sections of the book as well.

14. In the reading guide, the "civilizing mission" is exemplified by two quotes—one from the British prime minister Joseph Chamberlain and one from the Sierra Leonean F. Fitzgerald. In the graphic history as well, Brew is depicted as being a believer in the superiority of at least great benefits of British civilization, partly because of statements he made during his career that suggest that he harbored such sentiments. How do you account for the support given by some West Africans in this period for British "civilization" and even British rule in the region?

15. The author argues that Abina managed to overcome the historical "silencing" of people of her class by testifying in court, thus making her voice available to us today. Evaluate this argument. How were people of her class silenced in the period? Does this graphic novel reverse that silencing?

16. How do the author and illustrator read the transcript of Abina's testimony against the grain?

17. What does the author argue is Abina's "truth"? Do you agree or disagree? Why?

18. Although records exist of some 100 or more cases in which allegedly enslaved people testified in late nineteenth-century Gold Coast, Abina's testimony is unique in length and completeness. Can it be said that she is *representative* of a larger group of people, or should we treat her as *exceptional* and unique?

19. One of the measures of whether a historical work is *authentic*, according to the author and illustrator, is the affirmative answer to the question "Would Abina recognize herself in this story?" Is this a useful question for historians to ask themselves in producing a history? Why, or why not?

20. Consider Joe Miller's and Jerry Bentley's quotes in the section "*Abina* and World History." Can Abina Mansah's story be considered a "world" history in any way? Why, or why not?

ADDITIONAL QUESTIONS FOR ADVANCED UNDERGRADUATE AND GRADUATE STUDENTS

Answer the following questions by focusing on the original transcript and referring when necessary to the graphic interpretation.

21. What do the questions Melton ask tell us about his conception of "rights"?

22. Abina Mansah gives a whole series of statements that give us clues as to how it felt to be in her position. Interpret these statements in the context they appear in the testimony. What was Abina Mansah trying to tell the magistrate, and what do these statements tell us about her experiences and perspectives?

    a. "[W]hen a free person is sitting down at ease the slave is working that is what I know."

    b. "I had been sold and I had no will of my own and I could not look after my body and health."

    c. "As they were in defendant's house long before if the defendant had done anything for them I could not tell *but as for me he did nothing good for me.*"

    d. "I thought I was a slave, because when I went for water or firewood I was not paid."

The following questions are based largely on the reading guide, although you will find it useful to refer to other sections of the book as well.

23. Consider the arguments of Hayden White and others that historians merely construct the past based on plots available to them in their own culture. To what degree do you think the interpretation of Abina presented in this volume reflects Abina's "truths," and to what degree do they represent those of the authors and our society today? On what basis can you make this argument?

24. It is possible to suggest that by turning Abina's testimony into a graphic history, the author and historian have become the main voices, effectively marginalizing Abina's own voice in the telling of her story.

Do you agree or disagree? Why? Would it have been better to merely present the testimony as is and alone?

25. Some critics have argued that "deconstruction" is at times really "speculation," and that scholars read too much into sources. Can you find instances of speculation in the graphic history that are not sufficiently supported by evidence in the transcript? Is this a problem? Why, or why not?

26. This graphic history can be read as a cultural history of the ideas of four or five individuals. Can it also be said to be a social history? Of whom and what?

27. The author has striven to represent Abina's story in this volume as more of a "forum" than a "temple." Do you think this volume succeeds as a forum? Why, or why not? What are the advantages and disadvantages of this approach?

TIMELINE

1300 —— ca. **1300** First major Akan-speaking state, the kingdom of Bono, forms in the forest region.

1325

1350

1375

1400 ┌— ca. **1441** Atlantic slave trade begins.

1425

1450 ┌— **1471** Portuguese rent land from the ruler of Edina, Kwa Amankwa, to build Elmina Castle. It becomes the first European presence on the Gold Coast.

1475

1500

1525

1550

1575

1600

1600

1610

1620

1630

1640 — **1640s** The town of Cape Coast emerges as a major political and military player in the region as the capital of the state (*oman*) of Fetu.

1650

1660 — **1650s–1710s** Danish, French, British, Dutch, and German merchant companies arrange to lease or buy land, or seize it forcibly, to compete with the Portuguese for control over trade with the region.

1670

1680 — **1680s–1700s** Earliest known *asafo* companies emerge, mostly in the interior but also on the coasts.

1690

1700

1710

1720

1730

1740

1750 — **1745** Richard Brew, paternal ancestor of James Hutton Brew, arrives in West Africa.

1760

1770

1780

1790

1800

1800

1805

1810

1807 Britain criminalizes the Atlantic slave trade due to pressure from abolitionists, including Afro-Britons like Gustavas Vassa (Olaudah Equiano).

1815

1807 Asante invades the coast, establishing control over most trade between the region and Europe.

1820

1825

1823–1824 Conflict between British and Asante results in the death of Sir Charles Macarthy, reaffirming Asante supremacy in the region.

1830

1835

1834–1835 Slavery is abolished throughout the British Empire.

1840

1843–1844 British and some coastal rulers sign the "Bond of 1844," which formalizes relationships between them.

1845

1850

1855

1865 Administrator Edward Conran exiles the ruler of Cape Coast, Joseph Aggery, effectively imposing direct British rule over the town.

1860

1867–1871 Dutch abandon their forts on the coast, leaving British as sole European power in the region. Citizens of Cape Coast and neighboring states form the Fante Confederation. Leaders include James Hutton Brew.

1865

1870

1875

1873–1874 Anglo-Asante war results in the creation of the Gold Coast Colony and Protectorate.

1880

1885

1875 British antislavery laws are applied in the Gold Coast Colony and Protectorate.

1890

1876 Abina Mansah's case is brought to trial.

1895

1900

1896 A second Anglo-Asante war ends in defeat of Asante armies and the establishment of British control over much of the former Asante state.

1900

1905

1910

1915

1920

1925

1930

1935

1940

1945

1950

1955

1960

1965

1970

1975

1980

1985

1990

1995

2000

1902 British take control of Northern Territories, establishing final boundaries of the Gold Coast Colony.

1925 Constitution of 1925 establishes a "council of chiefs" to advise British governors.

1948 Veterans returning from Second World War march for new rights. Several are shot, and six leaders are detained, giving rise to a mass movement for independence.

1957 British Gold Coast Colony becomes independent state of Ghana.

1979 Cape Coast Castle named a UNESCO World Heritage site.

2011 *Abina and the Important Men* published.

FURTHER RESOURCES

ABINA MANSAH

So far as we can tell, Abina Mansah appears in the official archives of the Republic of Ghana only once—in the old, moldering court documents, book number SCT 5-4-19, case of *Regina* (Queen Victoria) *versus Quamina Eddoo*, 10 Nov 1876, and again a few days later for a final verdict.

Like most other poor Africans who happen to be written into the archives of a colonial court—indeed, like most other poor, "everyday" people in any archive—she was ignored during the period of the great political and economic historians that dominated the last century. When she finally found her way into a scholarly work, it was in a "social history" as, literally, a footnote. I (Trevor) was the author of that social history, *Slavery and Reform in West Africa: Toward Emancipation in Nineteenth-Century Senegal and the Gold Coast* (Athens: Ohio University Press, 2004), and at that stage in my career I was more engaged with putting together evidence about the "experience" of a group of Africans than focusing on the perspective of a few. Abina's case, along with those of other Africans claiming to have been enslaved, supported my wider arguments about social change in the region in the late nineteenth century.

Yet Abina's case was haunting, partly because of her insistence that she be heard in court. Still, the process of understanding what she was saying was difficult, partly because the "important men" in the case were so loud. My first step in excavating her voice was therefore to understand the position and views of men like Melton, a task that culminated in the research and publication of "British Courts, Slave-Owners, and Child Slaves in Post-Proclamation Gold Coast, 1874–1899," in *Child Slaves in the Modern World*, edited by Gwyn Campbell, Suzanne Miers, and Joseph C. Miller (Athens: Ohio University Press, 2010), first written for a 2004 conference in Avignon, France.

I was ready now to write about Abina, but the opportunity really only presented itself when I was invited to a conference put on by four leading scholars of the history of slavery in Africa—Alice Bellagamba, Martin Klein, Sandra Greene, and Carolyn Brown. The conference, entitled "Finding the African Voice: Narratives of Slavery," was held in Bellagio, Italy, in 2007. Two volumes have emerged from the conference of collected papers. The first, *African Voices on Slavery and the Slave Trade*, is being published in 2011 by Cambridge University Press. This volume reprints the full sources with brief interpretations for students, and includes the article "Interpreting Gold Coast Supreme Court Records, SCT 5/4/19: Regina (Queen) vs. Quamina Eddoo." The second, forthcoming from Africa World Press and provisionally entitled *Looking for the Tracks: Essays on African Sources for the History of Slavery and the Slave Trade*, focuses more on interpretations and includes a chapter that I wrote about the case, "Abina Mansah and the Important Men: Contesting Definitions and Experiences of Enslavement in Post-proclamation Gold Coast Courtrooms."

It is accurate to say that by telling her story in court back in 1876, Abina gave me both inspiration and work. I hope to repay her by retelling her story in this volume to as wide an audience as possible.

SLAVERY AND ABOLITION ON THE GOLD COAST

There are many volumes about slavery and abolition in Africa and elsewhere that deserve mention in this brief bibliography, but I will confine myself to a short discussion of those focusing on the Gold Coast.

Among the superior works on slavery in what is today Ghana are Peter Haenger, *Slaves and Slave Holders on the Gold Coast: Towards an Understanding of Social Bondage in West Africa* (Basel, Switzerland: P. Schlettwein, 2000); Benedict Der, *The Slave Trade in Northern Ghana*, (Accra, Ghana: Woeli, 1998); and Akosua Perbi, *A History of Indigenous Slavery in Ghana: From the 15th to the 19th Century* (Accra, Ghana: Sub-Saharan, 2004).

The debate about abolition on the Gold Coast, specifically, includes a number of articles and books, including Raymond Dumett and Marion Johnson, "Britain and the Suppression of Slavery in the Gold Coast Colony, Ashanti, and the Northern Territories," in *The End of Slavery in Africa*, edited by Suzanne Miers and Richard Roberts (Madison: University of Wisconsin Press, 1988); Gerald McSheffrey, "Slavery, Indentured Servitude, Legitimate Trade, and the Impact of Abolition in the Gold Coast, 1874–1910: A Reappraisal," *Journal of African History*, 24 (1983), 349–

68; Kwabena Opare Akurang-Parry, "The Administration of the Abolition Laws, African Response, and Post-proclamation Slavery in the Gold Coast, 1874–1940," *Slavery and Abolition* 19, no. 2 (1998), 149–66; and Trevor Getz, "The Case for Africans: The Role of Slaves and Masters in Emancipation on the Gold Coast, 1874–2000," *Slavery and Abolition* 21, no. 1 (2000). I also look forward to forthcoming work from the German scholar Steffen Runkel.

There are a number of wider studies of slavery in Africa that deserve mention here as well. These include the classics by Paul Lovejoy, *Transformations in Slavery* (Cambridge: Cambridge University Press, 1983); Martin Klein, ed., *Breaking the Chains: Slavery Bondage, and Emancipation in Modern Africa and Asia* (Madison: University of Wisconsin Press, 1993); and Suzanne Miers and Richard Roberts, eds., *The End of Slavery in Africa* (Madison: University of Wisconsin Press, 1988). Others deserve mention, but I will limit myself here to saying that anyone wishing to research further should look at Joseph Miller's fabulous *Slavery and Slaving in World History: A Bibliography—Vol. 2, 1992–96* (Armonk, NY: M. E. Sharpe, 1999).

ABOUT COLONIALISM AND THE GOLD COAST

There are numerous histories of the Gold Coast, several of which cover the colonial period particularly well. In order of complexity, these include F. K. Buah, *History of Ghana* (London: Macmillan, 1998); and Roger Gocking, *The History of Ghana* (New York: Greenwood Press, 2005).

There are also numerous more specific works that may be of interest to readers. For a gendered history, Victoria B. Tashjian and Jean Allman, *I Will Not Eat Stone: A Women's History of Colonial Asante* (Portsmouth, NH: Heinemann, 2000), is essential. Also recommended from the same series is John Parker, *Making the Town: Ga State and Society in Early Colonial Accra* (Portsmouth, NH: Heinemann, 2000). One intriguing analysis of how Europeans saw the Gold Coast is Seth Quartey, *Missionary Practices on the Gold Coast, 1832–1895: Discourse, Gaze, and Gender in the Basel Mission in Pre-Colonial West Africa* (Amherst, NY: Cambria Press, 2007).

One special item of note is the spectacular reprinting with commentary of Asantehene (King of Asante) Prempeh II's writings. This volume is an interesting companion to Abina's story, and is available as A. Adu Boahen, Emmanuel Akyeampong, Nancy Lawler, T. C. McCaskie, and Ivor Wilks, *The History of Ashanti Kings and the Whole Country Itself' and Other Writings* (Oxford: British Academy, 2003).

GENERAL HISTORIES OF AFRICA

Although Africans have long been aware that Africa has a history—despite assurances from professional historians that it did not—it was not until the 1960s that large-scale scholarly histories of the continent came to be published. A generation later, the field had advanced to such a degree that a group of African, European, and American scholars led by luminaries like J. F. A. Ajayi, Joseph Ki-Zerbo, and Ali Mazrui could edit the multivolume *UNESCO General History of Africa* (Berkeley: University of California Press, 1981–1997). The *GHA* remains one of the foremost comprehensive studies of the African past, but numerous useful syntheses have followed. These works have struck out in new directions. For example, Jonathan Reynolds and Erik Gilbert successfully argued for Africa's place in a global narrative in *Africa in World History*, 2nd ed. (Upper Saddle River, NJ: Prentice Hall, 2011). Joe Miller and Suzanne Blier are in the process of producing a humanistic history of the continent that aims to focus on Africans' own understandings of the world around them over time, to be entitled *African Worlds: The Human Experience in Africa* (New York: Oxford, forthcoming). Finally, the many methodological innovations and issues in the study of African history are surveyed in Esperanza Brizuela-Garcia and Trevor Getz, *African Histories: New Sources and New Techniques for Studying African Pasts* (Upper Saddle River, NJ: Prentice Hall, 2011).

IMPERIALISM AND COLONIALISM

The study of empire comprises a vast literature, even if restricted to just the late nineteenth and early twentieth centuries. Over the last century or so, scholars and activists have put forward sociological, economic, cultural, political, and pathological explanations for why massive empires formed during that period. Many of these are described and explored in David B. Abernethy's *The Dyamics of Global Dominance: European Overseas Empires, 1415–1980* (New Haven, CT: Yale University Press, 2000). It is also worth looking at Trevor R. Getz and Heather Streets-Salter, *Modern Imperialism and Colonialism: A Global History* (Upper Saddle River, NJ: Prentice Hall, 2010).

Aside from these two surveys, it is impossible to list all of the important volumes involved here, but a couple bear particular importance in relation to this volume. The first is Ronald Robinson and John Gallagher with Alice Denny, *Africa and the Victorians: The Climax of Imperialism in the Dark Continent* (New York: St. Martin's Press, 1961). This was one of the first explorations of the origins of the tropical British Empire to suggest that events in Africa itself played a role in the development of the empire. Another is Frederick Cooper and Ann Laura Stoler's edited volume *Tensions of Empire: Colonial Cultures in a Bourgeois World* (Berkeley: University of California Press, 1997). This book brought together many of the cultural historians working on empire in the 1980s and 1990s and helped to develop a broad understanding of cultures of empire that now cannot help but pervade books like this one.

Certainly one of the great edited series on empire is the *Oxford History of the British Empire*. Readers of *Abina* will especially be interested in the excellent *OHBE, Volume III: The Nineteenth Century*, edited by Andrew Porter (Oxford: Oxford University Press, 1999). They might also like to read a companion volume edited by Philippa Levine, *Gender and Empire* (Oxford: Oxford University Press, 2004). This is just one of several recent works that help to expose the ways in which gender perspectives and the gendering of colonial projects were important parts of imperialism and colonialism. Finally, one of the great volumes on the legacy of colonialism in Africa is Mahmood Mamdani's *Citizen and Subject; Contemporary Africa and the Legacy of Late Colonialism* (Princeton, NJ: Princeton University Press, 1996).

GENDER AND AFRICAN HISTORY

For much of the history of History, both women and the paradigm of gender have been largely ignored. It is now widely recognized that this has both limited historians' capacities to understand the past and rendered many of our findings inaccurate. This is nowhere truer than in Africa, where Western historians long ignored the role of gender and the presence of women. Both their assumptions and their ignorance have been overturned in the last quarter century by some very serious scholars. Chief among these are the Nigerians Ifi Amadiume and Oyeronke Oyewumi. Amadiume's *Male Daughters, Female Husbands* (London: Zed Books, 1987) showed the world the ways in which the flexible gender systems of Ibo speakers created a very different reality than those of their British colonial rulers. Oyewumi showed how among the Yoruba, even so basic a category as *woman* is both more complex and more absent than in modern, Western societies in *The Invention of Women* (Minneapolis: University of Minnesota Press, 1997).

The work of scholars like these is chronicled in Nancy Rose Hunt's article "Placing African Women's History and Locating Gender," *Social History* 14, no. 3 (1989), 359. Since its writing, a generation of scholars has begun to firmly gender the study of the African past. Two especially recommended works are Lisa Lindsay and Stephan Miescher, eds., *Men and Masculinities in Modern Africa* (Portsmouth, NH: Heinemann, 2003); and Cole, Jennifer and Lynn M. Thomas, eds., *Love in Africa* (Chicago: University of Chicago Press, 2009).

WEB RESOURCES

Historians have only belatedly recognized the value of the web both as a research tool and a place to disseminate their findings. Moreover, many of them are still wary of a medium so friendly to disinformation and error. However, there are several web resources that are worth visiting if you are interested in the topics, places, and times discussed in *Abina*.

The first website is the official *Ghana at 50* site (http://www.ghana50.gov/gh/) put together by the government of the Republic of Ghana to celebrate fifty years of independence, and containing several historical narratives. Additionally, Cape Coast Castle museum has its own website (http://www.centralregion.gov.gh/castle.php), which was developed with the assistance of historians and other scholars.

Readers who are interested in the Atlantic slave trade should look at the website developed by Manu Herbstein to accompany his novel *Ama* (http://www.ama.africatoday.com). Herbstein has collected a variety of resources to help his readers that are of value to everyone. If you are looking for primary sources, the *African Times Online* site contains digital versions of this nineteenth-century newspaper (http://diva.sfsu.edu/users/Trevor.Getz0/AfricanTimes).

Finally, if you are interested in contemporary Ghanaian issues, the Ghanaian expatriate community has developed a great site at GhanaWeb (http://www.ghanaweb.com) for keeping in touch with issues at home and around the world.

PRELIMINARY SKETCHES

THE PROBLEM OF REPRESENTATION

How do you sketch people who lived more than a century ago, and for whom we have no photographs, drawings, or other visual evidence? How can we know how Abina would have dressed when we possess no pictures of her, and the historical record includes precious few pictures of any Ghanian women of Abina's status who lived in the last half of the nineteenth century? As the authors of this book, we shared our individual expertise areas in history and design to best approximate what Abina would have looked like and what clothes she would likely have worn, and we did the same for Melton, Davis, Brew, and Quamina Eddoo. Throughout the making of *Abina*, we debated the kind of clothes each character would have worn—the design and cut of the cloth, jewelry and other adornments, and physical features. There were countless questions for which we sought answers. We wished to ascertain whether Melton would have worn a judge's wig (he would have not), whether rural men went shirtless (yes, they did), and how common was the practice of wearing head wraps (quite common, and still so today). We pored over dozens of pictures—newspaper illustrations, missionaries' photographs, and even woodcuts—to get a feel for both the village and urban environments that would have formed Abina's world. We found that many of these sources contradicted our own assumptions as well as the typical way this period of West African history has been commonly depicted. Of course, we will never really know whether we drew Brew's suit or Abina's beads correctly, but like all historians and artists with good intentions, we based our decisions and our interpretations on the sources that were available.

ABINA MANSAH

Liz Clarke 2010

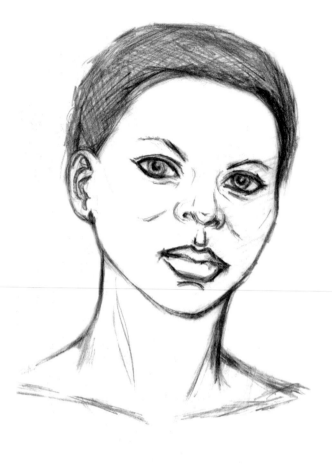

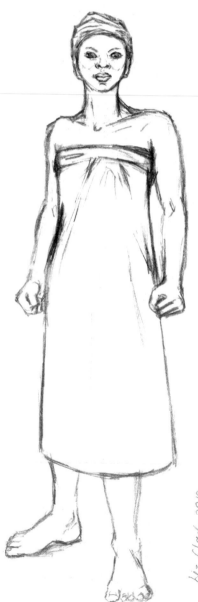

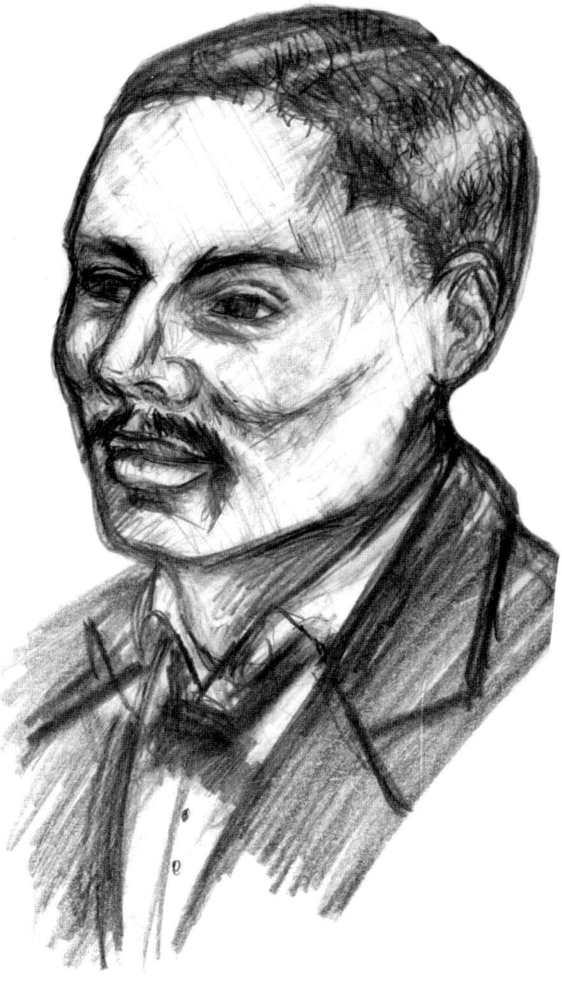

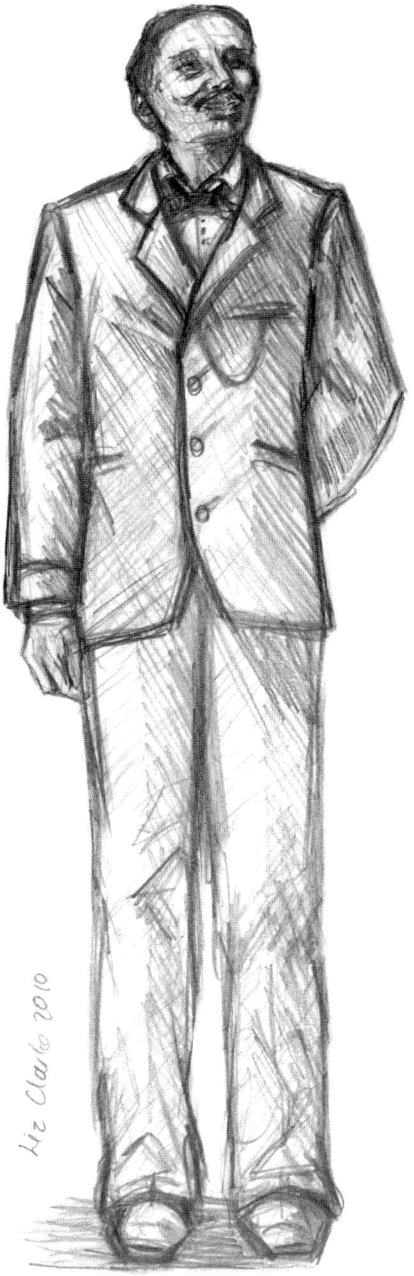
Liz Clarke 2010

JAMES HUTTON BREW

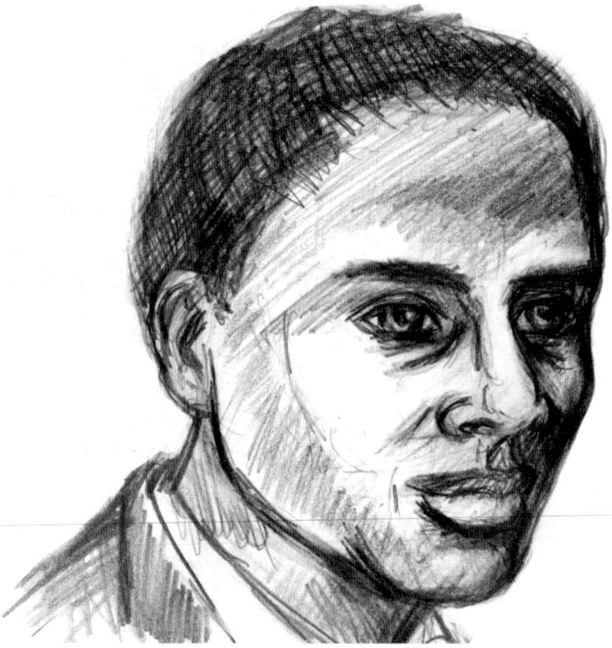

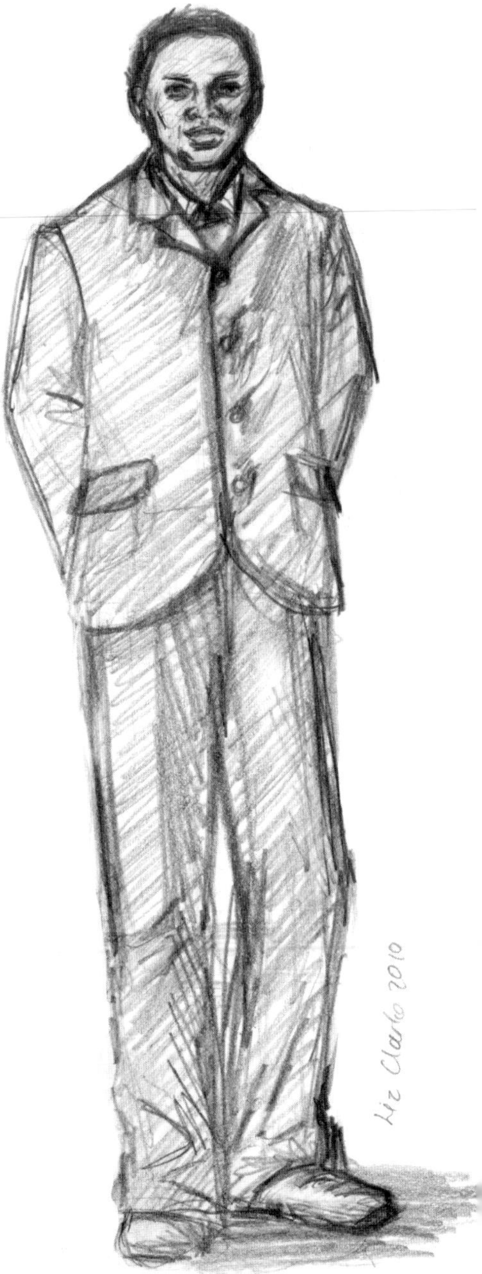
Liz Clarke 2010

JAMES DAVIS

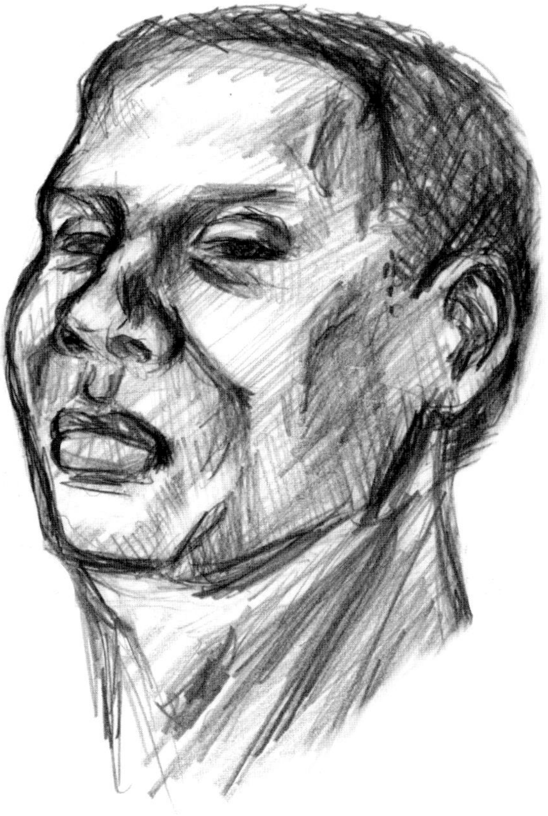

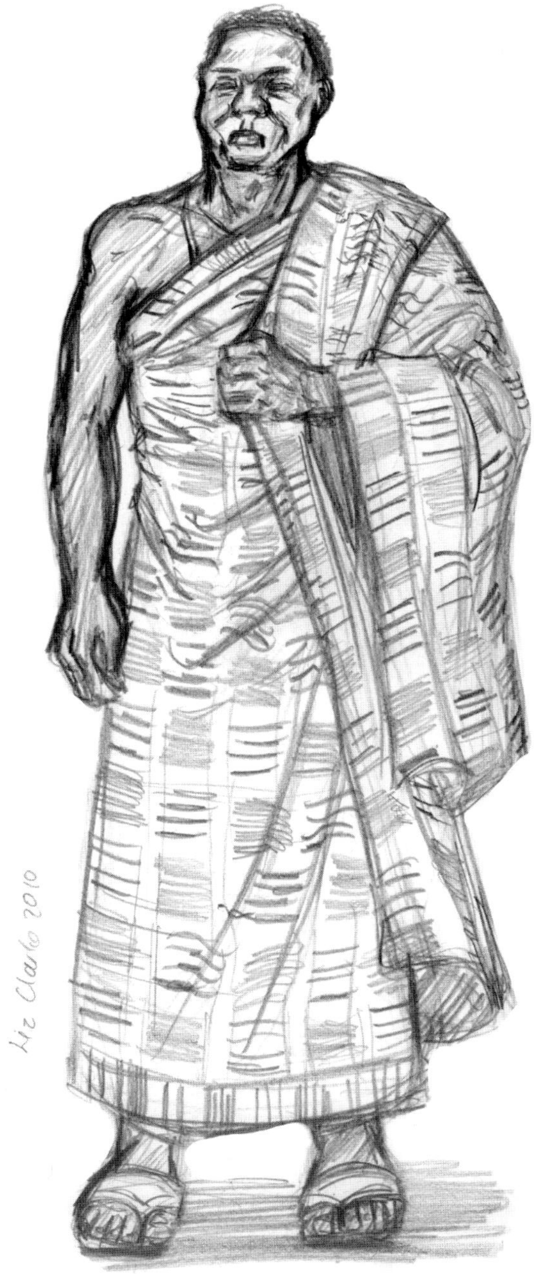
Liz Clarke 2010

QUAMINA EDDOO

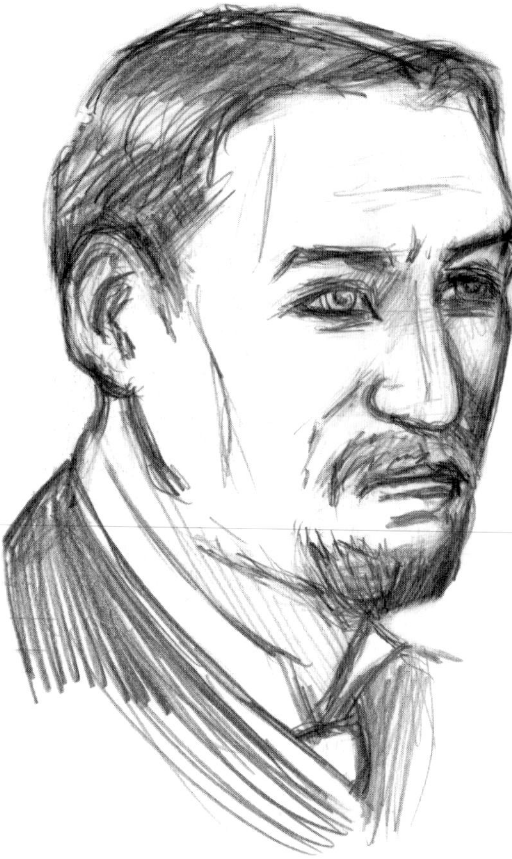

WILLIAM MELTON

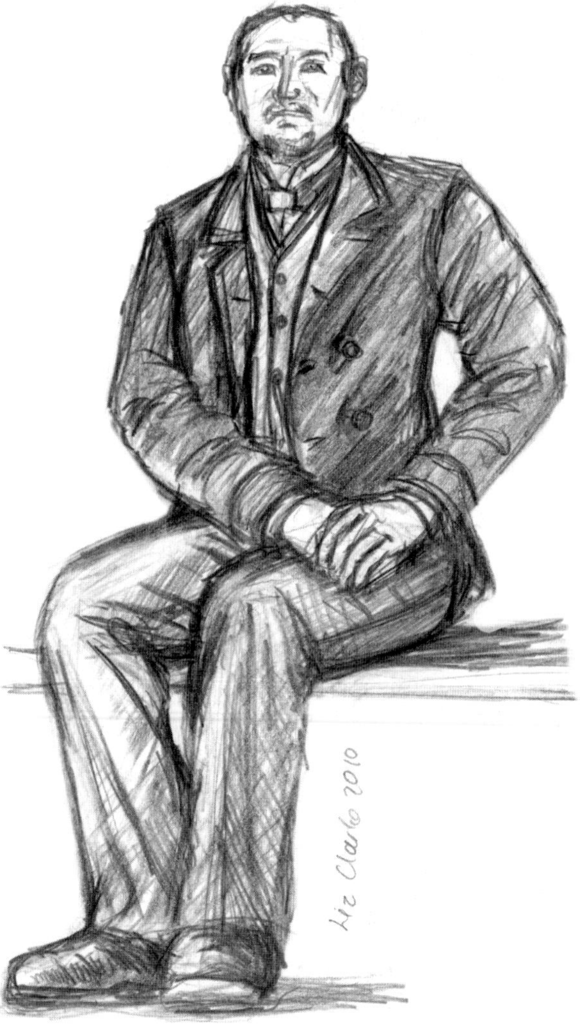
Liz Clarke 2010

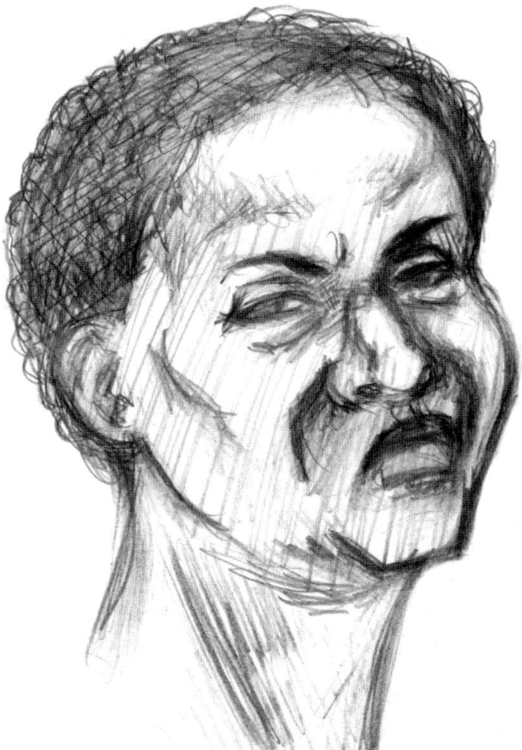

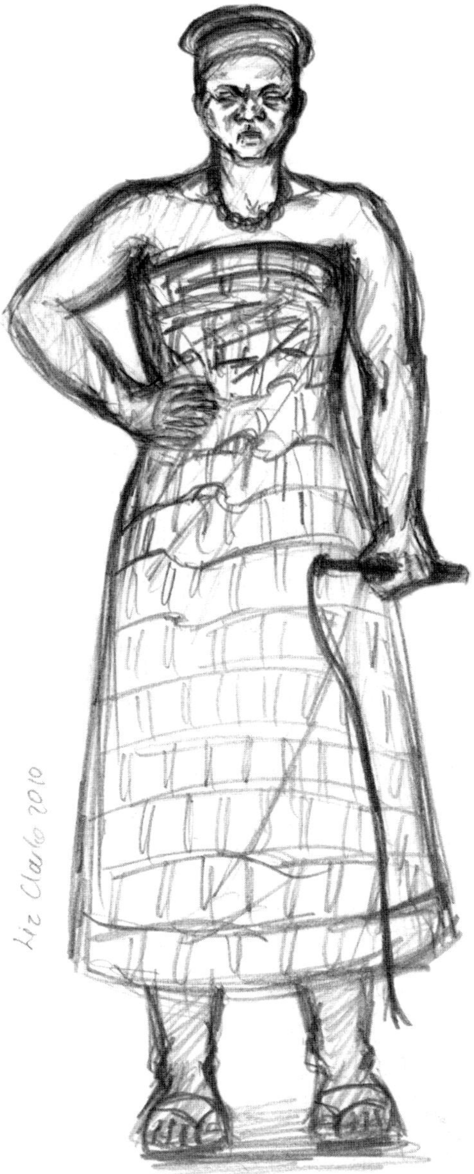
Liz Clarke 2010

ECCOAH

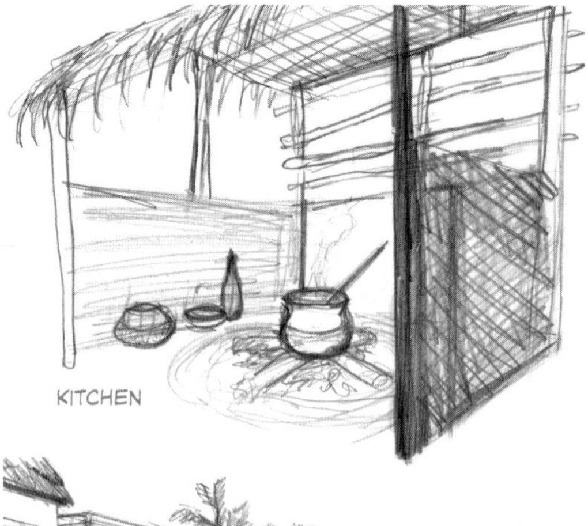
KITCHEN

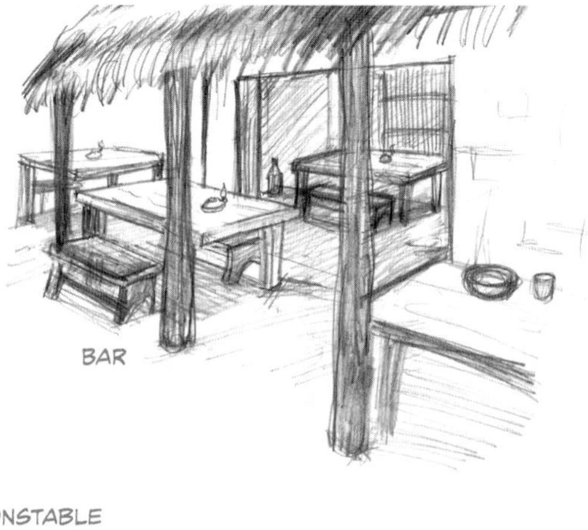
BAR

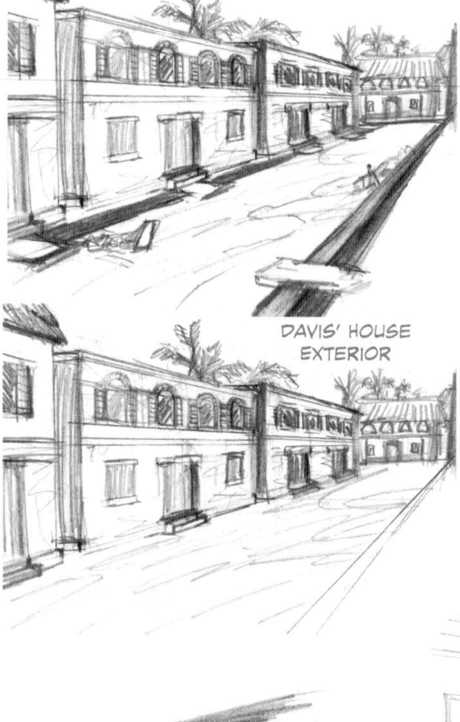
DAVIS' HOUSE
EXTERIOR

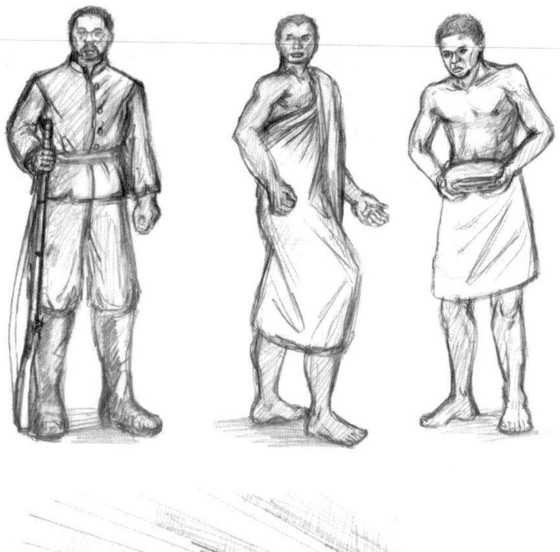
CONSTABLE
MOOSA
YAW AWOAH
TANDO

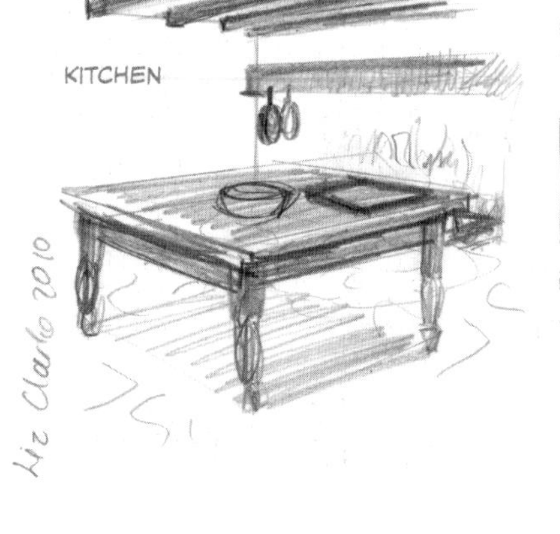
KITCHEN
Liz Clarke 2010

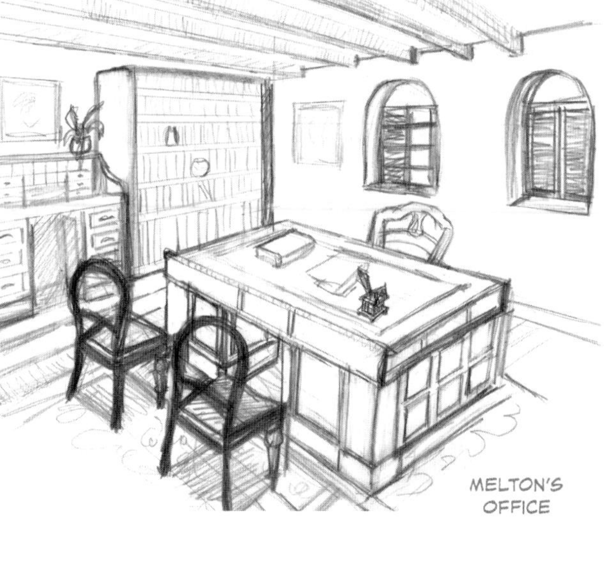
MELTON'S
OFFICE

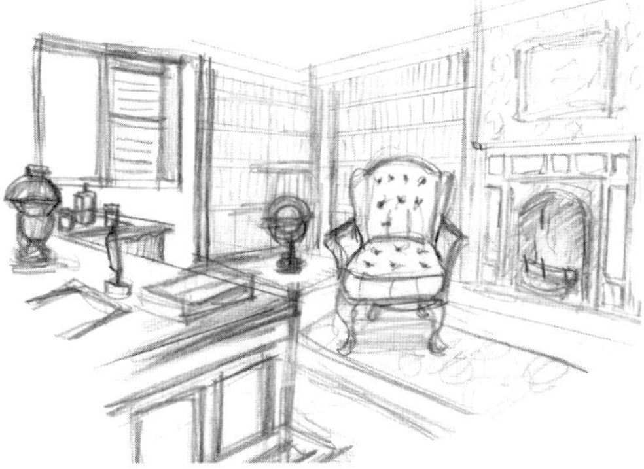

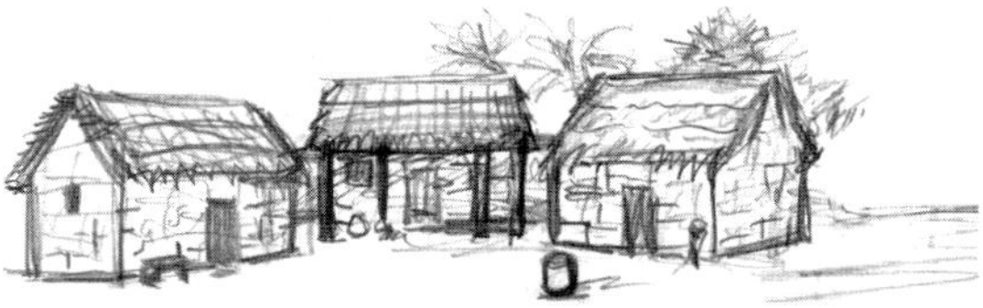

VILLAGE

BREW'S OFFICE

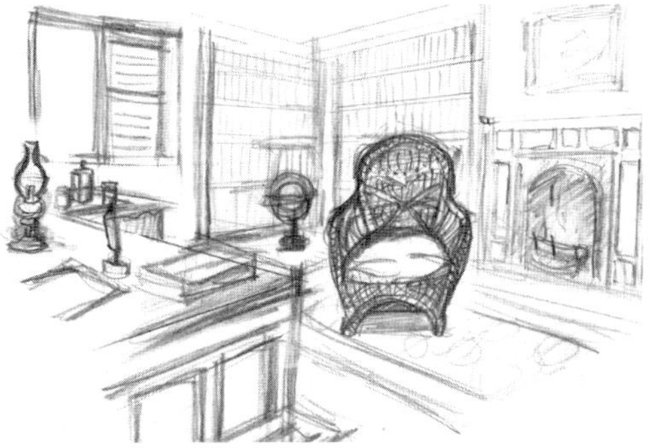

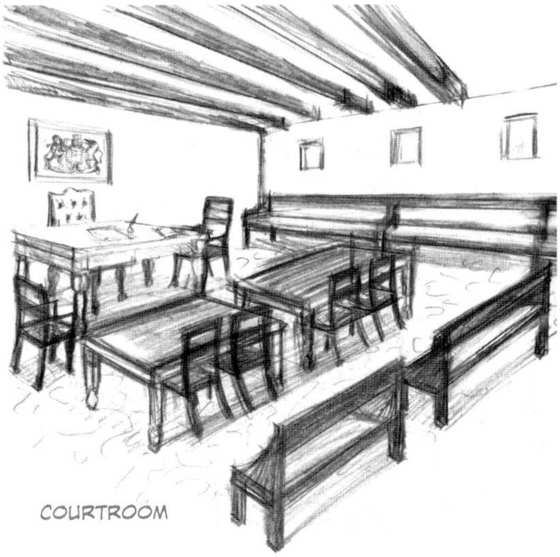

COURTROOM

DAVIS' HOUSE INTERIOR

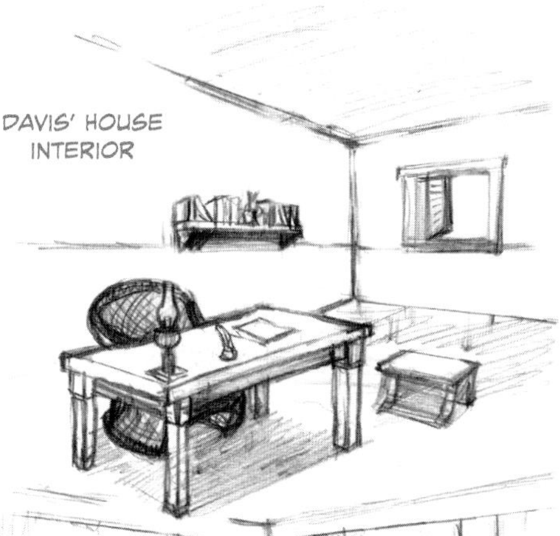

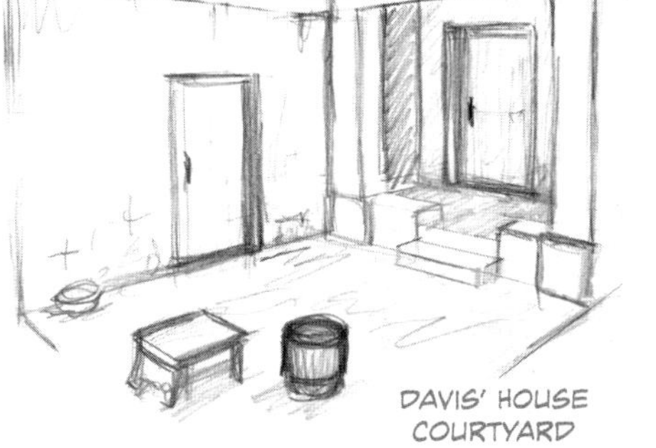

DAVIS' HOUSE COURTYARD

NANA AMPOFA

THOMAS AMINISSAH

JONATHAN DAWSON

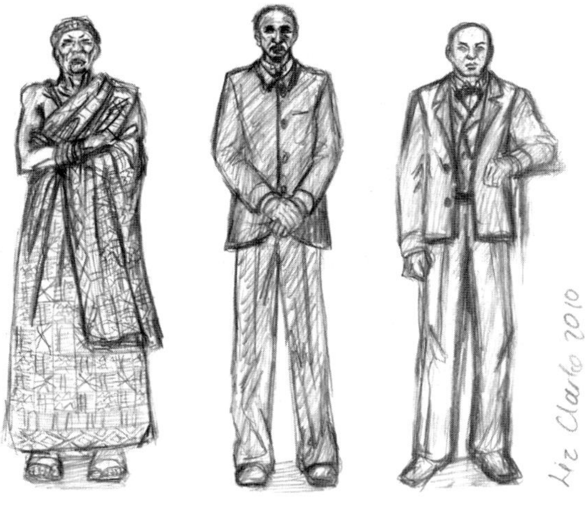
Liz Clarke 2010

QUAMINA EDDOO'S
HOUSE

GLOSSARY

ABUSUA *(ah-boo-sue-wa)* The matrilineal (traced through the mother) kin group that formed a core part of the identity of Akan-speaking people like Abina and Quamina Eddoo. Abusua (plural *mmusuatow*) may have developed as early as the fourteenth century as the key support structure for individual members of society. In the nineteenth century, slaves were generally not recognized as belonging in an abusua. *(see pages 99–101)*

ADINKRA *(ah-din-kra)* Akan ideograms, or visual symbols that convey concepts and meanings. Adinkra probably predate Arabic and Latin (English, French) script in the Gold Coast region. *(see page xv)*

AKAN *(ah-khan)* The name given to a collection of peoples speaking related languages and sharing a number of cultural institutions. The Akan make up the majority of the population of modern-day Ghana, and historically dominated a number of states including Asante and the Fante Confederation. *(see page 99)*

ASAFO *(ah-sah-foe)* Brotherhoods (and possibly sisterhoods) that have existed since at least the seventeenth century in Akan-speaking society. Membership is largely based on descent on the father's side. Asafo companies also had a paramilitary function in protecting the community from tyrannical rulers as well as outside invaders. *(see pages 101, 105)*

ASANTE *(ah-san-tee)* The multiethnic state that emerged from Akan-speaking peoples of the West African forests in the seventeenth century. Asante went on to dominate a region roughly the size and shape of modern-day Ghana. Note that the modern pronunciation and spelling "Ashanti" is a product of sloppy British colonial spelling of the state in English, beginning as "As-hantee" but quickly becoming "Ashantee." *(see pages 101–103)*

COLONIALISM In late nineteenth-century West Africa, colonialism referred not so much to the presence of European settlers as to the imposition of formal authority or informal power by Europeans, including the British, over African peoples. Colonial rule destroyed or twisted preexisting power structures and social organizations, and replaced them with a new set of ideas and relationships that placed European values and people at the top of a social hierarchy. *(see pages 145–146)*

COLONY *(Gold Coast)* In 1876, the Gold Coast Colony was a set of small territories surrounding the major British forts and trading positions (including Cape Coast) that were formally claimed as part of the British Empire and administered directly by British administrators. *(see pages 103, 105–106)*

CONSTRUCT In the context of historical methodology, construction is the task of putting together a narrative of the past using evidence but also relying on the ideas and worldviews of the historian. *(see pages 115, 120, 122–125, 129–130)*

CULTURAL HISTORY A school or field of historical research that focuses on identifying and seeking to understand the perspectives of people who lived in the past rather than the causes or experiences of major events. Cultural historians rely on the method of deconstruction and tend to explore relationships between individuals and society as a whole. *(see pages 132–133)*

DECONSTRUCT In the context of historical methodology, deconstruction is the task of decoding the meanings hidden within a text or source by reading it with and against the grain. It is the search for assumptions made by the author and messages encoded in his/her writing or artistry in order to understand the ways he or she thought and possibly to reveal the worldview shared by his or her contemporaries. *(see pages 126–129)*

FANTE CONFEDERATION A movement that emerged in the late 1860s to establish an African state in the region around Cape Coast modeled upon European states of the period. The Confederation's leaders were mostly formally educated men like James Hutton Brew, and they tried to tie together small states that had a long history of alliance against Asante invasion. The Confederation eventually failed when the British defeated Asante and declared a Protectorate over the region. The name is also applied to a much longer tradition of alliance among the states of the area round Cape Coast. *(see pages 103, 142)*

GOLD COAST This region of West Africa was named by Europeans in the sixteenth century on the basis of its population's production and sale of gold. The region, which had previously been known to at least some of its inhabitants as Wangara, was not politically unified other than briefly in the late eighteenth and early nineteenth centuries under Asante rule, and later as a British colony after 1902. *(see pages 99–105, 160–162)*

GRAPHIC HISTORY A graphic representation of the past, but also a history in that it purports to represent past events and experiences through the interpretation of sources from that period. Graphic histories are not meant to be fiction, although most authors and illustrators recognize that the narratives they are creating must at times venture into speculation. *(see pages 115–116)*

HERITAGE For our purposes, heritage is a way of thinking about the past that is different from history. Whereas history strives to be critical, heritage is generally a celebration of identity that draws upon past suffering or glories for its legitimacy. Heritage is often openly used to bring people together around a cause or identity. *(see pages 134–136)*

HISTORICIZATION The act of placing a source in the context of its time and location of origin. This process of relating a part (the source) to the whole (its historical context) is vital to deriving any accurate sense of the meaning of the source. *(see page 97)*

MATRILINEALITY A system in which ancestry is traced through the mother and maternal ancestors. *(see page 101)*

NOBLE SAVAGE One of the dominant ideas applied to Africans since the early colonial era, the "noble savage" concept both glorifies Africans as unspoiled "primitives" and degrades them as uncivilized and childlike. *(see page 144)*

OHENE *(owe-he-nay)* The *ohene* (plural *ahenfo*) is the ruler of an oman. In the nineteenth century, this chiefly officeholder's power was generally held in check by a network of elders, advisors, and even royal slaves. *(see pages 101, 142)*

OKYEAME *(owe-chee-ah-may)* In Akan-speaking societies, okyeame are professional linguists. They are court translators and often function as advisors or historians as well as interpreters of the law. *(see pages 131–132)*

OMAN *(owe-mahn)* An oman (plural *aman*) is an Akan state. The term may signify a very small but independent territory such as Saltpond, but is equally applied to vast confederacies like Asante. *(see page 101)*

PATERNALISTIC Paternalism indicates a belief in the power and authority of the father, and it is used in the case of British relations with the Gold Coast in the nineteenth century because it was the primary way that British officials, missionaries, and others viewed their relationship with the local population. It implies both a sense of a right to dominate and a duty to discipline the locals for their own good. *(see pages 111, 147–148)*

PEOPLE WITHOUT HISTORY Another of the ways in which Europeans judged Africans. Following the evolution of a formal discipline of history in late nineteenth-century Europe, people without written documents were seen as being outside of "history" and therefore also having no claim to civilization, ownership of land, or any of the other rights of people who had "history." *(see page 144)*

PRIMARY SOURCE A document, image, oral tradition, or other record produced during or in the general period of the event or trend it is describing. *(see pages 97, 115, 164)*

PROTECTORATE *(Gold Coast)* The large southern region of modern Ghana, over which the British claimed some authority following the 1873–1874 Anglo-Asante War on the basis of agreements and alliances with local rulers. Although the British did not directly rule these territories at first, they gradually extended their legal, economic, and military power across the region. *(see page 103)*

READING AGAINST THE GRAIN This is the practice of reading a text to discover ideas and concepts inadvertently placed within it by the author. *(see page 126)*

READING WITH THE GRAIN The practice of reading a text in order to discover the author's purpose and intended message to his/her audience. *(see page 126)*

RECONSTRUCT In historical practice, the process of putting together evidence to discover "what happened" in a past time, place, and series of events. *(see pages 97, 115)*

SECONDARY SOURCE Any source that is intended to be an account of an event of which the author or teller is not an eyewitness, whether oral, written, or visual. *(see page 115)*

SOCIAL HISTORY A school of history that focuses on interpreting evidence from the past to reveal the experiences of large groups of people rather than focusing on the biographies of individuals or causes of events. *(see page 132)*

WHIG Named after a British political movement, supporters of this "liberal" view of the world tend to believe that humans are making progress toward a more enlightened future, which they frame largely in middle-class, late nineteenth-century European terms. *(see page 127)*

WORLD HISTORY A school of history that focuses on the connections among societies and the networks and systems by which these connections operate. *(see pages 141–143)*

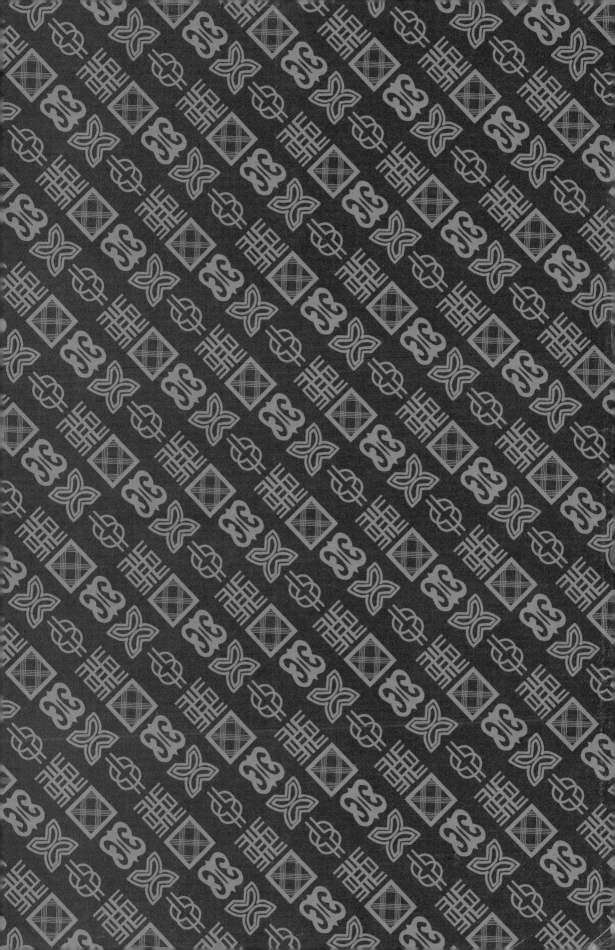